ECO-IMPACTS AND THE GREENING OF POSTMODERNITY

ECO-IMPACTS AND THE GREENING OF POSTMODERNITY

New Maps for Communication Studies,
Cultural Studies, and Sociology

Tom Jagtenberg
David McKie

SAGE Publications
International Educational and Professional Publisher
Thousand Oaks   London   New Delhi

For information address:

SAGE Publications, Inc.
2455 Teller Road
Thousand Oaks, California 91320
E-mail: order@sagepub.com

SAGE Publications Ltd.
6 Bonhill Street
London EC2A 4PU
United Kingdom

SAGE Publications India Pvt. Ltd.
M-32 Market
Greater Kailash I
New Delhi 110 048 India

Printed in the United States of America

Library of Congress Cataloging-in-Publication Data
Jagtenberg, Tom, 1950-
    Eco-impacts and the greening of postmodernity : new maps for
communication studies, cultural studies, and sociology / Tom
Jagtenberg and David McKie.
        p.   cm.
    Includes bibliographical references and index.
    ISBN 0-8039-7406-X (acid-free paper). — ISBN 0-8039-7407-8 (pbk.
: acid-free paper)
        1. Sociology—Philosophy. 2. Environmentalism—Social aspects.
3. Postmodernism. 4. Culture—Study and teaching.   I. McKie,
David, 1947-   . II. Title.
HM24.J33 1996
301'.01—dc20   96-35625

This book is printed on recycled and acid-free paper.

97 98 99 00 01   10 9 8 7 6 5 4 3 2 1

Acquiring Editor:	J. Alex Schwartz
Editorial Assistant:	Jessica Crawford
Production Editor:	Astrid Virding
Production Assistant:	Sherrise Purdum
Copy Editor:	Marilyn Scott
Typesetter/Designer:	Danielle Dillahunt
Indexer:	Will Ragsdale
Cover Designer:	Lesa Valdez

Contents

Introduction

Possible paradigm shifts, and various postulates of different kinds of post-1945 worlds, constitute subjects for debate in most branches of sociology, communication studies, and cultural studies. Although aligning with the view that some kind of postmodern great divide does exist (see Huyssen, 1986), we contend that the twin eco-impacts of environmental consciousness and environmental degradation need to be directly addressed as an integral part of an ongoing transformation. From our perspective, continuing planetary deterioration and contemporaneous social changes require remapping in conjunction with each other. Throughout *Eco-Impacts*, we delineate the decline of nature both environmentally, as a potentially catastrophic biospheric event, and discursively, as interlinked with social theories, communication discourses, and cultural practices (all of which have material force).

Taking initial bearings from Frederic Jameson's (as quoted in Stephanson, 1987) "locus of our new reality [as] space" (p. 40) and our positioning of the fields of sociology, communication, and cultural studies as generally pre-ecological, we seek to draw the biosphere into reflexive critical theory. Indeed, we identify that whole spectrum of our nonhuman physical environment as the theoretically undermapped spatial context. We acknowledge it as so central to sustainable life that it undermines the very idea of space and the biophysical world as a context for human activity. Spaces are places where different life forms compete and cooper-ate for the right to exist biologically and discursively; ecologies are not contextual in nature. Even in exclusionary disciplinary discourses, the bracketing of ecological interests is an artifice—an extreme deferral, to put it in poststructural terms. *Ecology* needs to be understood as a multidimensional concept that can enrich all academic fields. Ecologies are about interaction, flows, fields, systems, and space-time as well as the private spaces, worlds, and value systems of individual organisms. Space, time, and the biophysical world are embedded in all our human worlds and concepts. Ecological thought is holistic. It requires the strategic bracketing of human centeredness and the development of lan-guage and concepts that can draw in the interests and activities of other species and their ecologies.

Ecological holism is more alchemical than Cartesian-Newto-nian: We see macrocosm and microcosm as dialectically related and time and space as also structured by the rhythms of nature. In our desire for different cultural critiques and paradigm change, we do not wish to simply reinstate the remains of past dominant paradigms such as Buddhism, shamanism, or any other holistic premodern worldviews. Valuable as their insights may be, the present ecological crisis is post perennial wisdoms as well as postmodern and definitely changes the possibilities of previous cosmologies. In this book, we are attempting to break away from habits of thought and patterns of analysis that have had no absolute necessity to account for global environmental decline. In making the break, we can only grapple with the fields we know and subject them to our locally generated critiques.

In writing of eco-impacts on the environment and discourse, we are speaking metaphorically, as if ecological disasters and decline had a life outside the material and discursive worlds they affect. Of course we know better, but have doubts about our ability to write other than metaphorically: We stress that the map is not the territory. One small step we have taken, however, is to situate eco-impacts on our environment and on our cultures as central phenomena in the new realities of the "post" era. In particular, we argue for a cartographic shift in our specific academic spaces—the fields of sociology, communication, and cultural studies—and the creation of more eco-sensitive maps. Although we believe such reorientation contributes toward a greener planet, our concerns here are with academic theory and popular culture rather than eco-activism.

To enable our fields to engage more directly with eco-impacts, we realign their existing critical work with more ecocentric per-spectives and make tentative proposals for what greening might entail in academic terms. Specifically, we propose four interre-lated shifts: repositioning the environment as the fourth dimen-sion of social space alongside the traditional concerns of gender, race, and class; intensifying interdisciplinism (especially in rela-tion to science) to reduce binarism; making space for critiques of anthropocentrism; and reformatting enlightenment-based eman-cipatory projects in line with current knowledge-power configu-rations.

In responding to the identification by Jameson, and many others, of a new reality for the second half of the 20th century, we acknowledge a debt to those who established the idea of *post* conditions and mainstreamed that rather chaotic set of methodo-logical and political preoccupations. Of course, descriptions of the contemporary condition still vary and are still contentious: do we live in post-Cartesian-Newtonian, postcolonial, posthis-tory, postindustrial, post-Marxist, postmodern, or postscarcity worlds? As each description remains fiercely contested, the strug-gles impinge on every aspect of theory and practice. Their recon-figurations extend from academic fields to routine communica-tion in everyday life worlds.

Following the lead of radical communication scholars from
James Carey (1993) in the United States to Robyn Penman
(1994) in Australia, we propose that more ecocentric views also
emphasize active involvement in "communicatively constructing
a more differentiated and less constraining environmental reality" (Penman, 1994, p. 37). In our view, the classic communication questions of who says what to whom in which channel
occupy a smaller subset in the changing context and need to be
broadened beyond human centeredness. But again, we stress
that ours is a text of the break, not a new paradigm for ecocentrism. New paradigms, such as the green paradigm we discuss
in Chapter 4, are emergent gestalts and cannot be simply defined
as foundational premises. At best, as we discuss further in
Chapter 2, the changing patterns of discourse can be mapped.
Accordingly, our reorientation encompasses traditional communication questions with less narrowly human centered ones
more attuned to contemporary ecological and social conditions:

- What kind of world do we live in?
- How are humans positioned in relation to the rest of it?
- Where is knowledge-power about it situated?

As well as helping to characterize the contemporary social
world, these three questions also raise environmental concerns
and focus our case for a greener sociology, communication studies, and cultural studies. Prior to addressing the first question,
we wish to signal some of our other positions. In accepting the
contemporary world as the outcome of a great social and cultural
divide after 1945, we have questioned many conventional divisions: nature and culture, economy and ecology, mind and
emotion, reason and nature, and science and culture. In debating
these dualities, as in much else, we have drawn particular
inspiration from the example and strategies of the women's
movement. Besides borrowing heavily from many of its individual
eco-theorists, we follow pathways already taken by the movement
as a whole and seek perceptual shifts both akin to, and, we hope,
in alignment with, what they have already achieved.

WHAT KIND OF WORLD
DO WE LIVE IN?

From Australian land degradation to polluted Californian beaches and transnational acid rain, a specter is haunting the West. In extreme form, it is the specter, sometimes impending, of nature's so-called death. It casts a shadow across all genres of environmental representation—from advertising and bestselling novels, through eco-issue films and children's cartoons, to postmodern pundits and television news. These diverse visual and verbal discourses combine tellingly to convey, at best, a beautiful planet facing differing degrees of threats and, at worst, a planet virtually dead or dying. Although recognizing the wide diversity of responses, we contrast the relatively high visibility of environmental matters in popular culture, especially media, with their low profile in the social theory of academic culture, especially sociology, communication, and cultural studies. Elaborating on that contrast, we question existing configurations of scholarly knowledge and popular communication and propose reconfigurations to adjust the imbalance.

Science-based research and broader ecological studies deliver parallel warnings about the famous four horsepeople of the environmental apocalypse: ozone depletion, global warming, toxicity, and population growth (with its accompanying land and biodiversity loss). Doom-laden titles on global warming, the greenhouse effect, population explosions, and extinction epidemics proliferate. Edward O. Wilson (1992), reflecting from amid "the assembly of life that took a billion years to evolve" in the Amazon basin, poses the question, "How much force does it take to break the crucible of evolution?" (p. 15). Despite the variety and multitude of these expressions, we argue that social theory, communication, and cultural studies remain too implicated in Western modernization, too unaware of, or unconnected with, developments in science, and too narrowly human centered to engage adequately with actual environmental threats and other eco-impacts. Environmental apocalypse now, or in the foreseeable future, still struggles for a place on the current agendas of these fields.

To begin to reprioritize those agendas in Chapter 1, "The Death of Nature?" we focus more on the discursive than the biological to construct a historical and philosophical context for the so-called death. In the process of conceptualizing social and natural systems as part of a dynamic interaction, we consider death, the human emotions, and spirituality—which are all connected to the terminal condition we describe. We also take the death of nature as a metaphor for the end of dualistic hegemony and a questioning of the scientific and economic rationalism that commands contemporary social institutions.

Chapter 2, "Ecological Exclusions: Mapping Disciplinary Change," is broadly concerned with the exclusion and marginalization of ecological interests in academic disciplines. We begin our analysis with a discussion of academic disciplines for three reasons: first, because these institutional concerns have largely determined the kinds of issues and audiences we address in the book; second, they explain our concern to develop an interdisciplinary account; and third, this starting point prioritizes a postmodern reflexivity. Our initial examples are mainly drawn from Australian social sciences and humanities, but the logic of dualism and its exclusionary politics are present in Western texts and institutions internationally. By expanding Jameson's (1988) concept of *cognitive mapping* into a broader *cultural mapping*, we attempt to plot zones of exclusion, marginalized territories, and hidden dimensions.

In Chapter 3, "Readdressing Postmodernity and the Eco-Post," we give our position on the postmodern condition, including what Wernick (1991) calls its *promotional culture*. Preferring a postmodern to a late-modern approach, we outline three versions: postmodernism (a), whose key features we identify using popular television genres; postmodernism (b), which we characterize through diverse academic critical approaches (including potentially postmodern sciences); and postmodernism (c), which we locate through a temporal fix on its historical coordinates. In reidentifying the core characteristics of post-1945 society to locate the postmodern era historically, we argue for the present as an age of ecology.

Chapter 4, "Changing Paradigms: The Greening of Social Movements," reviews the role of social movements in promoting social and cultural change. Historically, social movements have contributed to major decenterings: The labor movement and the women's movement provide good examples of the power of activist networks and the institutionalization of opposition. Of particular interest is the continuing popular support for the development of women's struggles and environmental activism. In this chapter, we review the emergence of new social movements: post-1960s processes that have moved away from dogmatic institutions toward the recognition of grassroots contributions and the need for institutions to accommodate popular awareness and an increased demand for democracy. The ongoing greening of social movements opens possibilities for a further radical decentering and a more ecocentric green paradigm in academia and popular culture. Partly a reaction against entrenched left ideology, partly sustaining the decentering critiques of feminism and the counterculture, these new social movements embrace radical critiques, particularly of patriarchy and Cartesian-Newtonian frameworks, and provide fertile ground for ecological writing and activism.

In arguing that ecological location is fundamentally neglected in social theorizations of identity, Chapter 5, "Living in the Biosphere: Eco-Selves and Decentered Identities," explores what might be involved in the construction of a more ecological self. Continuing to analyze social movement theory and its failure to create a space for the private worlds of individuals, this chapter extends subjectivity and agency into ecology. We argue that social theory needs to develop concepts of an ecological self and that a postmodern interactionist perspective can provide some guidelines. We also value the expanded self of deep ecological critiques and explore the possibility of a theoretical domain that is postmodern and deeply ecological.

Sketching out ideas about what greener curricula of media texts might entail, Chapter 6, "Greening Media Studies: Natural Histories and CS (Communication Studies) Theory Zones," expands the existing idea matrix to accommodate other previously discredited knowledges. In addition, we analyze specific texts and genres as sites where social theories and controlling imagery vie for public acceptance, and we contrast diverse factual and fictional material with the ecocentric time scale and more generous biopolitics of natural histories. To better articulate animal, human, and physical forces as ecological, we conclude that historians and media critics as well as communication, cultural, and social theorists might all dismantle some of their disciplinary boundaries to extend their spatiotemporal dimensions.

Media texts and how they are studied help erect, maintain, and shift parameters of understanding across a number of divides and borders. Chapter 7, "Aligning Media: Debatable Divides and Boundary Crossings," considers media eco-advocacy, and some of its discontents, across different areas. In addition, we promote a move toward a more ecocentric approach by interrelating media criticism with diverse eco-texts to blur 10 symbolic and practical boundaries and explore their less bipolar borderlands. The chapter also tackles some of the difficulties in seeing (and being) green by examining concepts of citizenship and approaches to media audiences.

Chapter 8, "Contours of Knowledge: Science and the Death of Economics," traces where knowledge-power about the world is situated as a key communication, cultural, and environmental question. It crosses the imaginary chasm between C. P. Snow's (1964) (in)famous "two cultures" and explores the ecological potential in the mooted death of economics. Whereas humans generate both science and culture, the nature of the world they map or the way they map the same world invests that illusionary binary divide with material consequences. The resultant mappings also fissure the organization of knowledge about the earth, and we contend that the fields of communication and cultural studies do not keep in sufficient touch with the other side of the divide. Last, in considering economics in line with so-called post changes in the sciences and elsewhere, we contemplate the potential for a metamorphosis influenced by Chaos and Complexity to make space for women, the environment, and other exclusions of the neoclassical paradigm. (We capitalize *Chaos* and *Complexity* to distinguish the specialist usage of these terms in scientific fields).

Chapter 9, "Decentering Cartography: Scientific Futuremaps and Ecological Projections," develops our earlier argument that two communities, the scientific and the nonhuman, feature too infrequently in communication and cultural studies' interactions. In this chapter, we connect the two through ideas and maps derived from recent scientific cartography. With the new charts, we reassess mapmaking's role in the academic imperialism of the Birmingham Centre for Contemporary Cultural Studies and develop an ecological and postmodern decentering project. Taking additional bearings from the human genome project, genetic engineering, and science fiction, we extend future projections beyond the confines of traditional politics and the limits of high-tech, anti-organic cyborg configurations. Aligned with both ecoculturalist and scientific cartography, this final plotting of all these diverse coordinates further dethrones the human subject, widens our fields' community relations to encompass aspects of the nonhuman, and reprises the main trajectory of our greening.

Acknowledgments

M uch of my work on this book was completed during a study leave in 1995, and I would like to thank the University of Wollongong for funding me and Edith Cowan University and Griffith University for hosting me. I thank my colleagues and friends in the Media Studies Department, Edith Cowan University—in particular Robin Quin, Norm Leslie, Michael O'Shaughnessy, Kevin Ballantine, Max Pam, and of course, David McKie. At Griffith University, I thank Roy and Sally Rixon for their continuing support and friendship and also many other friends and colleagues in the School of Australian Environmental Studies, the School of Australian Comparative Studies, and the Faculty of Humanities—including Georgina Murray, David Carter, Mark Finnane, Paul Saffigna, and Richard Sanders. At Wollongong University, I thank the Centre for Research in Textual and Cultural Studies for a small grant in support of the project.

My partner, Becky, has contributed most to my work on the project—her research assistance and editorial work has been invaluable. Her love and support kept me going. My parents, Pat and Tom, have been patient and understanding. Thanks also to all my friends—Lenore, Sophie, Robert, and Tim in particular.

TOM JAGTENBERG

*   *   *

I gratefully acknowledge the support and friendship of my surrogate family in the Media Studies Department at Edith Cowan University and my many friends on the Joondalup and Mt. Lawley campuses as well as the magnificent Western Australian coastline, which also helps to sustain my life. Individuals who must be mentioned include Robyn Quin, Brian Shoesmith, Norm Leslie, Michael O'Shaughnessy, Kevin Ballantine, Linda Jaunzems, Doug White, Deb Westerberg, Michael Bennett, Ann Manning, Marie-Louise Hunt, Sonia Walker, and too many students to mention, Ian Hutchison, Alan McKee, and Hilaire Natt. I'm also grateful for the help received from my extended network in the Australian and New Zealand Communication Association and in communication, cultural, and media studies throughout the world. Again John Corner, Robyn Penman, Sue Turnbull, David Sless, Phil Bell, Andrew Tolson, Scott Allan, Mica Nava, Jennifer Slack, David Buchan, Ian Murray, Ann Good, Douglas Mack, David Skilton, Donald Low, Ken Buthlay, Judy Motion, and Shirley Leitch have more than earned specific mention. Special thanks, too, to Jenny Lee and Roslyn Petelin who proved the most encouraging and attentive of editors at critical times. However, given the provocative nature of some of the views that follow, none of them deserve to be rounded up as the usual suspects. They, of course, bear no responsibility for what was finally written.

Above all, I thank my partner, Jyoti, for her warmth, love, and gift of precious time over the intense period of creating *Eco-Impacts* and hope that my daughter Anna, granddaughters Abbie and Mhairi, and other future generations will be free to continue enjoying this wonderful healing planet as much as we do.

DAVID MCKIE

1

The Death of Nature?

Humanity is confronting both ecological decline and an explosion of discourse about nature. Although there is an unprecedented shift in public awareness about ecological issues, this does not guarantee a return or regeneration of the nature of old. At the same time as nature and ecology become the center of attention, they are transformed in ever more radical ways. The effects of exploding human populations and their material and cultural infrastructures—from agriculture and industry to administration and popular culture—are remorseless. In this complex dialectic, culture and communication have material force: They are material processes as well as also being symbolic and imaginary.

Communication, culture, and society have always been intrinsically ecological—that is, they do not stand outside the stream of life of which they are part. Furthermore, because these human processes dominate the interests of other species, they can be said to have a tangible impact on systems of which they are part—in many cases, profoundly degrading them. The semiosphere and the biosphere, as we argue, are entwined. When we act on the world in a planned way, we operate symbolically: We cut, dig, gouge, hack, build, enclose, and otherwise shape the environment in ways that reflect cultural norms, myths, archetypes, and ideologies. Such action is intrinsic to being in the world; it is also communicative. Conversely, all communication is biospheric in its action. From the molecular exchanges of sensory organs and the passage of electromagnetic fields to the vast industrially based infrastructures that support communication industries, communication and culture are material forces.

In this book, we try to reveal something of the complex dialectic between semiosphere and biosphere, between industries and ecologies. These we register as *eco-impacts.* We explore eco-impacts in a world that is both material and cultural. *Eco-Impacts* is therefore a multivalenced title. We are as much interested in deconstructing the paradigms that allow us to dichotomize nature-culture-society (and that allow us to speak of the "impacts" of one or the other) as we are in promoting the idea that human culture and society have impacts on the planet and the sustainability of our species' diversity and current human lifestyles. Indeed, the whole point of so-called green ecological theorizing is to persuade us of the intimate interplay among all components of complex systems—be they colloquially real or imaginary. Behind our academic concern to preserve pluralistic analysis, there is also a real measure of apocalyptic anxiety. Could this be the end of the world? The question needs to be given some priority.

The end of the world as a human-created ecological disaster and decline was registered as a serious possibility as early as 1962 with Rachel Carson's best seller, *Silent Spring.* In 1980, the death of nature was uttered in academic circles. By then, the general optimism of activists and academics appears to have sufficiently cooled to allow Carolyn Merchant (1980) to title her book, *The Death of Nature.* A decade later, Bill McKibben (1990) reconfirmed that "we have killed off nature—that world entirely independent of us which was here before we arrived and which encircled and supported our human society" (p. 88). Writers in various genres have lent support to these fears, from cyberpunk to the more strident critics of technology out of control—such as the North American neoluddite Jerry Mander (1991), who writes of the complete takeover of nature by bigger and bigger technological forms.

In this tide of grim concern, the death, end, or decline of nature is occurring biologically and culturally. McKibben's (1990) claim, and his book, *The End of Nature,* convey two prominent features of contemporary attitudes to environmental issues: ambiguity about the character of the corpse, "there's still something out there, though—if you look out of the window there's probably a cloud" (p. 88), and an apocalyptic tone. Popular culture amplifies the tone's volume and multiplies the points of dissemination registering different degrees of alarm at an environment in danger.

Environmental novels, from the certifiably serious and upmarket Iris Murdoch to the determinedly popular and seriously comic Ben Elton, now occupy prominent spaces on the shelves of libraries and book shops, respectively. Green themes have mass audiences and mass markets. In this multigenre appropriation of the environment, advertising acts as a barometer of the extent to which popular and commercial cultures have been greened. Advertisers of everything—from dolphin-safe tuna to greenhouse-friendly nuclear power—circulate messages that mingle various versions of doom with qualified hopes and utopian fantasy. Television ecology program titles echo advertising ambiguities by simultaneously celebrating *A Most Remarkable Planet* (1990); alerting viewers to ecological fragility, *It's a Matter of Survival* (1990); and counselling various strategies for *Turning the Tide* (1986) (of environmental deterioration). In feature films, Sean Connery's *Medicine Man* (1992) constructs a fictional cancer cure to suggest that rain forest loss may negatively affect the future of Western medicine; in the animated cartoon, *FernGully* (1992), Robin Williams's zany bat gives voice to development as the real-life bloodsucker of natural flora and fauna. With typical U.S. modesty and puritan ethics, Ted Turner's *Captain Planet and the Planeteers* have worked from 1990 to save the whole planet in regular episodes of children's television cartoons.

At the pessimistic end of the spectrum of perceived death, McKibben (1990) attributes humanity's loss of faith in nature's "essential strength" to "the idea of nature" being unable to "survive the new global pollution" (p. 54). Although attributing new global pollution as a biospheric factor, McKibben has recorded more of a semiotic than a biospheric death—as the title of his 1993 sequel, *The Age of Missing Information*, also suggests. Humankind, he concedes, "have not ended rainfall or sunlight" but the "*meaning* of the wind, the sun, the rain—of nature—has already changed" (McKibben, 1990, p. 44). McKibben's perception of nature's end also serves to announce what Frederic Jameson (1991) calls the birth of the postmodern: "what you have when the modernization process is complete and nature is gone for good" (p. ix).

In part, this simultaneous end of nature and birth of the postmodern, like so much else, is anticipated in the processes of modernity but not articulated as such. For instance, in the recent history of social theory in the humanities and the arts, alienation and humanism have been more dominant concerns than the radically decentering processes of postmodernism, deep ecology, or eco-feminism. These former concerns are predominantly centered around the imperatives of science, technology, progress, and economic growth and are significantly pre-ecological. The alienation of modernity's human subjects has been so widely portrayed in art, literature, philosophy, and the social sciences that it has become almost natural for social theorists to portray humanity as angst ridden, fractured, exploited, oppressed, and, in many other ways, off center. The fate of the individual in modernity and postmodernity are subjects we take up in later chapters where we move toward more ecocentric positions and attempt to get beyond alienation.

Our position on nature's reputedly terminal condition also takes off from Iain Chambers's (1986) claim that "it is perhaps unjust and imprecise to suggest that postmodernism merely entertains the idea of 'the end of the world' " (p. 100). Instead of the death of all nature, we see the beginnings of the end of the dominance of Eurocentric, patriarchal paradigms and world views. We see an end to the dominance of ethnocentrism and a de-scribing of that discursive empire that colonized reason as the exclusive province of the Scientific Revolution, the European Enlightenment, and their scientific and philosophic successors. In this shifting of controlling imagery, there are many deaths, including the alleged death of materialism (Davies & Gribbin, 1992, p. 4). This gives scientific verification to a demise that has been reported since at least the time of the counterculture. In their broad interest in paradigm change, post-1960s social movements, particularly the counterculture, have been widely concerned to counter the dominance of the Cartesian-Newtonian universe and rationalizations based on an endlessly exploitable nature. The death of these paradigms may come too late to save the biosphere as we know it, but a history of changing ideas of nature remains critical as we move into a so-called risk society and contemplate the condition of postmodernity.

IDEAS OF NATURE:
A HISTORICAL REVIEW

Raymond Williams, the eminent pioneer of British cultural studies, has provided a coherent summary of centuries of cultural change and shifting dominant categories of Western European usage of the word *nature*. The kind of typification and peace building introduced by Williams is particularly relevant to the understanding of ecological postmodernism and its registering of a variety of worldviews and paradigms. Williams's work is also important for the way it articulates a view of nature that is informed by neo-Marxist critical social theory. It represents something of a benchmark for theoretical orthodoxy in cultural studies. It also provides an introduction to the work of Carolyn Merchant, which continues in the tradition of a progressive post-Marxism but opens more directly into postmodern spaces.

In a chapter titled "Ideas of Nature," Williams (1980) gives us an interesting summary of dominant European representations over the past several hundred years. In following a fairly conventional historical declension, Williams notes a movement from early cultures that give us images of nature spirits or nature gods "which embody or direct the wind or the sea or the forest or the moon" (p. 69) to the instrumentalism of contemporary expressions. At some point in a progression from animism, nature becomes "singular, abstract and personified" (p. 69). Nature as Goddess, as divine Mother, then gives way to monotheistic religion in which God is absolute, with Nature as his minister and deputy. In this process, although Williams did not say it, Nature became spiritually disempowered, paving the way for the death of nature in the scientific positivism to follow in later centuries.

By the time of Shakespeare's *Lear*, Williams notes that there were a wide range of cultural meanings available for nature: nature as a primitive condition before human society; nature as a state of original innocence from which there has been a fall and a curse requiring redemption; nature as a quality of birth (i.e., our "original nature"), through to themes of nature as a personified goddess—"Nature herself." Williams might have been intrigued to see that these ideas are still to be found in various guises in contemporary cultures—in subcultures and the discourses of eco-feminism and deep ecology; in Goddess worship, shamanism, and paganism; and in the eclecticism of investigators of the Gaia myth and its extensions in science fiction and science fantasy.

To complete Williams's (1980) schema, nature, in 17th-century to 19th-century European thought, becomes a less imposing figure. Nature becomes in effect a constitutional lawyer, or at least an accumulation and classification of cases expressing laws of nature. Evading personification in this modality, nature becomes a secularized object, "even at times a machine" (p. 73). After the constitutional lawyer, we have nature as the selective breeder by the late 18th and early 19th century. Agricultural improvement and the industrial revolution finally deliver us nature as the lonely places, the wilderness, the place "where industry was not"—"in Wordsworth and beyond him, there came the sense of nature as a refuge, a refuge from man; a place of healing, a solace, a retreat" (p. 80).

One might contest the abstraction of such a neatly defined, linear, and high cultural account. But of more relevance to our discussion of the cultural variability of ideas of nature is the structural point that Williams (1980) is making: Although perception and representation of nature is historically and culturally variable, particular ideas have dominated at particular times. Williams' history amounts to an account of paradigm succession. Today, there are still dominant ideas and cultures of nature, but the heterogeneity of these fields is part of what we see as the prevailing condition of postmodernity. Today, we find most of these different ideas of nature still at play in the ongoing construction of nature in different institutional sites. They can be seen not only in the routine processes of the sciences and technology and in the discourses of the humanities and social sciences but also in the constructs of fields and social movements that are becoming more ecologically reflexive.

Williams (1980), like Carolyn Merchant and social ecologists generally, sees the alienation and domination of nature—its otherness—as a reflection of problematic relations between human beings:

Out of the ways in which we have interacted with the physical world we have made not only human nature and an altered natural order; we have also made societies. It is very significant that most of the terms we have used in this relationship—the conquest of nature, the exploitation of nature—are derived from real human practices: relations between men and men. (p. 84)

Williams (1980) concludes with the observation that if man(kind) alienates the living processes of which we are part, we necessarily alienate ourselves. We need, he says, "different relationships, . . . different ideas, different feelings, if we are to know nature as varied and variable, as the changing conditions of a human world" (p. 85). By implication, only when we have developed ecological relations between human beings and human society will we be able to transform our relations with other species.

True as all this may be, it is also easy to read Williams's essay as sexist and human centered. Williams is certainly correct in addressing "men" as prime movers in the creation of dominant social and cultural forms, but one has to wonder about the underlying phallocentrism of his whole account—gently ironic as it may be. Merchant (1980) is certainly a more gender-aware critical theorist. Williams's (1980) key idea, however, is that knowledge of nature is a projection of our human social relations. This construction of the history of ideas is paradigmatic for all left theory and is pre-ecological, pre-post structural and pre-post modern. His linear history needs to be placed in a broader context of cultural production and the politics of textual production, themes we take up in Chapter 2 via consideration of the exclusion of nature. We also subject paradigmatic human centeredness to further critique when we review the dominance of left and neo-Marxist theory in Chapters 4 and 5.

OFF-GROUND

The vocabularies of social theory are limited when it comes to characterizing the relationships between humanity and other species and ecologies. This is evident if we apply the logic of Williams's social ecology to the social relations of capitalism to understand our position and our relationality in an ecology. In modern times, social relations in a capitalist order have been regularly described by critical theorists in terms of *alienation, exploitation, domination, control,* and even *repression.* This is the broad legacy of Marx and Freud but is expressed throughout the classical canon of critical theory. These concepts find their mean-ing in the dominant dualisms of nature-culture, male-female, mind-matter, reason-emotion, and master-slave. The possibili-ties of these dualistic frameworks are obviously limited, but they do locate a number of key sites and differences that ecological theory needs to transgress.

For instance, Chesneaux (1992) has recently given the concept of alienation a decidedly more ecological and postmodern spin with the notion of *off-ground*: "a general category of modernity, the state of being radically dissociated from the natural, social, historical and cultural environment" (p. 13). In more popular usage, off-ground finds echoes in *offshore* for tax havens and cheap labor production; *off-world* for science fiction (especially

Blade Runner); *cyberspace* from science fiction, now in use for actual Internet communications and financial transactions; to, above all, what Douglas Rushkoff (1994) calls the *datasphere* whose "ever-expanding media has become a true region—a place as real and seemingly open as the globe was five hundred years ago" (p. 4). In effect, whether we like it or not, we are all virtual realists now.

Currently, "off-ground" features as only one of many semantic variants that serve to emphasize the denial of organic life and ecology in the transformations of late modernism or postmodern society and culture. These transformations now include such semantics as the *deconstruction* of poststructuralism and the *hyperreality* of Baudrillard (1988) and Eco (1987). These textually centered worlds of the post era are critically located to challenge many of the dominant assumptions of contemporary and modern societies with their constitutional belief in science and truth, progress and perfection, democracy and freedom, and so on. In playing with the dominant dualisms that support patriarchal, Eurocentric cultures to date, poststructuralism and postmodernism have alerted us to the need for transgressing these dominant dualisms. Typical of academic endeavors, however, they do not actually deliver an ecologically (or even an ontologically) grounded viewpoint. Nevertheless, they do sensitize us to excess in society and culture and facilitate the critical and ironic eye so necessary to deal with the media, advertising, and the new virtual worlds of the datasphere.

WAYS OF DYING, WAYS OF AVOIDING

Unfortunately, humankind's superhighways to excess may lead to the place of extinction rather than the palace of virtual wisdom. In a world where simulations reign and phenomena demonstrate the increasing permeability of reality to representation, it is hard to know which way to face or which time frame to adopt. Believing in the need for a time frame longer than modernity, we opt for the centuries-long span adopted by both

Williams's (1980) "Ideas of Nature" and Carolyn Merchant's (1980) *The Death of Nature*. Unlike Williams, Merchant is quite confident that a significant death occurred. Merchant sees nature as still alive in the 1500s and relates its loss to the Scientific Revolution and the subsequent subjugation of the natural world. What died, for her, was the idea of nature as a living organism "binding together the self, society, and the cosmos." She views the "change in controlling imagery" as "directly related to changes in human attitudes and behavior toward the earth" (pp. 1-2). These are the longer-term frameworks that are necessary to understand the roots of modernism and its anti-ecological tendencies.

To illustrate how such frameworks of imagery and explanation implicate us in value judgments, Merchant (1980) assembles an impressively vast selection of pre-death-of-nature examples. On the still contentious issue of mining, she observes how Roman writers and Stoic philosophers openly opposed it as an abuse of the earth as their mother. She recounts a late 15th-century allegorical tale opposing mining encroachments on German farm-lands in which "Mother Earth, dressed in a tattered green robe and seated on the right hand of Jupiter, is represented in a court case by 'glib-tongued Mercury' who charges a miner with matri-cide" (pp. 32-33). Merchant argues convincingly that such an organic framework proved sufficiently powerful, for a time, "to override commercial development and technological innovation" until "the acceleration of such changes throughout western Europe during the sixteenth and seventeenth centuries began to undermine the organic unity of the cosmos and society" (p. 5).

This kind of animated defense continues to come from indige-nous cultures that are centered on the earth as a living deity. Tribal ecocultures remain a source of cosmological renewal, for some people, indigenous or not—for example, in shamanism, paganism, New Age cultures, and the associated renewal of Eastern cosmologies. Many fragments of these premodern cos-mologies today circulate in the fictions of the media. For example, however diluted and recycled in the wake of nature's death, traces of the earth goddess Gaia can be found in Western popular and scientific cultural notions of the earth. The television special for Earth Day 1990 features a bedraggled Bette Midler in tattered green robes adorned with litter as Gaia. In a frenzy of intertextuality, she is treated in intensive care by medics and scientists who include television's Dr. Doogie Hauser, Nurse Colleen MacMurphy from *China Beach*, film's mad scientist Christopher Lloyd from the *Back to the Future* movies, and Murphy Brown reporting Bette's (and Gaia's) possibly terminal condition from the hospital steps. We refer to this example to show both the continuity and difference between the circulation of pre-1700 and post-World War II imagery: the former as a respected and an integral part of the whole cultural fabric, the latter as a comedy-based attempt to alter eco-attitudes through a one-off television special. In addition, the Earth Day Special coalesces popular science (through a lecture by Carl Sagan), ecological information (through questions on environmental pollution being asked in a quiz show format), and entertainment (through sitcom and cinema stars sending up anti-environment perspectives)—see Chapter 7 for a more extended analysis. This humor does not extend through academia. *Homo Academicus*, as Bourdieu (1988) terms academic knowledge workers, tend to keep disciplinary mixes more hermetically sealed and to be allergic to entertaining communication.

Merchant (1980) stresses the nature-culture dichotomy as an integral part of disciplinary separations. Based around "the distinction between nature and culture fundamental to humanistic disciplines such as history, literature, and anthropology," it acts as "a key factor in Western civilization's advance at the expense of nature" (p. 143). This dichotomy and its disciplinary matrix has fed into communication and cultural studies and, although it is beyond the scope of this book to detail such influences, one very important figure has been the structuralist anthropologist Claude Lévi-Strauss, whose work provides an important bridge between Cartesian-Newtonian orthodoxy and poststructuralism. Stating that "all problems are linguistic ones" (as quoted in Pace, 1986, p. 158), Lévi-Strauss took the turn to language so central to both fields, simultaneously employing distance as his basic epistemological approach—whereby knowledge was "always the result of encountering an 'Other' " (p. 57). Lévi-Strauss's structuralism is akin to Derrida's better known formulation: there is nothing outside the text. Both theorists have continuing ecological possibilities, despite their methodological prioritization of language. We understand the former's *language* and the latter's *text* as also social (con)text—an interactive and semiotic weaving of human subjects with external others that does not exclude animals and the nonsentient world.

In addition, through his structural anthropology, Lévi-Strauss helped to guide both fields around the influential "structural turn." He has had far fewer followers in the high priority he assigns to the nature-culture divide:

> The terms "reactionary" or "revolutionary" made sense only in relation to conflicts which oppose one group of men [sic] to another. Now, today, the chief peril for humanity does not prove to be the enterprise of a regime, of a party, or a group or a class. It is humanity itself, in its entirety, which reveals itself as its own worst enemy and, at the same time, alas, that of the rest of creation [sic]. It is that of which it is necessary to convince mankind [sic] if one hopes to save it. (as quoted in Pace, 1986, p. 191)

One of his interpreters, David Pace (1986), categories the passage as "this depoliticization of public issues" (p. 190). On the contrary, we want to argue that such human centered narrowness, which classes population impact on the globe's inhabitants as nonpolitical, remains dominant in the social theory of communication studies, cultural studies, and sociology. Going back in time with Merchant to advocate a more ecocentric approach, we want to retain what is valuable in linguistic and structural turns and, at the same time, maintain a critique of viewpoints that exclude the rest of the planet from what counts as politics.

TOWARD ECOCENTRISM

Merchant is exemplary in filling out Eckersley's (1992) definition of ecocentrism as "based on an ecologically informed philosophy of internal relatedness, according to which all organisms are not simply interrelated with their environment but also constituted by those very environmental relationships" (p. 49). The viewing of historical change as ecological change goes beyond acknowledging that existing environmental conditions have a history. Merchant's (1980) more ecosystemic model, as well as featuring specifics of European "farm, fen and forest" (p. 42) and land management changes in detail, establishes three major related aspects: the philosophical shifts accompanying, and powering, the Scientific Revolution; the enclosure movement's physical separation of people from their traditional land; and the commercial commodification of nature.

The legacy of the first of these, the Scientific Revolution's intellectual will to dominance, and especially dominance of the natural world, still remains prevalent. Many of the contemporary discursive positions we will go on to critique have their origins, if not their clearest statement, in those 16th-century and 17th-century thinkers. The instrumentalism of the philosopher-scientist Francis Bacon typifies this revolutionary shift in culture. In the advancement of his kind of learning, Bacon (as quoted in Marshall, 1992) expressed the convergence of excessive anthropocentrism with humankind's separation from the environment and through the idea that the rest of the planet exists solely for the use of humans:

> Man, if we look to final causes, may be regarded as the center of the world; insomuch that if man were taken away from the world, the rest would seem to be all astray, without aim or purpose . . . and leading to nothing. For the whole world works together in the service of man; and there is nothing from which he does not derive use and fruit . . . insomuch that all things seem to be going about man's business and not their own. (p. 184)

Bacon's instrumentalism may sound extreme, but it captures a human centered arrogance still prevalent as its nemesis, global ecology, "forces us to admit that the current process of industrial development is destroying the very ecological foundations of all humans and non-humans simultaneously" (Chatterjee & Finger, 1994, p. 50). Many social theorists after Bacon and his contemporaries have shared and supported Descartes's (as quoted in Rifkin, 1991) intent to "make ourselves masters and possessors of nature" (p. 32). Even contemporary modernists have done little to counter Locke's (as quoted in Strauss, 1953) assertion that the "negation of nature is the way to happiness" (p. 315). The Scientific Revolution and the Enlightenment project remain central to any understanding of the disempowerment of nature.

The second of Merchant's major aspects similarly prefigures current issues. Although now in a more so-called advanced form, the tragedy of the commons occurred first in medieval Europe when the enclosure movement began to remove rural workers from their traditional land and to abolish their traditional land rights. An early kind of privatization of this separation of common, or ordinary, people from their common, or communal, farming and grazing grounds has since escalated, but what one historian called this "revolution of the rich against the poor" (as quoted in Rifkin, 1991, p. 39) first dismantled the social use of the land as a means of subsistence. Instead of the residual feudal system, whereby peasant farmers exchanged part of their crops—or their labor—for cultivating the land, a money economy commercialized the process so that rent or taxes were required for permission to farm, and the enclosure movement enclosed areas with fences, hedges, or ditches to prevent access to the common ground surrounding villages. Legal and political changes further consolidated the commodification of land over the next few centuries and helped transform the nature of the relationship among people and between people and nature as it displaced millions of rural workers from the land. These movements have now spread over the whole planet's land mass, beneath its seas, and above its skies to outer space as the desire for profit drives privatization and commodification further and further in search of exploitable ecological regions.

Merchant's (1980) third factor records "how the resource of soil fertility affects population growth and decline, peasant-landlord conflict, and market expansion" (pp. 67-68). For her, history that excludes these fails to comprehend "democracy and capitalist economic institutions in Europe and America" that were "directly dependent on the exploitation of natural resources" (p. 68). "The disruption of associated ecosystems (forests, prairies, marshes, lakes, oceans) and their human components" (p. 68) affects the constitution, health, and psychology of societies. In later chapters, we update Merchant's three major factors, contrasting the philosophical shifts accompanying the Scientific Revolution with the conditions of postmodernity. We also contrast the enclosure movement's physical separation of people from their traditional land with the ongoing spread of the tragedy of the commons through the globalization of industry and agriculture and the genetic enclosures of biotechnology, and contrast the commodification of nature with the hypercommodification of promotional culture. As a further development of these lines of analysis, we will also explore the growth of more ecocentric movements.

ROUTES OF RESISTANCE

We devote so much space to Merchant, and argue for consideration of her work and methods to be expanded within sociology and cultural and communication studies, for a number of reasons. Historically, her version of what is now called a more ecocentric approach was early, thorough, and still provides a sound base for more ecologically informed studies. Moreover, she has continued to develop her early perspectives (see Merchant, 1989, 1992, 1994) without ever losing touch with interlinked issues of class, gender, and racial justice. In particular, in a manner that anticipates our later arguments, she deployed Western and non-Western intellectual knowledge traditions nonhierarchically—as in *Ecological Revolutions* (1989), where she examined "how different human cultures—native American and Euroamerican—occupied the same geographic space in close succession with differing effects on the environment" (p. xiii). More recently, in her editing of a 1994 ecology anthology, she has maintained these perspectives, all of which we see as fundamental to more ecologically aware and engaged disciplines. Demonstrating characteristic breadth of scope, her collection places pieces on eco-feminism and deep ecology alongside socialist ecology and material on spiritual ecology and postmodern science. This scope raises new possibilities in the identification and positioning of key concepts in critical theory. For Merchant

(1994), the central insight in such an assemblage is emphatically that domination is "one of our century's most fruitful concepts for understanding human-human and human-nature relationships" (p. 1).

Finally, the extended time frame of Merchant's more ecocentric history of nature's death also draws in another set of politics we regard as seminal: the 1960s, with their triple impetus of countercultural revolution, women's liberation, and the ecological movement. Focusing on the last two movements as being the instigators of her first book, Merchant (1980) constructs a project that fuses both movements' goals to "suggest new values and social structures, based not on the domination of women and nature as resources but on the full expression of both male and female talent and on the maintenance of environmental integrity" (p. xv). In fully supporting her aims and highlighting her work, we do not want to imply that Merchant stands alone. She participates in and draws from other discourses about nature-environment but is centrally feminist in her orientation.

Feminism is particularly important in the context of our book because it reveals that the construction of nature is a gendered process and that the textual politics of feminism and the environment have similarities. The environment has been marginalized in discourse through similar techniques mobilized against women. Relevant, too, are the discourses about other marginalized others, especially indigenous peoples, but the fate of women has been most thoroughly documented and is so thoroughly implicated in thought about nature and the environment that we have made gender and feminist analysis a stronger focus in the book. At one level, the death of nature is a "gendered fiction" (cf. Cranny-Francis, 1992).

OTHER DISCOURSES,
OTHER DEATHS

On this as on many other matters, sociology, communication, and cultural studies still have much to learn from feminists. Patricia Mellencamp's (1992) honesty about her own body and aging, for example, places her personal history as part of second-stage feminism, "replacing self-hatred with acceptance and self-regard" (p. 250). Her reflections differ from the usual association of Mother Earth with the feminine but are interestingly suggestive about possible similarities and differences with perceptions of the earth as growing old. What equivalent personal linkages might exist in the face of ecological death is an easier question to ask than answer, but we see Mellencamp's self-reflexive account of her subjective interaction with controlling imagery as indicating a route that will need to be followed. It adds significantly to the more commonly circulated affinities between women and nature as metaphoric; as mythological; and as exploited, objectified, and repressed.

Although noting these commonly circulated distinctions, we have no wish to reaffirm them. Nature is polysemous and although women have been positioned alongside nature, women still suffer alienation from nature for many reasons shared with men. Much good analysis of processes of exclusion in feminist literature, for example, is ecologically valuable to both genders and to nonsentient life. Beverley Thiele (1986), for instance, has catalogued "vanishing acts" in social and political thought. In her analysis, these "tricks of the trade" have rendered women invisible in an androcentric sociology of "male stream thought" (p. 30).

Not that exclusion is the only mode of repression in operation. Nature is also rearticulated and given new nuances in all these discourses. We routinely see the so-called naturalization of nature occurring, as nature and the environment are continually commodified and recirculated as image, sign, myth, and product. From advertising to zoology, we see the steady rearticulation of nature. In response, the social sciences, communication studies, and cultural studies have increasingly focused attention on the ideological deployment of things supposedly natural. In this discursive twist, the naturalization of gender differences to fundamental biological imperatives has been of particular concern to feminists and other analysts of discourse (e.g., Fiske, 1990; Grosz, 1989; Williamson, 1978). The essentializing of culturally measured differences to biological causes has a profoundly repressive history in patriarchal orders. It is not surprising that the articulation of sociobiological and related reductionist perspectives should stimulate so much concern. In no longer accepting that they are "naturally" inferior, women have seen the importance of exposing so-called natural orders as patriarchal stock in trade.

Thus, nature (as naturalization) has frequently resurfaced academically as another negative term. The idea that anything humanly connected could be natural is probably anathema to new generations of social theorists, armed with the acid of debunking, ideological analysis, and deconstruction, and may have inadvertently further reified the nature-culture distinction. There is a lot at stake in the representation of nature. Overshadowed by an impending millenarial ecological spasm, struggles over its definition and construction will undoubtedly intensify. Other more positive connections remain to be made.

Nirvana and cosmic connection, for example, can now be cast in terms and symbols not so patriarchal, perhaps even gender neutral or ambiguous. Collectively, we can develop spiritual and material identities that are not off-ground. Words are central to this project. The semiosphere is part of our connection with nature, and it is polysemous. As Williams, Merchant, and many others (e.g., Berman, 1984; Roszak, 1973) have indicated in their historical studies, Western perceptions of nature have varied widely. They still vary in subcultures and marginalized and underground cultures as well as in the burgeoning diversity of multicultural postmodernity. But today, there is evidence for a more systematic shift of viewpoints in Western culture. We may be presently undergoing another major paradigm shift with the emergence of oppositional social movement cultures, interdisciplinarity, and postmodernism.

SEMIOTIC DEATH AND EMOTIONS IN A RISK SOCIETY

In the context of death and dying, cultural issues tend to have strong implications for individual and social psychology. Our selves, our bodies, and our whole sensuous engagement with the world are culturally mediated and, to an extent, culturally constituted. In his account of the changing cultural significance of death in European life, Philippe Aries (1974) documents how death changed from being an omnipresent familiarity to being something shameful and forbidden. Death became enclosed by the institutions of State and Church and taken away from more popular culture and the affection of the people. In the process, death has become sanitized and disenchanted. Fear of death became institutionalized and death became something of a taboo subject. An eco-psychoanalyst might surmise that the cultural repression of interest in death sustains the denial of the severity of the decline of other species and their habitats. Fear of death entails fear of life (cf. Grof & Halifax, 1977; Kübler Ross, 1969). Human emotion is particularly vulnerable in this changing appreciation of death. Furthermore, the rationalistic revolution of the sciences only compounds the inability of human emotion to deal with death—our own and that of the earth. The rise of science saw a much reduced status for discourse about the emotions.

At the level of the individual, recent neurological research has identified Descartes's mind-body split as an error. Its findings endorse Pascal's claim that it is on "knowledge of the heart and of the instincts that reason must establish itself and create the foundations of all its discourse" (as quoted in Damasio, 1994b, p. 116), to propose a positive role for emotion in a post-Cartesian scientific world. Reporting on the research in *Descartes' Error: Emotion, Reason, and the Human Brain*, Antonio Damasio (1994a) attributes the absence of emotion to be at least as pernicious for rationality as excess of emotion and argues that rationality is less likely to come from language or intellect than from the biology of living organisms determined to survive. He concludes that these findings might have particular implications for the planetary survival of the human species (Damasio, 1994b, p. 116). Damasio's research is certainly worth bearing in mind when environmental groups and supporters are accused of excessive emotionality. It provides justification for advocating a more emotional response at both personal and planetary levels, not only because "the action of biological drives, body states, and emotions

may," in fact, "be an indispensable foundation for reason"
(Damasio, 1994a, p. 200), but because

> The idea of a disembodied mind also seems to have shaped the
> peculiar way in which Western medicine approaches the study
> and treatment of diseases. . . . The Cartesian split pervades both
> research and practice. . . . Versions of Descartes' error obscure
> the roots of the human mind in a biologically complex but fragile,
> finite, and unique organism; they obscure the tragedy implicit in
> the knowledge of that fragility, finiteness, and uniqueness. And
> where humans fail to see the inherent tragedy of conscious
> existence, they feel far less called on to do something about mini-
> mizing it, and may have less respect for the value of life. (p. 250)

Dying raises many emotions. In the case of our personal selves,
Kübler-Ross (1969) has drawn attention to different stages of
dying and exposed a previously hidden emotional progression:
denial and isolation, anger, bargaining, depression, and acceptance. If these stages are present generally as a kind of syndrome
determining institutional and collective response to catastrophes
such as the death of nature, we hypothesize that humanity is still
more or less at the first stage of engagement with the mortality of
other species, habitats, and ecologies. The killing of nature and
ecological decline resist comprehension because the effects are
so deeply personal, affecting what we eat, our leisure activities
. . . and, of course, much more. If at all possible, death and decline
are things to be denied or avoided.

Each of us faces death in many ways. If we "think local," our
personal experiences become relevant. Speaking personally, one
of us grew up in Australia among laminex, lino, Hills Hoists,
Victor lawn mowers, and other icons of modernity, which even
then seemed to prefigure the death of something; the other, in
Scotland where the end of distinctive Scottishness (monarch,
parliament, and culture) seemed to have been happening for
centuries but where a contemporary west coast, said to glow in
the dark because it housed so many nuclear warheads, promised
a potentially final solution to perennial crises of national identity.
For both of us, aspects of sex, drugs, and rock' n' roll; social justice;

feminism; counterculture; and alternative religions for a time took our minds off the ongoing decay of the planet of progress. That was before increasing satellite-generated knowledge of ecodegradation, Gulf war "ecocide,"[1] Chernobyl-style eco-catastrophes, AIDS, and a riskier world encompassing everything from financial Black Octobers to possible planetary destruction by passing meteorites (see Davies, 1994). Some sociologists now refer to a *risk society* (Beck, 1992).

Environmental consciousnesses raised in the wake of Rachael Carson's (1962) *Silent Spring* and the Club of Rome reports on impending systems collapse now face having to accept, and perhaps grieve over, a radically changed world. We share a great sadness for the loss of a natural world that seemed to be a birthright. Gone are the tropical forests, palm trees, and golden beaches as uncomplicated utopian safe havens—they are now all potential health hazards in an increasingly toxic environment. Formerly deified as the universal source of life, the sun has become such a high cancer risk that many Westerners take refuge in the artificial environments of the so-called global condominium: that highly mobile technospace that contains us all in some way. Indoor surfing marks one ultimate in containment and attempts to develop "teledildonics" or "erotic telepresence technology" enabling "sexual experiences with machines" (Rheingold, 1992, p. 345), another.

Because nature can be linked to everything, the ideological potential is vast: nature and health, nature and leisure, nature and escape, and nature and spirituality. Almost endless possibilities can circulate. In institutional practice, these semantic and ideological possibilities are limited. But for a corpse, nature maintains a vigorous afterlife as a signifier as complex as its previous semiotic history. For the natural sciences and for the social sciences, which are still ultimately dependent on empiricism and some kind of scientific methodology, nature still serves as a touchstone of reality. In advertising, images of pristine nature are still a dominant attraction, but images of unspoiled beauty are only one set of fantasies. Elsewhere, the authority of nature is in negotiation. We now have a culture of hypernature flourishing along highways from east coast Australia to west coast United

States. Big Bananas, Big Prawns, Big Potatoes, Big Oysters, and Big Cows blend in with natural theme parks and shopping mall simulations—not to mention zoos, oceanariums, natural museums, and all the other ways we preserve, protect, trade in, and relentlessly domesticate nature. In these promotional cultures, nature is symbolically reconstructed and transformed. In practice, genetic engineering and controlled breeding deliver us ever bigger and juicier foodstuffs. Bigger bananas are only a genetic snip away.

Killing nature, therefore, involves more than a physical or biological process, more than the unintended consequences of an industrial society. The death of nature is simultaneously a process of cultural construction in which images and ideas of a transformed nature circulate as part of an ecologically suspect hypernature: a realm driven by images and only limited by human imagination. The ecological effect of fantasies of control is profound, but the material impact of industrial pollution is no fantasy: Its effects are everywhere to be seen. What remains "is like the old nature in that it makes its points through what we think of as natural processes (rain, wind, heat), but it offers none of the consolations" (McKibben, 1990, p. 88). Instead, "each cubic metre of air; each square foot of soil, is stamped indelibly with our crude impression, our X" (McKibben, 1990, p. 89). The physical and biological are clearly marked by the X of human excess, this X is a material sign and an unfolding text. The simultaneous explosion of discourse about nature into fragmentary specialisms, coalescing cross-disciplinary activity and consumer culture, all of which are highly mediated, are part of the X we inscribe in the world. If nothing else, one might say that there is already an excess of meaning about nature in contemporary culture. As Baudrillard might say, nature has become obscene in its excess.

Such contemporary constructions of nature contribute to a syndrome that simultaneously enables and disables a confrontation with death. Because the death of nature is also our own death, it is doubly unthinkable. Death is public spectacle (the media) but personal taboo (the fear of death). Strong personal identification with a dying planet is not likely under these conditions. Nonetheless, the death of nature is an identity crisis, our own potential death, and an ongoing hedging of bets in a risk culture. How else do we explain the relative academic silence, Bette Midler's popular reincarnation of our dying goddess as comedy, and the West's sustained commitment to unsustainable ways of living as being business as usual?

As we approach the millennium, it is not only religious cults that are in the habit of announcing the end of the world. Media news has kept us in a state of high anxiety about the future for decades. It certainly has been, to use the titles of the Glasgow University Media Group, *Bad News* (1976), *More Bad News* (1980), and *Really Bad News* (1982). Perhaps cyberpunk is more on the money with its up-front preoccupation with death: "Conventional 'old-wave' science fiction of the Star Trek type has it all wrong: death, not space, is the final frontier of the imagination, beyond which only the most innovative adventurers boldly go" (McHale, 1992, p. 267). Charlene Spretnak (1991) puts current denials as the latest in a long history of "patriarchal culture's brutal and self-destructive divorce from the body—the Earth-body, the female body, the body of the mother" (p. 260). Outside of the West, from the perspective of a perennial philosophy such as Buddhism, the associated death denial has possibilities of being transformed through nondual awareness into a mere death of the ego—a deconstruction of "the separate, defended, illusion-ary self that prevents people from regaining transcendent aware-ness" (Zimmerman, 1994, p. 200). As heirs to a less meditative Enlightenment tradition and now the captives of a global news media, the West may instead be "precessing" (Baudrillard, 1983) into unsustainable ecological modes. We may be at risk of confusing ecological simulacra with the real thing—a declining biosphere.

One does not have to be a postmodernist to appreciate that the semiotics of nature are complicated by the simultaneous feedback and feed forward of the media. When politicians depend on the media for their knowledge of world affairs, we should expect some strange decisions created by the process of multiple feedback. In any case, nature has become an overloaded signifier, fragmented into specialisms as well as production, consumption, and promotional culture. Nature is dead as a singular order. It is now one of a multiplicity of orders marked by gravestones commemorating those other notables: God, Man, and the Author. These deaths may have been disturbing episodes in the history of ideas, but nature's death has yet to fully register as the incremental fulfillment of the Enlightenment dream of a nature that could be known, tamed, conquered, and brought into a fully commercial relationship with humanity. It has yet to register as our own demise. As well as emotional avoidance of death, another great escape is occurring—a collective and personal escape from ecological realism. As advertisers subliminally tell us with their utopian images: As long as consumption can be separated from the ecological consequences of production, profit margins will stay up.

DECADES OF DISCONTENT, CONSTELLATIONS OF KNOWLEDGE

The rise and rise of commodification has not gone unchallenged. As with much contemporary discourse about feminism and ecology, Merchant's personal watershed interweaves with other emancipatory movements of our time to confront racial equality, peace, and personal freedoms. The full benefits of these post-1960s new social movements have yet to affect social theory, as we argue in later chapters. For us, things certainly got wilder after the 1960s: For the hippies and other counterculturalists, nature blossomed as a part of us all. Nature was perceived as a realm of limitlessly unfolding potential and the resolution of illness and conflict. Spectacular in their celebration of life, the 1960s and early 1970s revitalized discourse about nature and the natural through radical challenges to prevailing orthodoxies informed by everything from lysergic acid through Eastern religion and occultism, to new science (see, e.g., Berman, 1984; Roszak, 1969, 1975; Toulmin, 1982b; Watts, 1973, and our more extended treatment in Chapter 4). This great vortex of cultural differences established a new sensitivity to the integrity of the planet and opposed "the bias against nature in western religion" (Worster, 1985, p. 58) with pagan and non-Western spiritualities of nature. Nature was resocialized, albeit tenuously, and installed in popular culture as something that could meaningfully qualify all the important things in life: health, food, healing, medicine— even lifestyle itself. Nature and culture achieved considerable reconciliation in celebrations forgotten since the ascendancy of the Scientific Revolution.

The joy of throwing out that very conservative Cartesian-New-tonian orthodoxy, along with its mind-body and culture-nature splits, was celebrated widely. At the same time, even the anar-chistic-pagan eclecticism of hippy culture stayed centered on a very traditional set of assumptions about nature, even if couched in so-called New Age terms. Spaces for women still tended to cluster around sex, nurture, domesticity, and reproduction: Being closer to nature never was an antidote for sexism. Neverthe-less, nature was still simultaneously present in all the different declensions defined by cultural historians. Merchant has charted the shift in controlling imagery from respect for an organic female earth to domination of earth as mechanistic inert matter explica-ble in terms of physics and chemistry. Others have recorded similar shifts in cultures in European history when nature, perceived as spirits or nature gods, gave way to conceptions of nature as singular, abstract, and personified. Williams (1980) followed nature's move from Goddess to Divine Mother, then to God the Father of the monotheistic religions, and on to neo-Darwinian concepts. These shifts of meaning have continued. To the strata of codified European conceptualizations described by Williams and others, the 1960s' counterculture inserted multicultural layers from Eastern religions, mysticism, occultism, and innu-merable New Age perspectives.

In a multicultural postmodernity, any contemporary unity of nature exists more as a mythological theme than an epistemo-logical and methodological principle. Nature is dispersed and divided in complex discursive fields, in disciplines, in technologi-cal practices, and in everyday activities. Despite the overwhelm-ing evidence that nature is not the unitary phenomenon that

Alexander Wilson's (1992) title, *The Culture of Nature*, might imply, discursive colonizing persists. In North America, for example, Wilson's book demonstrates, in effect, a dominant "culture of nature" driven by the imperatives of the development of capitalism. Such common senses of nature would appear to be strongly commodified and extend well beyond Canada and the United States. Commodification entails market orientation, with profit as the bottom line, and is part of an increasingly globalized capitalism. These developments are in tension with ecologically sustainable values and lifestyles. Furthermore, the somewhat restricted visibility of the toxic downside of this culture in the West depends heavily on an asymmetric distribution. Although not totally invisible, the hidden hand of the market allocates a disproportionate amount of polluted eco-fallout to the third world and sections of Western cities heavily populated by the rising urban underclass and disadvantaged ethnic groups.

In the 1990s, negative images of nature diminish into the euphoria of ecotourism and the hypernature of artificial simulations as just one set of possibilities among a number of potentially profitable virtual environments. The fact that many have labored mightily in the services of planetary ecology has not delivered us from our difficulties in maintaining a nature with safe air to breathe, clean water to drink, and uncontaminated food to eat. Although that ecological nature has not been entirely excluded from the discourses that matter, it has been marginalized as "other" in the cultural landscapes of the capitalist text. For this to continue, whole constellations of meaning and practice have been, and continue to be, excluded, marginalized, or both. In sociology and communication and cultural studies, we may help to reshape the construction of earth's realities, but we are simultaneously configured by a long history of cultural practice and strong institutional forces. Despite the fact that we have access to many so-called objective factors that go into the creation of a scenario of ecological decline, we know very little about how particular institutionalized sites, such as the sciences, social sciences, and humanities, participate in the ongoing death of biospheric nature in a promotional culture.

NOTE

1. Although guiltier than most in coining eco-prefixed terminology, we find this usage damagingly ambiguous in that it encompasses both ecological suicide and ecological murder and can confuse agency. It is also important not to add eco-crimes to the demonization of Saddam Hussein because nearly all modern wars are wars against the environment, and the forces of the New World Order were not particularly eco-sensitive (see Ross, 1994).

2

Ecological Exclusions

Mapping Disciplinary Change

Academic disciplines and their institutionalized processes constitute the often unstated ground of intellectual work. The possibilities of professional discourse take shape within these constrained spaces, and the present work is no exception. This book has been framed within the spaces of academic disciplines—Australian social sciences and humanities and our industrial institutional locations provide the broad local context for our work. From any ecological position, these are restricted spaces, and our challenge has been that of finding greener pathways, often against the tide of established practices.

Our professional activities and interests lie across the fields of communication and cultural studies and sociology. This is where we teach and find our primary intellectual orientations. In their exclusion and marginalization of ecological interests, these fields illustrate our general argument about the constraints of disciplinary analyses. Nonetheless, our choice of focus reflects our particular disciplinary locations rather than our nomination of these fields as paradigmatic.

This chapter builds on Chapter 1 to address the silences and exclusions in academic disciplines that allow the death of nature to occur in relative silence. Our efforts to introduce ecological themes to subjects and curricula have compelled us to confront the limitations of our discursive locations and those of the humanities and social sciences generally. From our interdisciplinary work, the idea that interdisciplinarians are particularly focused on mapping their contextual fields emerged as a useful metaphor for thinking about the creation of new discursive spaces. We start by taking a few soundings from institutional divides and go on to develop the idea of *mapping* as a methodology.

We reaffirm poststructuralism's interest in exclusionary processes in text and society by looking at institutional and cultural constraints and the exclusions they impose. We do so less to define another position than to review a range of positions and to take our bearings amid a proliferation of discourse in the social sciences and humanities. We see ourselves as mappers of cultural diversity and collaborators in the creation of new spaces for the articulation of ecological concerns. We see our efforts to map disciplinary change as part of a proliferation of maps from all disciplines and mass media. In this, we are part of the reflexivity of modernity and postmodernity. These processes also clearly indicate that many paradigms are in a state of change and confusion. Ecological crisis is undermining modernity and stimulating broad interest in change, including ideas about change.

INSTITUTIONAL CONSTRAINT

Although environmental concern has taken root in university cultures, these cultures are still strongly divided along traditional lines that go back through medieval scholasticism to the Greek academy. There is a constant pressure for new interests to institutionalize in traditional intellectual forms. New disciplines and multidisciplinary activities have to win their ecological niches among serious competition. The establishment of environmental science as a discipline, for example, occurs in symbiosis with physics, chemistry, biology, and all the traditional hard sciences. In general, the establishment of interdisciplinary units with ecological mandates does not guarantee that ecology will be studied in an interdisciplinary fashion. Environmental research in this paradigm is often more determined by the quest for funding than by cross-disciplinary enthusiasm. From commercially based professional cultures to the universities that support them, the same old science-versus-nonscience hierarchy still defines the agenda—often marginalizing the humanities and social sciences. The dominant research cultures in Australian universities are still resolutely modern in their regard for the power and privilege of science and technology. The cutting edge of academic research is today a high technology edge. From the heartlands of Cartesian-Newtonian rationalism—pure mathematics—to the intellectual turmoil of poststructuralism and postmodernism, new communication technologies are creating major change in the methods, objects, and media of research. Computers have revolutionized academic production, office work, and scholarly communication generally. Today, much of the office is in cyberspace.

Euphoric as our present encounters with the expanding Internet may be, there is a worrisome social obsession and fatal attraction that drives the process of modern technological innovation. This is the now fairly universal desire to be carried away by any available means—in contemporary terms, the technological determinism identified by sociologists of technology (McKenzie & Wajcman, 1985; Winner, 1977) and the associated desire for seduction (Baudrillard, 1990), sexual power (Easlea, 1983), and the thrill of the chase. The development of the nuclear industry, for instance, with its extraordinarily short-term and decontextualized horizons of ecological meaning, has depended on the seductiveness of new technology and the phallocentric allure of control over the universe's fundamental energies. The same blindly optimistic appreciation of technology and progress underpins the rapid entry of computers into daily life. The sweetness of technological innovation, the strange beauty of techno-landscapes, and all the aesthetics of seduction and conquest surround the computer as an obscure object of desire (Galvin, 1995).

Newby (1991) and Redclift and Benton (1994) have argued that social scientists must challenge the technological determinism that has dominated environmental debate and policy formulation. The same should be said for those working in the humanities and interdisciplinary fields, such as communication and cultural studies—fields where new communications technologies are both the means and ends of analysis and its legitimation. In any analysis, however, ecological problems are bigger than single disciplines and current interdisciplinary mixes. This raises one of our central themes: To what extent can ecological concern become interdisciplinary, in theory and practice, such that crosscutting discourse can green academic cultures?

There are some signs that academic cultures are becoming more ecologically aware and redirecting energy toward interdisciplinary and ecological decline. The number of specialist publications dealing with ecological issues, for example, has flourished as part of the institutionalization of ecologically focused research in traditional discipline-based activity, in newer disciplines, and in cross-disciplinary activity (e.g., environmental studies and women's studies). Environmental research institutes have also been created in universities and consultancies arranged with business and government. Although these are all signs of a greening of academic culture, we should also note that there are already major institutional constraints in place. Even if the immediate subject matter of disciplines changes as they attempt to follow new cultural fashions and attempt to become creatively involved in crisis management, the old dualistic social processes and intellectual traditions that sustain them remain largely intact. For instance, although many of the ideas contained in the decentering social movements of environmentalism and feminism (and Marxism before them) appear to contain radical implications for disciplinary processes, the humanities and social sciences in Australia have managed to accommodate these potentials for subversion and transgression within established disciplinary frameworks. Furthermore, the politics of disciplinary formation and university funding remain hierarchical, male dominated, and respectful of tradition—just like the processes of the major political parties and government bureaucracies.

Any hopes for the greening of academic cultures needs therefore to take account of the necessarily conservative nature of institutional processes and the time it takes to create new structures and ways of thinking. In practice, the themes of academe may appear greener as disciplines seek to take advantage of new priority areas, but the greening of academic culture is differentiated, or variegated, across a range of institutional locations and processes. We cannot assume it to be a homogeneous process; nor should we assume that all academic cultures are open to the cultivation of ecological themes. Interdisciplinary processes may draw differences together and eventually create new specialisms, but this need not occur in a particularly reflexive or ordered manner. Academics, too, are driven by the logic of funding markets and their own passions: They are mobilized by crises; and they work under the contested sign of postmodernity.

Disciplines are by their nature exclusionary. They are part of a division of nature and the universe into different domains and activities, and they create their own discursive spaces. There is a considerable tension involved in this institutionalized partitioning of analytical space and in the negotiation of which constituency can speak for particular social groups, animal species, or ecologies. There is therefore a desire in many academics for both a looser partitioning of disciplines and a reassessment of their foundational rights. There is much support for the idea of a more open-textured debate about ecology and our possible futures.

POSTMODERN CHAOS?

Superficially, the disciplinary ferment we are experiencing in Australia might seem somewhat chaotic. If the postmodern premises of declining metanarratives, rising relativism, multiple identities, intertextuality, and complex referentiality are (as we argue in later chapters) correct, it will not be easy to sustain the notion that ideas or methodologies have a natural home or location in one particular discipline. Nor can we confidently predict what texts will be taken up in particular disciplines. The ideas generated by texts and images are today highly mobile and find relevance in new and sometimes surprising ways. Social theory, for example, now cuts across many disciplines and is no longer something that belongs to sociologists. The same could be said of semiotics and semioticians and Chaos theory and mathematicians. This loosening of established structures is fertile ground for interdisciplinarity and other transgressions, such as the intrusion of ecological concern into previously unreceptive disciplinary processes.

In this changing environment, the idea of chaos is gaining currency as a kind of postmodern emblem. As the world speeds up along infobahns and continuously adjusts to new technologies, as global politics emerges as a frighteningly unpredictable field, and as global ecology declines, an idea like chaos resonates with the unpredictability of change. There is a new spin to the word in the late 20th century, however. The classical dichotomy of order and chaos becomes transgressed in the chaos of late 20th-century mathematics and computer programming. Chaos theory as it emerges in these discourses is not about chaos in its colloquial sense of being the opposite of order. We now see subtle order in the random fluctuations of large systems, a fractal order (Gleick, 1987; Lauwerier, 1991). This is a non-Cartesian-Newtonian and unpredictable order and one that demonstrates surprising isomorphism with natural forms, blurring distinctions between science and art, semiosphere and biosphere.

Curiously, the search for graphic techniques of rendering complex data meaningful has generated lifelike forms on the plane of complex numbers. Self-powered complex numbers can be made to generate endlessly unpredictable mappings of the complex plane. Fractal landscapes, Mandelbrot's monsters, and Pickover's biomorphs are the better-known examples.[1] About biomorphs, Pickover says, in some sense, the mathematical creatures exist. The objects inhabit the complex plane, though they resemble microscopic organisms that we could easily imagine flourishing in a drop of water (Dewdney, 1989). In our view, the new mappings of Chaos theory offer new possibilities for the analysis of disorder and fluctuations in texts and society. They may serve to calm some fears about the nihilistic and hopelessly relativistic chaos that new science and postmodernity appear to represent. New mappings provide new metaphors and new analytical possibilities, but discourse usually continues in traditional ways also. Chaos speaks to order, relativism speaks to certainty, and nihilism speaks to connection as postmodernism unfolds. Katherine Hayles (1989), for example, has argued that there are parallels between deconstruction and mathmaticians' Chaos theory (which is distinct from common sense usage of "chaos"); McKie and Bennett (1992) have argued that Chaos theory is relevant to communication and cultural studies. There is even strong interest in the chaotic fluctuations of stock markets (Gleick, 1987).

The emergence of new fields, such as Chaos theory, certainly encourages speculation about the general causes and contexts of new ideas. Sociologists of knowledge would suggest that there are always determinate connections between culture and society. As far back as Marx's classic base-superstructure model, it has been understood that new ideas and new paradigms reflect something about the social context of their formation. Cultures encode the circumstances of their production. They express worldviews (see Berger & Luckmann, 1972; Remmling, 1973). Under conditions of rapid and revolutionary social and cultural change, it may therefore not be surprising that Chaos theory should emerge as a new idea about order—it resonates with perceptions of risk, catastrophe, and disorder. A contemporary Max Weber might speculate that there is an emerging elective affinity between doctrines of chaos, uncertainty, and risk and the emerging social forms of postmodernity. The metaphoric possibilities of chaos need, however, to be distinguished from the technological infrastructure that enables its graphic representation and practical application. Viewed as a technological artifact, a techno-space, this chaos is actually part of the dynamics of large systems and a product of highly systematic processes. As the work of Chaos mathematicians so clearly demonstrates, there are algorithms and logic machines at work in the seeing. Chaos is only revealed after a great deal of number crunching and the mediation of many screens and machines. On this basis, it would appear that order and chaos (or disorder) are mutually implicated; they are a semantic dichotomy that now appears to be blurring. There is order in chaos and random fluctuation, which takes us beyond relativity theory and quantum mechanics into new scientific paradigms and whole new worlds of metaphoric possibility. What if disciplines bifurcated as butterflies flapped in the upper echelons of administration? What if whole semantic structures were capable of transformation by the excessive repetition of the same idea?

As semiotics, institutional analysis, social theory, and ideas like chaos are brought to bear on the many worlds and multiple realities contained in an ecology, a highly complex field unfolds. This complexity is a condition of postmodernity and a possibility for postmodernism—an articulation of biosphere and semiosphere together. This complexity provides an interface between semiotics, institutional analysis, and the many worlds we now see revealed under conditions of postmodernity. In this framing, the coexistence of real worlds, imaginary worlds, hyperreality, and now chaotic worlds with a fractal order, is ecologically resonant. Here we draw on the metaphoric possibilities of this complexity, and in our discursive mappings, try to reveal ecological implications and possibilities—we have an interest in the ecology of discourse as well as in the location of ecology in discourse. We seek to reveal the biosphere and the semiosphere as a complex interconnection involving communication, interaction, production, consumption, and discourse.

The articulation of ecological ideas in new contexts is critical for the success of this project. We might start with the idea of ecology itself and note that the postulation of many coexistent worlds is a basic premise of all ecocentric worldviews. Biospherically speaking, an ecology is a complex balance of different life forms and their habitats. The differences are critical and a measure of an ecology's health. We might also extend this principle to discourse and speak of the ecology of discourse and the extent to which difference is articulated. We might also look to processes of evolution and selection at work and the way in which different networks territorialize space and fold back in on themselves. The metaphoric possibilities are again endless.

TAKING BEARINGS

Faced with this complexity, we can only make a modest beginning to the task of decoding the ecological signs of postmodernity. To begin with, we need some methodological guidelines that avoid the unreflexive rearticulation of the same old dualisms. In this chapter, we would suggest that the apparently simple idea of mapping can become a suitably postmodern methodology for introducing a broader discussion of ecological considerations. If we start with some appreciation of postmodern ideas about complexity as well as preserving a poststructural interest in dualisms and exclusions, there is a space for what we would call an *ecoculturalist postmodernism* that maps cultural change in a more reflexive and relativistic mode than Cartesian-Newtonian cartography.

The intrusion of new considerations such as ecology and gender into the structures of disciplinary relevance has already created considerable complexity. As multiplicity and complexity dissolve the solidity of worlds taken for granted, is it still even possible to think of mapping as a reliable procedure for finding one's way around in unknown spaces, places, and fields? If there is no unmediated correspondence between representation and reality and no acceptance of a correspondence theory of truth, then maps need to be considered as interpretations that are relativized by their sociocultural contexts. Maps create their own spaces and also reproduce structures, processes, and interests. Maps also change, and in today's context of complexity, risk, and chaos, we need to look at maps and signs as containing multiple possibilities. We need to look for absences as well as presences, exclusions as well as inclusions, and we need to return to the semantic algorithms that so strongly determine the possibilities of what can be expressed—that is, the dominant dualisms of patriarchal Cartesian-Newtonian logic.

Processes of exclusion and marginalization, and their mapping, are particularly important in disciplinary development and hybridization—their margins and edges define frames, cores, and zones of exclusion. These are critical considerations because processes of disciplinary development and change are contested, particularly in times of low and zero growth in universities, where new developments come at the expense of prior developments and tend to be resisted by the status quo. This forced conservatism creates a risky climate for those interested in new developments—such as communication studies, cultural studies, environmental studies, and women's studies—where there may not be secure institutional support. It becomes particularly important to know the reasons for what's in and what's out and to be able to negotiate the maze of possibilities presented as disciplines unfold. Processes of closure create risks for those interested in disciplinary innovation. They frame texts, institutions, and the goals of social action. They are a point of origin for lines of flight and nomadic excursions.[2] Their points of application may be loosely chaotic, but the logic of closures is ordered by dualisms and the priorities of host institutions, their power brokers, government policies, and market pressures.

These processes do not present fields of possibility that are entirely random and untraceable. There is an interface between semiotics, institutional analysis, and the many worlds we now see revealed under conditions of postmodernity. The coexistence of real worlds, imaginary worlds, hyperreality, and now chaotic worlds (with a fractal order), is suggestive of a postmodern ecology. In this shift, humanity's ecological place is relativized by the blurring of modernism's dominant dualisms—nature-culture, mind-matter, male-female, reason-emotion, and so forth. Human exposure to the many different worlds in ecologies is a critical shifting toward ecocentrism. This is a process in which many of the divides between disciplines need to be crossed. We need new and bigger maps.

EVERYBODY'S MAPPING

Indeed, the only way most academics can survive in an explosion of cultural diversity and crosscutting fields is to ever chart the surrounding cultural environment for relevance and difference. The sheer quantity and conceptual density of information available through all media has never been so great. With the continuing information explosion driven by new communication technologies, academics and intellectuals are forced increasingly to become mappers of cultural differences and intellectual terrains. There are ever-increasing sorting and classification processes that now accompany academic work. More and more, this processing of information is mediated by electronic databases and computer-generated searching processes. These complex codings and decodings are, as ever, human constructions but are now frequently driven by networked systems and machine algorithms. In the end, we are all forced to be mappers of complexity.

Intellectual cartography is a routine task of academics. Map making, map reading, map revising, and perhaps even map burning, are all part of daily routine. Mapping is basic to the territorialization of academic space. Teaching, research, administration, and the induction of neophytes necessarily involve the routine demarcation of territories and the policing of boundaries. Mapping (or *cultural mapping*, as we develop the term) is, however, an attempt to develop a routine process into a reflexive methodology. This is critical mapping rather than commonsense mapping. The idea is a development of Jameson's (1988) suggestion of a cognitive mapping and, in critical processes, relativizes disciplines by juxtaposing their differences. This focus exposes foundational dualisms that create zones of exclusion and the structured spaces in which interdisciplinarity arises as an antidote to artificial constraint. The construction of such global perspectives challenges the hierarchization of intellectual territories—because, in addressing a system, or an ecology, individual differences are relativized as part of an emergent whole, provisional as that may be.

The mapping of difference and disciplinary development is subject to the same methodological constraints as social science research which attempts to describe cultural fields. In all social science research the primary problem is differentiating between map and territory and ensuring that significant phenomena are not ignored or distorted by the researcher's bias. At the same time, it is generally agreed that research and writing can never be neutral. The best resolution of this dilemma is a degree of reflexive intellectual movement—that is, the cultivation of different perspectives and theoretical and methodological options. We need multiple maps because any maps, models, or representation can only be provisional—Heisenberg's uncertainty principle has a macroscopic analogue here: The observer and the observed define an interactive system. The observed and reality encode the processes of their observation. In a similar vein, the poststructuralists Diprose and Ferrell (1991) write that the political reality of the changing map of the world, its allegiances, exclusions, and oppression, is testament to cartography as a relevant metaphor. Mapping as representation is inextricably caught up in the material production of what it represents.

The idea of mapping clearly has many recent disciplinary precedents. These range from classical sociology of knowledge, through Thomas Kuhn's (1962) work on paradigms in the history of science and the idea of cognitive institutionalization in the sociology of science (Jagtenberg, 1983; Whitley, 1974), to Foucault's archaeology and genealogy, to Fredric Jameson's appropriation of the term *cognitive mapping* from human geography, and our own recent work in mapping Australian social sciences as four dimensional social space. Indeed, mapping has a history relevant to any reconfiguring of cultural studies, communications studies, and the social sciences in general. Mapping has become far more than a cartographic metaphor. Territorial conquest, surveillance, bureaucratic control, and market manipulation are now understood to be part of modern map making. Processes of social control conspire to regulate and order our maps, and create the likelihood that our maps contain missing continents and hidden dimensions.

THE EVOLUTION OF MAPPING

Mapping has been a recurrent theme and metaphor in poststructural and postmodern analysis. As the Diprose and Ferrell (1991) title, *Cartographies: Poststructuralism and the Mapping of Bodies and Spaces*, suggests, new paradigms and theories provide possibilities for new mappings. Texts, discourses, language, and culture can generally all be construed as maps by which we find our way around in life and through which social power is encoded, regulated, and reproduced. Even the body can be seen as a map—cultural practices are inscribed onto and into the human body. Tattooing, ritual scarring, body piercing, body building, dieting, and exercising are effectively a mapping of cultures and subcultures. They produce cultural icons that circulate in the media. Dietary cultures become part of our bodies, which in turn can be read as a mapping of social practices.

This interest in maps and mapping in cultural studies and social theory has arisen, we think, as a corrective for the widely observed suppression of space and privileging of time in social theory (Soja, 1989). In the postmodern era, our cultural languages are dominated by categories of space rather than time. Docker's summary of Fredric Jameson's (1984) well-known reaction to the lobby of Portman's Bonaventure Hotel in Los Angeles captures the typical spatial angst of critics of postmodernism:

> Here you experience a feeling of packed emptiness, a bewildering immersion in a kind of postmodern hyperspace, immersed up to your eyes and your body. In such a state of bewilderment and immersion—presumed by Jameson to be experienced by everyone there—you lose a sense of distance that enables perception and perspective. The result is that the individual human body can no longer map its position in a mappable external world, and such forced incapacity is symbolic of the wider incapacity of our minds to map the great global multinational communicational networks of the postmodern world. (Docker, 1994, p. 118)

Recent writing in cultural studies continues to emphasize spatiality. For instance in referring to music, Jody Berland (1992) reminds us that "in theoretical terms, we need to situate cultural forms within the production and reproduction of capitalist spatiality. How does one produce the other: the song, the car, the radio station, the road, the radio, the town, the listener?" (p. 39). Quoting David Harvey, Berland also reminds us of the impermanence of capitalism in which there is a perpetual struggle in which capital builds a physical landscape appropriate to its own condition at a particular moment in time, only to have to destroy it, usually in the course of crises, at a subsequent point in time. (p. 45)

Donna Haraway's (1992b) essay, "The Promises of Monsters," develops the idea of spatiality with her use of maps as generative machines in a brilliantly creative analysis. She explores newly emerging techno-spaces and their inscription as ecological, as gendered, and as also marked by class and ethnicity. Her methodology is playful: She invents "a little time machine that also functions as a map, an artificial device that generates meaning very noisily: A. J. Griemas's infamous semiotic square" (p. 304). Haraway is concerned here to apply "a structuralist engine to a modern [sic] purpose," a project in which she allies herself with Bruno Latour, a sociologist of science. The spaces she generates, and the objects she finds in them, are totally artifactual, nothing "natural" here—just "monsters" like imaginary cyborgs and other social constructions. Nature, according to Haraway, is not a physical space, it is a topos, "a place, in the sense of a rhetorians place or topic for consideration of common themes; nature is, strictly, a commonplace" (p. 296). Whatever nature's ontology is deemed to be, Haraway's paper demonstrates that theoretical analysis can never exhaust ecological devastation, the injustices of inequalities, gender oppression, and racism. There are promises and challenges in all four quarters. In Haraway's work, these spaces are not completely decentered, however: They rotate around the binary opposites in language and the possibilities of Griemas's square; they are intelligible in the frameworks of cultural studies, feminism, and science studies; they are interdisciplinary spaces, and they can be creatively mapped.

COGNITIVE MAPPING

The clearest exposition of mapping as a methodology comes, however, from Fredric Jameson (1988) and his paper, *Cognitive Mapping.* As might be expected from a contribution to a volume dedicated to the project of a unified Marxist cultural studies, Jameson's work is subverted by its own logic: its privileging of concepts, its silences and exclusions. Jameson's popularization of the term *cognitive mapping* derives from his efforts to develop a "post-Althusserian, post-Marxism" (p. 354). Jameson introduces the term in various ways: as a "spatial analysis" of culture (p. 348), as "a slogan" (p. 353), as "a pretext for an essay" (p. 356), as "an aesthetic" (p. 353), and as a methodology. About its origins he says,

> I understand this concept as something of a synthesis between Althusser and Kevin Lynch—a formulation that, to be sure, does not tell you much unless you know that Lynch is the author of a classic work, *The Image of the City,* which in its turn spawned the whole low-level sub discipline that today takes the phrase "cognitive mapping" as its own designation. Lynch's problematic remains locked within the limits of phenomenology. . . . Lynch suggests that urban alienation is directly proportional to the mental unmappability of local cityscapes. (Jameson, 1988, p. 353)

In Jameson's (1988) project, cognitive mapping becomes "an integral part of any socialist political project" (p. 353). Cognitive mapping is to be part of a social mapping that can analyze the totality of class relations "on a global (or should I say multinational) scale" (p. 353). This project does appear to confuse means and ends and subjugates methodology to the goal of socialism. As John Docker (1994) reminds us, Jameson remains a Marxist with more sympathy for modernism than postmodernism (p. 116). Today, this is a problematic location, and we seek to define mapping as a more reflexive and less value-laden project. Mapping and the pursuit of any global view needs to be able to accommodate cultural change and difference as part of the mapping strategy. We also need to know what is excluded and why.

As we develop the idea, mapping strategies begin from the concept of discourse rather than any particular concept of social structure, or gender, or ecology. Because dominant concepts shape all discourse, ideas such as value neutrality and objectivity only exist as ideals that may guide practice. Maps can never be fully trusted—they change and may distort, deceive, and simulate. But they register a level of consensus, and we use them routinely. The sense of mapping we favor derives more from an interest in interdisciplinarity and crosscutting analysis than the resurrection of socialism. Nonetheless, our ideas about mapping have been influenced by contemporary political writing. Our development of the idea of cultural mapping takes particular impetus from feminist analysis of textual politics—the analyses of exclusions and marginalization by Beverly Thiele (1986) and Val Plumwood (1993) have been strongly influential on our work. But today's map makers may also benefit from more biospherically and culturally reflexive methods of mapping. In this last shift, we might finally come to revitalizing our species-centrism.

Jameson's idea of cognitive mapping is provocative because it opens up general issues about objectivity, referentiality, relativism, and reflexivity—issues that have been perennially interesting as part of the discourses of social science methodology, phenomenology, sociology of knowledge, critical sociology, and more recently feminism, poststructuralism, and postmodernism. These issues and paradigms challenge any separation of text and society, as has occurred in the notorious textualism of much discourse analysis. We go on to challenge textualism in Chapter 3, where we introduce a more biographically centered postmodernism. As we argue, the postmodern issues of reflexivity, referentiality, and relativism have become freshly prominent in the context of a communication revolution. The explosion in scope of publicly accessible texts and images has provided new conditions for the interpenetration of semiosphere and biosphere.

Cognitive mapping is particularly interesting because of its potential to resurrect methodological debate about the role different perspectives play in the framing of discourse and taken-for-granted realities. In this questioning, all disciplines need to be placed in the context of political and cultural difference and a range of methodologies. This is appropriate because the question of the most appropriate theory and methodology with which to know the world is often strongly contested in disciplines—and the contest is never so fierce as during revolutionary times in paradigm development (Kuhn, 1962). Although the changes being experienced in the humanities and social sciences may not be fully revolutionary in the Kuhnian sense, we argue that the social sciences and humanities are in a state of regular crisis and paradigm change and that they are no longer unitary formations. The impacts of increased awareness of class, gender, race, and now ecological crisis have in rough succession decentered these fields. Most recently, the rise of feminism, poststructuralism, and postmodernism have had profound effects on the shape of the contemporary social sciences and humanities and on levels of confidence it is possible to have about traditional methodologies. What this amounts to is that most of the social sciences and humanities are now even less able to specify their own fields and best methodologies as coherently as the less reflexive fields of the natural sciences.

CULTURAL MAPPING

In the light of all these considerations, we prefer the term *cultural mapping* to signal a broadening of Jameson's idea. Jameson's formulation of mapping is too limited for fields oriented to multiple realities and differences. If Jameson was facing ontological spinout because of the lobby of a busy hotel, we wonder what he makes of the Internet! Finally, Jameson's use of the word *cognitive* is difficult to sustain because of the recognition that dualistic formations, such as society-culture, reason-emotion, and mind-matter, need to be transgressed if difference is to be cultivated rather than repressed. The word *cognitive* has an uncomfortable rationalistic bias, given the breadth of Jameson's concerns.[3]

Jameson's thinking is resonant with the critical theorist Adorno, who was also interested in global, post-Marxist, multidimensional analysis. There is a strong precedent in the work of Adorno for the kind of multidimensional formulation we are exploring. His thoughts on the relationship between psychology and sociology, for instance, raise the problematic of a dialectical global analysis in a way that does not totalize the whole and that does not lose sense of the whole because it is fissured and fragmented. Martin Jay (1984) has captured Adorno's position well:

[Adorno] argued that the fissures and contradictions of the real world meant that no harmoniously conceived methodology could be adequate to its object. Thus, although empirical techniques could register certain limited truths about, say, the reactions of listeners to certain kinds of music; they could never reveal the underlying implications of the music itself. The whole may be the "untrue," but it was still necessary to combine approaches to grasp its shattered dimensions. The combination should not be that of a smoothly unified mediation of these approaches, but rather that of a force field or constellation which registered the unresolved tensions behind the facade of harmony. (p. 50)

The key intellectual context of that globalizing methodology, we might note, was the impending controversy about positivism and phenomenology (see, e.g., Bryant, 1985). This contextual difference aside, Adorno's desire for a "constellation which registered unresolved tensions" remains metaphorically relevant. In the social sciences and humanities, all documents can be seen to reveal unresolved tensions because any facade of harmony has long since disappeared in media portrayals of war, poverty, and social inequality, not to mention ecological devastation.

More recently, the critical sociologists Best and Kellner (1991) have suggested the idea of a *multidimensional critical theory* that is dialectical and nonreductive, institutionally focused, and concerned with mediations and interconnections. This is, in fact, a general concern of much Australian social science. Best and Kellner, however, are focused on an analysis of capitalism where commodification, reification, and fetishism are the noteworthy features. And indeed, these are noteworthy features—but we need to extend the multidimensionality of this analytical domain. Ecology is still other to their discourses.

Fortunately, the issues of textual politics have become more widely appreciated with the advent of poststructuralism and postmodernism in academic cultures. In this wave of influence, the writings of Foucault, Derrida, and poststructuralists have particularly encouraged academics to look at their work as being about the manipulation and construction of texts. For us, this also raises questions about the positioning of self and others. Exclusion, marginalization, and the endless deferral of meaning impose a necessary reflexivity about authorship. Texts and disciplines are collectivities, they are institutional (cf. Weber, 1987). They are maps in the sense of recording traces of all these processes and absences. Rather than dissolving authorship or recording the death of the author in endless textuality (Barthes, 1977), we prefer to preserve a certain sense of authorship (or textual agency), with the idea that authorship is a process of mapping or finding one's way in a symbolic world. We intend cultural mapping to be a postmodern methodology directed toward the creation of new discursive spaces and the preservation of an embodied authorship. The term signifies a concern to record difference, reflexivity, complex referentiality, relativism, and the endless intertextuality of authorship.

THE MAPPING OF FOUR DIMENSIONAL SOCIAL SPACE

There can be no precise rules for the processes of cultural mapping. In the production of text books, for instance, the process of interaction between authors, editors, and the marketplace is just as much guided by the serendipity of everyday life and the rhizomic process of network growth as it is by the authority of traditions and the interventions of academic gatekeepers. As an example of the mapping that occurs in the production of foundation study textbooks, we can provide some observations about the production of *Four Dimensional Social Space* (Jagtenberg & D'Alton, 1992), which attempts to map Australian social sciences along the dimensions of class, gender, ethnicity, and nature-environment. The idea of mapping is particularly germane here to the kinds of tasks involved in that kind of survey work and in the devising of curricula generally.

The mapping that occurs in a large edited text is both a descriptive and a reconstructive process. Through discussion and interaction with the book's users and critics, the representation of academic fields changes to reflect the needs of the market and other factors. The production of such a text includes feedback gained from interaction, communication, and debate about relevance. In our case, it needs to be sensitive to processes of textual exclusion and manipulation. The exclusion of nature and the environment from Australian social sciences was one of our primary concerns in *Four Dimensional Social Space*. In our survey of Australian social sciences, class, gender, and ethnicity emerged as dominant categories or thematic concerns reflecting the fact that these concepts are central structures and processes, or dimensions, of analysis, that provided considerable intellectual coherence as well as professional and cultural identity. The three categories signify major structural divisions in society and now fairly universally inform the conceptual basis for social science concerns. As demonstrated in *Four Dimensional Social Space*, Australian sociology can be mapped using these dimensions. One might speculate that, insofar as the humanities and social sciences remain concerned with social justice, social inequality, emancipation, and even progress, discourse will continue to take shape within a space structured by the social relations of class, gender, and ethnicity—a space structured, we might say, by a holy trinity of inequality.

These three categories define major boundaries for the kind of vision generated within disciplines such as sociology. It has to be said that this vision is not strongly ecological. The environment tends to remain sequestered in specialisms such as the sociology of agriculture and rural sociology and has only recently registered as a more general theoretical or substantive cultural interest. Although an ecological sociology is now emerging with the work of Redclift and Benton (1994), Martell (1994), and others, these writers all start by acknowledging the ecological silence in sociology and social theory from which they start. This silence extends across many of the humanities and social sciences. There is an uneasy tension between nature and culture in the institutionalization of the humanities and social sciences. Social sciences are dominantly three dimensional and other to the concerns of the natural sciences and new sciences, such as environmental science.

THREE DIMENSIONAL
SOCIAL SPACES

These three dimensions also permeate the field of communication studies as ontology and discourse. Class, gender, and ethnicity have come to define social structures and types of experience. They are a premise of most social science analysis and are absorbed into our models of communication. For instance, the semiotic school of communication studies that Fiske (1990) identifies presupposes a society structured by class, gender, and ethnicity. Semiotic analysis generally is a form of social analysis that seeks to articulate signs as a part of social life. Meanings are constructed socially and sustained in social relations and communication processes. The other major approach that Fiske identifies, the process school with its transmission model of communication, is arguably flawed, precisely because, as he and others have argued, it decontextualizes these considerations—see, for example, Kress (1988), Palmer (1994), and O'Sullivan et al. (1994). Without argument, social issues, culture, and communication need to be considered in the context of class, gender, and ethnicity; but these structural considerations do not exhaust the domain of the social. As suggested earlier, nature-environment-ecology provide a fourth dimension—another major perspective for the analysis of social space, culture, and communication.

This new dimension is, however, a challenge to the humanities and social sciences, whose current practices reflect classical disciplinary assumptions. This is even true where the poststructural and postmodern turns have been most strongly registered. Semiotics and sociology, for instance, both struggle to provide a space for ecological issues and ecological theory because their intellectual origins are so grounded in a logic of two cultures. In this dualistic paradigm, the environment is objectively out there and knowable through the research of biologists, ecologists, and other scientists. On the other side, the humanities and social sciences study far less tangible subjects, such as society and culture. In the positivist tradition, which is the dominant historical influence here, human consciousness and meaning (as they are handled by the arts and social sciences) are not scientifically knowable because they are subjective matters, as Kolakowski (1972) and others (e.g., Bryant, 1985; Luckmann, 1978) have discussed at length. The dichotomies of nature-culture, fact-value, inner-outer, real-imaginary, and reason-emotion prevail in this partitioning. Even with the advent of an apparently transgressive critical theory in the humanities and social sciences, ecology was never a priority. It has taken a concerted effort by environmentalists, rather than Marxists, to get ecological issues into the public arena. This is hardly surprising because the scientific materialism of Marxism was concerned with questions about economics, human values, and political power. It was not focused on systems that might transcend human interests in scope, power, and value—that is, ecological systems.

Even with the deconstruction of nature in poststructuralism and feminism, ecological considerations remain largely bracketed out. This is despite their extensive deployment of the word *nature* in these discourses. It has been widely argued (see Chapter 1) that the perception of things as natural in common sense or popular culture is problematic because there is inevitably a forgetting of history that facilitates such a recognition and often, a relegation of women to the domain of nature, away from reason and culture (Fiske, 1990; Grosz, 1989). Even when these concerns are placed in an ecological context, they are generally more in the province of a study of ideology than ecology per se (e.g., Plumwood, 1993; Ruether, 1975; Sydie, 1987). As Judith Williamson (1978) pointed out in her pioneering neo-Marxist study of advertising, that which is revealed as natural in the texts of advertising is constructed and is not a reflection of any underlying nature. In short, the legacy of critical theory and poststructuralism is that *nature* and *natural* have become particularly problematic terms. This may be theoretically warranted, but in the absence of more precise signifiers, it becomes that much more difficult to build ecological discourse in the humanities and social sciences. Our vocabularies are highly restricted and do not facilitate the theorization of an ecological discourse.

The Australian eco-feminist Val Plumwood (1993) has recently spoken of the need for better theory in ecological feminism: In *Feminism and the Mastery of Nature*, she begins by saying,

> We need a common, integrated framework for the critique of both human domination and the domination of nature—integrating nature as a fourth category of analysis into the framework of an extended feminist theory which employs a race, class, and gender analysis. (pp. 1-2)

The need extends beyond eco-feminism to the limited vocabularies of all social theory.

ANOTHER METANARRATIVE?

In describing *Four Dimensional Social Space* as a form of cultural mapping, we have not in that work shifted to any such integrated framework of analysis. We have been more concerned to present an overview than to prescribe a mode of analysis. The teasing apart of discourses around the dimensions of class, gender, ethnicity, and nature-environment is nonetheless still a kind of globalizing theory—an intellectual strategy directed toward the gaining of an overview—but one that is "tolerant of cross-cutting viewpoints and methodological differences" (Jagtenberg, 1992, p. 567). To echo Lyotard and other postmodernists: This is not the time for totalizing discourses, or Grand Theory, or a systematic theory of the whole in the tradition of a Marx, a Parsons, or a Habermas. There are too many legitimate and intransigent differences manifesting in our social and biological worlds. Too much is in question. There is no credible legitimating discourse for any new world order. Hegemonic discourses are still collapsing. Nevertheless, in the long run, we are optimistic that social research that remains committed to social justice, or at least to some reflexive analysis of power, can today hardly avoid decentering itself to an even greater extent than presently achieved.

But how permeable to ecological concern is the dominant three dimensional space of the social sciences? If disciplines such as sociology and philosophy have been slow to respond because of the two-culture syndrome, perhaps hybrids such as communication studies, cultural studies, and women's studies offer different possibilities. This question of the permeability of academic fields is best dealt with initially in terms of the closures of fields: that is, in terms of the exclusions and marginalizations in text and discourse—*discourse* as we understand the term, being inclusive of the social institutionalization of fields (Hartley, 1994; Hodge & Kress, 1988).

THE EXCLUSION OF NATURE

There are interesting precedents to be found in feminist literature for any analysis of exclusion. Feminist analysis is particularly important because the construction of nature and the natural is a gendered process and because the environment has been marginalized in discourse through similar techniques mobilized against women. Feminist textual analysis is particularly revealing of power relations and the often unconscious assumptions in all texts. Beverly Thiele (1986), for instance, following the work of other women such as March (1982) and O'Brien (1981), has catalogued a number of so-called vanishing acts in social and political thought that by analogy are helpful in understanding the marginalization of ecological thought. In her analysis, these tricks of the trade have rendered women invisible in an androcentric sociology, invisible in what she calls "male stream thought." She identifies three forms of invisibility—(active) exclusion, pseudo-inclusion, and alienation—and five tricks of the trade that bring about invisibility.[4]

We can readily apply Thiele's (1986) broad exclusionary framework to the representation of environmental concerns in the social sciences and humanities. This framework allows us to focus on the absent presence of nature, the environment, other

species, and the nonhuman generally. These interests are as
follows:

Active Exclusion. This occurs through the processes of disciplinary division of labor—which involves the bracketing out of
phenomena—and through the construction of nature as other. In
these processes, political agency is denied to other species, as is
their basic right to exist as knowable subjects in texts and
ultimately, by force of neglect, perhaps eventually in nature itself.
These exclusionary processes can be traced back to basic dualisms such as nature-culture and mind-matter.

Pseudo Inclusion. This is inclusion as a special case: a token
woman, a token animal, an empty gesture, a broken promise.
This is a space of potential transgression nonetheless. In this
spirit of pseudo inclusion, Lévi-Strauss (1979), for example,
devised the idea of transgressive categories to provide for the
ambiguous status of domestic animals and other phenomena that
do not easily fit into the polarities of dominant dualisms.

Alienation. If we can take the radical step of recognizing the inner
worlds or sentient nature of other species, we can extend the idea
of alienation found in Marxism and feminism to nonhuman
domains. For instance, just as women's experience is reinter-
preted and alienated in male stream thought, so are the experiences of other species presumed to be understandable through
human reason. In the texts of scientists, this is often taken to the
extreme of supposing that animals do not think at all (because
they do not have a human brain) and are held to be instinctive,
nonreflexive, and without language or culture. According to the
social scientist Marshall Sahlins (1976), culture was developed
in the hominid line about 3 million years ago. In this view, culture
is a new condition that arose because of the complexity of the
human mind-brain.

   The idea that culture is uniquely human was foundational in
sociology from Durkheim, through Mead and Parsons, to contemporary textbooks where it is taken to be common sense
(e.g., Haralambos & Holborn, 1990). Here, culture is understood

to be behavioral and reproduced through institutionalized socialization processes. On the other side of the divide, we have genres
and all the biochemical and evolutionary mechanisms that can
be studied through the reductive methodologies of the hard
sciences (e.g., Dawkins, 1976). This is the nature-culture dichotomy, and it is still foundational in the organization of academic
fields.

This dualistic logic is, however, under challenge. From both
sides, there are transgressions. Evolutionary biologist John Bonner
(1980), for instance, has written The *Evolution of Culture in
Animals* in which he argues for the desirability of hypotheses that
include both genetic and cultural components. His prejudices are
still reductive—"When a field is able to make advances by a
reductionist approach, the progress is most exciting and rapid.
. . . [I]t is not inconceivable that the same process might occur in
the social sciences at some time in the future" (p. 7)—but he
recognizes that many nonhuman animals experience culture. For
their part, communication scholars William Brooks and Robert
Heath (1993) now stress the continuity of animal and human
communication. Their text, *Speech Communication,* opens with a
section on the "amazingly efficient" communication of animals (p.
4). The communication problem they pose, however, is typically
parochial. What we need to do, they think, is to explain how and
why humans acquire "better skills" in communication (p. 5).

Their answer—the uniquely human process of personal and
social growth—may not have changed emphasis since the time of
George Herbert Mead and the birth of interactionism and social
psychology, but at least the presumption of no culture in nature
is challenged. We still await a better understanding of the languages and cultures of other species. So far, only some species,
such as whales, dolphins, prairie dogs, apes, and birds, are
credited with communicative ability of much sophistication, but
this ability is insufficiently cultural to pull them into deeper
community with humans. Nonetheless, if anthropocentrism is
considered problematic (as it should be), then we do have to
seriously address the phenomena of real communication among
other species and communication between human and nonhuman domains and agencies. These are still marginal concerns on

both sides of the disciplinary divide. Certainly, the idea of communication with other species and whole ecologies is an exotic proposition for the humanities and social sciences; yet this experience is what naturally underpins all indigenous tribal cultures and pre-Christian Europe. It is also what any deep ecological position proposes (Fox, 1990; Merchant, 1994; Tobias, 1985).

The exchange between humans and other species is perhaps one of the most exciting frontiers for nature-culture transgressions. Clarissa Estés's (1992) *Women Who Run With the Wolves* is particularly interesting in the way it gives authenticity to the myths and practices of ecocentric tribal cultures. Estés locates wolf nature as an archetypal source of human power; even so, we wonder whether this sensitivity will save wolves from extinction in the wild. We obviously can and do communicate in various ways with other life forms, but we await broader paradigms of communication to interpret the exchanges between humans and nonhumans. Estés's book is important because it continues premodern oral traditions, albeit on women's empowerment, that find community with animals.

We argue for developing the position of humanity in ecology along poststructuralist lines. We focus the debate as being about difference and the methodologies developed to communicate and cultivate difference. From this position, we argue that analysis of processes of the textual exclusion of women will cast light on the processes by which the environment is silenced, excluded, and made invisible. Val Plumwood's (1993) work is suggestive here. She argues that the general features of dualisms provide bases for various kinds of centeredness:

[They] provide the cultural grounding for class centred hegemony as discussed by Gramsci and others, for male-centredness, Eurocentredness, and ethnocentredness, and for human-centredness. The construction of otherness clearly has a logical pattern and corresponds to certain representations of otherness in logical theory. . . . It corresponds closely to features of classic logic, but not to the principles of logic *per se.* (p. 55)

In favoring Gramscian hegemony, Plumwood's categories avoid any returns to alienation or to the social psychology or phenomenology of experience. This enables Plumwood to sharply differentiate her critical ecological feminism (a discourse about human inequality) from deep ecology. Whereas we evaluate deep ecology more sympathetically in later chapters and distance ourselves from the structural Marxism that underpins Plumwood's account, her analysis of dualisms is particularly useful in understanding patterns of marginalization and exclusion. Furthermore, her foregrounding of patriarchal master-slave relationships as the key to understanding the logic of dualism opens up an important avenue for post-Marxist analysis (see also Chapter 8).

Plumwood (1993) sees the radical exclusion, distancing, and opposition between different social orders as deriving from a family of five features that are characteristics of dualisms: (a) backgrounding (denial), (b) radical exclusion (hyperseperation), (c) incorporation (relational definition), (d) instrumentalism (objectification), and (e) homogenization or stereotyping. These categories are introduced as typifying certain things about the hierarchal subordination of women in the perspective of the master. This logic systematically informs our way of "getting along" (p. 47) by providing a cultural framework. In Plumwood's analysis, the dualisms of master-slave and male-female are the deep structures of a dominant patriarchal system and rationality. Plumwood situates her work as a feminist social ecology, in the sense that the marginalization and exclusion of nature from text and society is considered to be a corollary of the marginalization and exclusion of women in patriarchy. This defines a clear ground for a critical ecological feminism. She is concerned to define this position carefully to deliberately frame out the more ethnographic and postmodern questions that now arise.

Plumwood's (1993) analysis defines an important position, but her essentially philosophical approach needs to be seen in the context of other positions—it needs to be mapped as part of a field of crosscutting environmental discourse. As a thoroughly oppositional paradigm, social ecology opposes patriarchal capitalism and certain varieties of environmentalism: deep ecology, counterculturalism, New Age, and other metaphysical and mythologically oriented subcultures—not to mention postmodernism. As we show in later chapters, this division in environmental philosophy and theoretical writing has roots in the historical differences between the left political arm of new social movements and the cosmologically oriented counterculture.

MAPPING SPECIAL
JOURNAL ISSUES

As the final mapping exercise for this chapter, we want to briefly review a selection of special issues that have appeared in current journals. We focus on special issues of scholarly journals because they are a good indicator of levels of interest and the state of the art in any selected area. In this section, we briefly review three issues from the fields of communication and cultural studies that have been substantially devoted to ecological issues. The journals—*Media, Culture and Society, Australian Journal of Communication,* and *Cultural Studies*—come from British, Australian, and U.S. cultural bases, respectively. The three issues were the only 1990s examples of such focused journal interest we were able to find in these fields. Of the three issues we review, only one—from the *Australian Journal of Communication*—is devoted entirely to ecologically related issues. The other two contain only substantial sections devoted to environmental issues. This is hardly a critical mass of ecological concern.

In surveying these examples, we find common themes among diverse approaches and ideas for future directions more than a substantial body of work. Many of the articles point to the need for further research, and certainly, no monolithic eco-view is discernible. In 1991, most of one issue of the British-based *Media, Culture and Society* (Corner & Schlesinger, 1991a) featured a range of work on media and the environment. The first article, by Anders Hansen (1991), locates "media-related research on environmental issues" as following much "the same path as media and communication research on any other social problem" with "many of the same weaknesses" (p. 443). On this topic, Hansen recognizes the need to redress those weaknesses by recognizing "the dynamic interaction" of "different fora of meaning production" and "the wider cultural contexts of the environment" (p. 443). He ends by placing the conceptualization of the media and a detailed study of British media within a "larger constructivist framework" (p. 454). In the second article, after finding it "somewhat surprising that few comprehensive sociological studies have been carried out," Alison Anderson (1991) reports her research on "how environment correspondents," again in Britain, see the green agenda developing and "the extent to which environmental pressure groups employ strategies in order to achieve media attention" (p. 459).

The journal's third article moves outside of Britain and national boundaries. In doing so, it illustrates the necessity for transnational modes of address for eco-issues, particularly in the wake of Chernobyl and other eco-catastrophes. Stig Nohrstedt (1991) charts how Sweden, in common with the rest of Europe, found itself unprepared for such a catastrophe happening beyond its borders and how that triggered a national "information crisis" (p. 477). The fourth and final piece, partly because it is by three academics in a geography department, demonstrates ecological interdisciplinarity of a less common kind. In addition, their article deploys qualitative audience research to probe "the consumption of news about nature conservation" (Burgess, Harrison, & Maiteny, 1991, p. 499). They conclude that "in its presentation in the media," nature conservation "is still experienced by 'ordinary' people as a dominant form of distant-public discourse—the voice of a scientific and elite culture opposed to their concern at the local-public level" (p. 517). The editorial, by Corner and Schlesinger (1991b, p. 437), reinforces such concerns with a pertinent quote:

> In relying upon risk assessment and risk management techniques, the belief in technocratic solutions also understates the extent to which ongoing judgments are inescapable in the complex process of identifying, ranking and regulating the bewildering array of potential hazards and their possible health and environmental risk. The belief in technocratic solutions is also dangerous

insofar as it can bolster the temptation to deal with environmental risks through dirigiste politics or by resorting to states of emergency and crackdown on the media. (Keane, 1991, p. 180)

Despite its considerable diversity, *Media, Culture and Society* sets out themes that recur in our other two journal examples: the value of constructivist frameworks, acknowledgment of the need for transnationality, and the need for an interdisciplinarity that engages with scientific discourse. Perhaps because of its intense media focus, *Media, Culture and Society* turns out to be less ecocentric than the other two journal issues.

In 1994, an issue of the U.S.-based *Cultural Studies* (Berland & Slack, 1994) had a substantial section on "Cultural Studies and the Environment." In observing how scientists and social scientists dealt with environments, that section's opening article develops a case for abandoning divides between nonhuman and human communities and between scientists and social scientists (Slack & Whitt, 1994). Others gave serious attention to eco-feminism and eco-valences (Stabile, 1994), technological colonialism and the politics of water (Cohen, 1994), and the ecological potential of computer simulations during the new estrangement of a third nature (Wark, 1994a). The seventh and final piece merges science and social constructivism to explore how the weather, with its "rhythms and irregularities" interacts with our "rituals" and "mediates between our physical and social bodies" (Berland, 1994, p. 99). In a very ecological fashion, Berland (1994) establishes that we are "related" to the weather, that we "affect it, and to that extent we are responsible for its well-being" (p. 112). She concludes that we now need "a way to write that on to the maps, in all the diverse ways that such inscription occurs" (p. 112).

The other articles are more conventionally human centered, and one of the few sustained pieces on media coverage of the environment, by political scientists Carpini and Williams (1994), will be dealt with at length in Chapter 7.

In 1994, a volume of the *Australian Journal of Communication* was titled "The Environment Issue" (McKie, 1994a). It is the only one of the journals to have all its articles directly related to ecological themes. Nevertheless, in demonstrating a pattern of distinct diversity surrounding common themes, it resembles its international counterparts—which it acknowledges as establishing an ecoculturalist agenda. In the first article, Jennifer Slack (1994) raises questions of theory and practice by addressing ethical considerations and our complicity in the exploitation and pollution of the planet. She provides a basic ground from which to begin, but as she points out, being complicit does not guarantee intervention, enlightened action, or policy making.

Some of the titles and contents of the articles that follow suggest the very different perspectives the issue offers: Robyn Penman (1994) brings knowledge from organic farming practices and recent communication theory into fruitful conjunction; two other scholars develop Foucauldian studies to look, respectively, at "The Administration of Life: Ecological Discourse as 'Intellectual Machinery of Government' " (Rutherford, 1994) and "Disciplining the Feminine, the Home, and Nature in Three Australian Public Health Histories" (Stratford, 1994); another looks at how print media framed local and regional nuclear issues (Lucas, 1994); another considers "The End of Nature" (Jagtenberg, 1994); another, the biopolitics of narratives (McKie, 1994c); and one contribution from Aotearoa, New Zealand (Jones, 1994), combines organization and cultural studies perspectives to analyze a unique indigenous people-environmental law nexus.

SUMMARY

Ecological issues have become more prominent in the media and in academic life, but there are reasons to question the ability of the disciplines to adequately respond to the complexity of these issues. Taking a lead from feminism's experiences of exclusion and marginalization, this chapter has traced part of the problem back to hierarchic dualisms and an academic establishment that is still dominated by modernist scientific rationality.

With a real world capable of being mapped and faithfully represented problematic, we wonder about the fate of the ecology after modernism. The pluralism and hyperreflexivity of postmodernity may well lead to a submergence of biodiversity in the excess of cultural simulacra and texts about nature. Might we not drift in an indeterminate nature, no longer able to respond to the rhythms and needs of the ecologies that sustain us? This is an unnecessarily alarmist reaction if we see postmodernity as a complex mix of paradigms, epochs, and eras and not some totalization of the possibilities of new technology (such as the Internet and cyberspace). In this complexity, we have argued that ecological concern needs to become a legitimate part of the reformulation of the priorities of the humanities and social sciences.

There would seem to be definite possibilities for postmodern mappings. We know that multiple realities, difference, and power leave their traces—even as the absences and silences that post-structuralists have drawn to our attention. Consequently, it seems possible to map ecological exclusions and transgressions: by going back to the generative logic of dualism and the social context of the institutions and practices that support them and forward to spaces that have ecological potentials. We think these spaces can be postmodern with an ecological spin. But as we have emphasized, postmodern maps need to be tolerant of different viewpoints and methodologies; they need to register the tensions behind facades of harmony and consensus, and they need to encourage pluralism and diversity.

This kind of critical mapping is a process of invention and discovery. There is no set form or prescription. It is an activity and adventure rather than an algorithm. However, just as Pickover's biomorphs can be seen to have an ambiguous location in nature (Are they simply artifacts? Can something in a complex mathematical space be said to exist as nature?) so, too, postmodern maps should lure us into an indeterminate unknown and at the same time relocate us in the known. As we discuss in the following chapter, postmodernism is playful about its referentiality; it encourages reflexivity and fantasy and it is relativizing. In post-modernism, the world of the known is folding back on itself, generating hyperreflexive images and techno-spaces in which the old agonies can be reiterated and new beauty found in the invention and mapping of ecological spaces. Postmodern maps may not all be as beautiful as Chaos mandalas, but they allow us to make some sense of a world of sliding signifiers and changing disciplinary formations. Ironically, there may be some comfort to be drawn from the work of mathematicians who have found order, and ecological simulation, in Chaos.

NOTES

1. Mandelbrot patterns, fractal landscapes, and biomorphs are typical examples of the often extraordinarily beautiful patterns in the fractal orders of Chaos mathematics. See, for example, Dewdney (1989), Pickover (1986), Gleick (1987), and Lauwerier (1991).

2. Deleuze and Guattari (1987) develop these ideas in *Mille Plateaux*. As Paul Patton (1995) has recently pointed out, these metaphors have purchase on contemporary political analysis. The recent Australian High Court Mabo judgment presents liberal political theory with a dilemma about equity that can be illuminated by poststructural ideas about difference, freedom, and change: "for Deleuze and Guattari, a society is defined less by its contradictions than its lines of flight. . . . [T]here is always something that flows or flees, that escapes binary organizations" (p. 10). We might note that Patton does not seek to distinguish poststructuralism from postmodernism. It also needs emphasizing that the texts of Deleuze and Guattari, Foucault, Derrida, and Baudrillard are all texts of a break with modernism and structural determinism. Texts such as these are deliberately transgressive and evasive.

3. The distinction between cognitive and social factors has been made by many sociologists and psychologists. It emphasizes the society-culture dichotomy and enables ideas to be distinguished from social relations—that is, the distinction gives some necessary autonomy to culture and is a corrective to overdetermined models of society. This was historically important in the sociology of science, which developed its own styles of cognitive mapping. See, for example, Whitley (1974) and Jagtenberg (1983), where the idea of cognitive institutionalization was introduced and developed as a mapping of programs of scientific research.

4. These are *decontextualization, universalism, naturalism, dualisms,* and *appropriation and reversal* (Thiele, 1986, pp. 34-39).

3

Readaddressing Postmodernity and the Eco-Post

For sociology, communication, and cultural studies to recognize the crucial contemporary issue of the environment, we see the need for the equivalent of a paradigm shift. Yet the major debate among social theorists is whether a paradigm shift, most frequently termed *postmodernism* or *postmodernity*,[1] has already taken place. These disagreements involve more than cultural frisson. Located in social movements as well as universities, they signify a contest over values, priorities, economic organization, and ultimately, the kind of future worlds we will construct. Many proponents of postmodernism, and associated movements such as postindustrialism and postcolonialism (often clustered under the term *the post* to characterize both the period and a certain commonality in their projects), argue that we already occupy a new social and cultural formation. We argue that a postmodernism-postmodernity of that stature would have to incorporate the impact of an ecological age.

LATE MODERNITY OR
THE THREE POSTMODERNISMS?

Many critics refuse to recognize postmodernism as anything significantly different. Influential dissenting voices (Hall, 1991a; Murdock, 1992) answer the question of what kind of world this is by identifying it as *late modernity*. They see us occupying what is predominantly a late-modernist world that displays more continuities with modernity's business-as-usual than would justify a new label. In owning our position as ecoculturalist postmodernists, we address this "post" phenomenon through three labels: postmodernism (a), whose key features we identify through popular television genres; postmodernism (b), which we characterize through diverse academic critical approaches; and postmodernism (c), which we locate through a temporal fix on historical coordinates. With typical postmodern disregard for modernism's boundaries and for definitive beginnings, we elaborate the philosophical and political issues of postmodernism (a) through the ethnic and ecological consequences of some contrasts between television news and television comedy. In fact, at this point in eco-history, we claim that the former's serious genre is a dangerously exclusive area, whereas the latter's light entertainment genre requires more serious consideration. By questioning the truth claims of so-called reality programming and the associated construction of an exclusive New World Order based on an outmoded scientific worldview, we advocate a greater range of knowledge traditions and a broader humor of inclusion to combat the false reassurance rituals of television news.

To clarify what we mean by postmodernism (a) and to make it accessible, we condense our version to the new three Rs of relativism, referentiality, and reflexivity. To make it pleasurable, a key and too-often neglected postmodern characteristic, we start by retelling an old Lone Ranger and Tonto joke. For those who have never heard of the Lone Ranger, let alone seen the television program, he is a North American cowboy who fights for unambiguous good against unambiguous evil in tight pants and a black mask in the same manner as Superman fights for truth, freedom, and the American way. The Lone Ranger has a Native American sidekick called Tonto—a kind of inferior, unpaid servant, since renamed Uncle Tom to by ethnic activists (Bataille & Silet, 1980)—whose destiny, even at the cost of his life, is to serve his superior selflessly.

In the joke itself, the dynamic western duo are trapped between two unscalable mountains with an uncrossable river in torrent behind them and three combined tribes of Native Americans armed with Winchester repeating rifles blocking the only way out. The Lone Ranger turns questioningly to Tonto, "Looks like we've had it this time, old friend?" Tonto stops watching the Native Americans, stares into his erstwhile master's eyes, and replies, "What do you mean 'we,' paleface?" Although this may be a bad joke, it prioritizes the politics of exclusion by putting relativism, particularly in terms of ethnicity, firmly on the agenda: Who do we speak for when we say *we*? Who are targeted, either directly or by implication, as *them*? And how appropriate is laughter?

SINKING TO NEW DEPTHLESSNESS, OR WHO LAUGHS AT POSTMODERN JOKES?

The joke also contextualizes postmodernism's three Rs: First, as an end to ethnocentrism by relativizing the single truth of the white, male, and universal project of modernism (Lyotard, 1984); second, as an attack on modernism's in-depth map of reality by showing that referencing, or representing, the world requires multiple maps and different levels of cartography (Appignanesi & Lawson, 1989); and third, as a demand for reflexivity (Lawson, 1985; Woolgar, 1988) by asking all questioners to reflect back on how their own position influences the construction and credibility of these different truths and multiple realities.

These three Rs, relativism, referentiality, and reflexivity, characterize postmodernism—dubbed the *new depthlessness* by some and *shallow* by others (Jameson, 1991)—and how it calls into question the superiority of depth analysis over surface meditations. For illustration, although staying resolutely superficial, we consider television news as a branch of show business and as a genre that defines an inclusive *we* through an excluded *they*, which Fiske (1987) has plotted into a set of systematic binary oppositions:

Allies	Enemies
Australians	Non-Australians
Victims	Villains
Management	Unions
Us	Them (p. 307)

Post-Gulf War commentators update the terms to confirm the ongoing centrality of the division. Mellencamp (1992) analyses how, in that television coverage, "'They' were a map without bodies or identities other than Saddam Hussein, 'We' were individuals, real people" (p. 126). Robins (1993) concurs by noting that "the not-me we used to embody the sense of catastrophic danger was Saddam, vilified as child-molester, rapist, murderer, monster" and "his scuddish evil, George Bush assured the western world, confirmed us as the guardians of enlightened and civilized values" (p. 324). The extent of the attachment to anchored "we-dom" and "they-dom" can be partially judged by the vitriolic reception given to Jean Baudrillard (1995) when he claimed that the Gulf War did not take place; that it was a simulation; and that, in an era marked by semiotic excess and mediated images, the violence and moral issues slide into spectacle. According to Baudrillard, the fight was "over the corpse of war" (p. 23) because the so-called Gulf War was won in advance against a so-called enemy who never had a chance.

REFERENCING REALITIES: INSIDERS AND OUTSIDERS

In the postmodern politics of media spectacle, events and numerical precision have been cut loose from empiricism and its motivation to represent the real. Numbers become a negotiable

part of the atmospherics dependent on the imaginative thresholds
of audiences. Through exaggeration, a news production team's
joke further exposes arithmetic ethnocentrism in the British
reporting of disasters: "One thousand wogs, fifty frogs, one
Briton" and "One European is worth twenty-eight Chinese, or
perhaps 2 Welsh miners worth one thousand Pakistanis" (quoted
in Schlesinger, 1987, p. 117). This example leads to the second of
the new three Rs—referentiality, or the relationships between
representation and things in general. Of particular concern here
are the degrees of virtuality in the virtual reality of television news.
At stake are "systems of expectation and hypothesis [that] involve
a knowledge of—indeed they partly embody—various regimes of
verisimilitude, various systems of plausibility, motivation, justification and belief" (Neale, 1990, p. 46).

Ironically, in a movement pledged more to surface, style,
pastiche, and wordplay, postmodernism has developed a politics
in its pleasures. Its critical edge consistently cuts into the precarious relationship of reality to celluloid representation. It questions the reliability of reference points, still coded around dominant binary oppositions, claiming to guarantee the transfer of
actual events to the news reels. Postmodernist interventions have
not replaced modernist popular narratives of sex and gender,
class, race, and ethnicity, but their playfulness can help alert
viewers to the constructed nature of the media. As Huyssen
(1984), Appignanesi and Lawson (1989), and others argue, postmodernism exists among the texts of modernism. Postmodernism
is part of the cultural phenomenon of multiplicity that charac-
terizes a post or a late modernity. John Hartley (1992) has
identified the critical role binary divisions play "in the analysis of
social phenomena, the opposition between public and private
domains, and in the analysis of texts, between reality and illusion" (p. 30). Developing on Chapter 1's division into semiosphere
and biosphere, we extend his insight to the assumed division
between so-called real news and illusionary comedy.

Our challenge to the high status and implicit truth claims of
news as verisimilar to outside reality has two targets: its assumed
high status in relation to matters of social importance and its
associated relegation of comedy to an inferior status vis-à-vis

representations of the nature of the world. As Todorov (1981) puts it, "the verisimilar is not a relation between discourse and its referent (the relation of truth), but between discourse and what readers believe is true" (p. 119). Television news's realism "as an ideology can partly be defined by its refusal to recognize the reality of its own generic status or to acknowledge its own adherence to a type of generic verisimilitude" (Neale, 1990, p. 48). Sold heavily as "real life"—real events, real people, real pictures with the real story of what happens in the real world—television news, all on the surface and before our very eyes, dishonestly creates virtual realities. These virtual realities have far more material force than currently fashionable obsessions with virtual reality as electronically constructed simulations of everything from architecture to global community.

In terms of showing things as they really are, news, as "a high status television genre" (Fiske, 1987, p. 281), attempts to distance itself from the obvious artifice and canned laughter of situation comedy: "Its claimed objectivity and independence from political or government agencies is argued to be essential for the workings of a democracy" (Fiske, 1987, p. 281). Yet it is also another heavily promoted entertainment genre that seeks ratings through jingles, billboard advertising, and newsreading stars (Bonney & Wilson, 1983). Nor, in its contestation of the real, does it always emerge well from comparison with sitcom versions of social relations.

In the 1990s, U.S. sitcoms, such as *Murphy Brown*, British ones, such as *Drop the Dead Donkey*, and Australian ones, such as *Frontline*, have all gathered critical acclaim for telling the so-called truths that serious news excludes. All acknowledge

how deviance is constructed by the powerful; how deviant categories, especially those with a marked racial component, are the
product, and thus the sole responsibility, of those whose interests
are further served by portraying themselves and their protectorate
as being threatened by deviance. (Ross, 1990, p. 32)

All these sitcoms provide scenes that foreground the institutional potential for complicit police-journalist relations and include, unless as in the Rodney King case, exceptional visuals become broadcast, what would normally be excluded. Although an abundance of media studies literature over two decades in Britain (Glasgow University Media Group, 1976), North America (Ericson, Baranek, & Chan, 1987; Tuchman, 1978) and Australia (Bell, Boehringer, & Crofts, 1982; Edgar, 1980) charts the institutional potential for just such distorting mutuality, it has little visibility on television and none on television news. Sitcoms provide a balance because they direct empowering laughter at a socially, and sometimes environmentally, dangerous lack of self-reflexivity among the serious media.

IS OUR WORLD SAFE?

Self-reflexive criticism cannot afford to overlook how television news functions as what Morse (1986) calls a regular ritual rather than an information provider. Night after night, the bulletins intone habitual responses to predominantly negative happenings. They don't so much inform their viewers about what has happened on any specific day as continuously replay variations on their one solitary question: Is our world safe? Television news keeps before us the idea that we live dangerously in what Ulrich Beck (1992) has termed *risk society*. Although a part of modernity's reflexivity, television newsreaders also perform a comforting ritual. Each night, they run an impressive list of troubles past us, and although these might not be immediately resolved, we are still invited to rest easy.

That ritual form includes times when the *we* might refer to all inhabitants of the planet and when a less ritualistic and more rational answer might be no, our world is not safe. Television, as national charities (Australian commercial television's annual Appealathon and Telethon events raise millions of dollars) and global appeals, such as Live Aid, illustrate, has enormous potential to mobilize. Yet caught in an automatic reassurance ritual, contemporary news more regularly lulls to a false sense of security. Too often assuming an identity of interest with the institutionally powerful, television leaves crucial criticisms to comedy. At this point in eco-history, we propose taking comedy more seriously and treating news as a dangerously frivolous exclusion zone. One typical sketch, in which British comedian Lenny Henry parodies a newsreader, neatly captures the point at the level of language and atomic power: "The nuclear power plant at Windscale has been renamed Sellafield because it sounds nicer. In future, radiation will be known as magic moonbeams."

That example of the third R—reflexivity, and particularly self-reflexivity—draws attention to the maker's role in constructing meaning, not just in news but in any activity. Communication and cultural studies focus strongly on identity politics: Who do we think we are? Where do we think we are? Why do we think so? And what does the way we study do to all this? We argue that we in universities, as a privileged part of mainstream Western society, need wider traditions of humor and philosophy. We haven't begun to relativize nearly enough. There's a Sufi story about that wise fool, Mullah Nasruddin, visiting the bank. When the teller requested proof of identity, he asked for a mirror, looked solemnly into it, and said "Yes, that's me alright" (as cited in Ornstein, 1986, p. 79).

Who do we see? Looking at surface phenomena with the three Rs, we see ourselves first, reflexively, as people with an environmental axe to grind; second, relatively, as part of a prosperous, yet still inegalitarian, society whose way of living contributes to keeping a large part of the globe at near or below subsistence level; and third, by referencing disproportionate Western resource usage, as people endangering the future of the biosphere itself.

BEYOND ANTHROPOCENTRISM

Sufism is only one of a number of enlightenment, and enlightening, traditions that use different forms of reflection, including meditation and technologies of the self. These often align well with suggestions from deep ecologists that ecological awareness needs to be experientially based (e.g., Devall & Sessions, 1985). In this context, although conceding that Sless's (1994) call for less theory has considerable merit, we propose not less theory per se but less theory from the same narrow temporal and spatial (basically modern Euro-Western) range of sources and more theories from other times and spaces. Without giving priority to the question of who we are, action minus awareness, for example, may not be the best way to respond to environmental crises. To explore different answers might require meditation—the "don't just do something, sit there" advice of Zen and other Eastern traditions. These excluded traditions now offer guidance to inner growth in the context of the failing dream of outer growth for all. In addition, they invite a perception-altering laughter that is valuable in itself, and they facilitate insights into other kinds of eco-identities.

Along with the cosmologies of Aboriginal and other indigenous people, these premodern traditions range beyond the West's current perceptual reach to encompass other sentient beings and the material world. Their extended empathy may yet, before "the modernization process is complete and nature is gone for good" (Jameson, 1991, p. ix), fuse with the ecological potential in postmodernist assaults on modernity's "contempt for the world of nature" (Fuller, 1988, p. 129). As emerging ecocentric approaches gain greater acceptance—in popular culture, postmodernism, and some social movements—such a fusion opens points of integration extending beyond exclusively human liberation movements. It threatens to breach "the species-barrier between human and animal" (A. Wilson, 1992, p. 154) and expand the sphere of human identification with nature toward caring "as deeply and compassionately as possible about the [Earth's] fate not because it affects us but because it is us" (Fox, 1984, p. 200).

Other very different writers reach similar conclusions via a different route. For some time now in art and literature, various writers have argued for extending or exploding the established canons (Ferguson, Gever, Minh-ha, & West, 1990). Cowan (1993) carries the argument beyond the galleries and curricula to push for the inclusion of that "canon of belief" of the "earth-wisdom possessed by traditional people throughout the world" (p. 3) and to heed their message that "every species; every genus and phylum; every breed, race and tribe are all inextricably linked . . .

part of bandaiyan, nature's 'big body' of which we, too, are an integral part" (p. 204). Nevertheless, in his argument, Cowan is still wedded to Western science. His recognition that science forms the rational undergirding of Western modernity may be uncontroversial, but his assertion that the West cannot "conceive of a canon of belief that stands outside of the current opus of science-based information" (p. 3) is out of touch with an emerging scientific paradigm. Simultaneous with Hartley's (1992) observation that the neat distinction between reality and illusion only "survives where reality is construed on the model of physical science, as comprising only empirically observable material objects and actions" (p. 30), Davies and Gribbin (1992) announce that, from the standpoint of physics, this so-called matter myth is scientifically outmoded.

SHIFTING PARADIGMS AND SICK GAIA GAGS

An allied deconstruction of Cartesian-Newtonian science's hegemonic dominance formed an integral part of what Morris Berman's (1984) book termed *The Reenchantment of the World*. In company with Charles Birch (1990) and other practicing scientists, he posited a postmodern science with ecological implications. Cowan's concerns with human exclusiveness and its exclusion of the natural world resonate with responses from decentered scientists and other cross-disciplinary travelers: Prigogine and Stengers (1984) have called for a new dialogue with nature; Mandelbrot (1982) and Birch (1990) attempt to learn from, rather than to dominate, the natural world; Margulis and Sagan (1986) promote evolutionary cooperation; Diamond (1992) and Haraway (1989) remind us of our important genetic and temporal proximity to primates; Druyan and Sagan (1992) emphasize the influencing shadows of animal ancestors; E. O. Wilson (1992) polemicizes our need to preserve the diversity of as many living forms as possible; and Lovelock's (1979) Gaia hypothesis generates congruent reconceptualizations, including global systems theory. Because, as Paul Davies (1992) further reminds us, the whole planet shares a common origin as "animated stardust" (p. 232), perhaps we humans should adopt a less exclusive and superior attitude to the subsequent shapeshifting of all life on earth.

In foregrounding relations with nonhumans, particularly given the clear relationship between Western economic development and species extinction, we don't want to downplay very real contemporary human suffering. Nor do we want to encourage environmental racism by shifting the burden for ecological destruction onto the struggle of developing countries seeking prosperity in conditions dictated by the first world. In the differential living conditions of the postmodern globe, it's obvious that, compared to many third world locations, the joke's not yet on many of "us." Ecologically though, everyone in this endangering and endangered species is running out of time to laugh at humor that isn't black. Imagine then, as the Australian ABC's comedy show (1990) *The Big Gig* did, comedian Wendy Harmer speaking as celestial landlady of planet earth. She's making an inspection at the end of humanity's tenure of Gaia as rented accommodation. Having kicked a hole in the ceiling, killed the owner's pets, turned the solar heating into a health hazard, poisoned the atmosphere, polluted both huge ponds and left some of the garden's remaining trees on fire, she asks rhetorically, "What tenants would have the nerve to ask for their bond back?"

In the final irony, sick Gaia gags might yet shake us into sympathy with other races, other species, and even the earth itself. The main *we* such humor threatens is our contemporary version of an exclusive New World Order based on an outmoded scientific worldview with accompanying technological imperatives. Shifting to the humor of inclusion, we—in the sense of we who inhabit the earth—may come to develop a postmodern humor not based on a racist they-dom or making animal others insignificant. The end of the world is more genuinely funny when humanity's dominance is relativized by laughing at our human arrogance.

POSTMODERNISM (B): ACADEMIC RESPONSES AND CRITICAL LISTINGS

Academically, postmodernism has had a more serious reception. It has been variously characterized as the dominant cultural form of "late capitalism" (Jameson, 1984, p. 91), a post-metanarrative mode of philosophical inquiry (Lyotard, 1984), self-reflexive language games with important consequences (Appignanesi & Lawson, 1989), a politics of referentiality (Hutcheon, 1988, 1989), a celebration of differences (Hebdige, 1988), a transformational hypercommodification (Wernick, 1991), and a void of self-congratulatory chronology (Anderson, 1988). Such thematic listing offers a more useful way than definition for constructing and working with the diverse academic responses of postmodernism (b).

To make the list manageable and to continue to play off these themes, we concentrate on a few theorists—Jameson, Hebdige, Lyotard, Wernick, and Anderson—who convey a significant range of responses to the phenomenon of the postmodern.[2] They are also selected to allow us to continue our dialogue about science as the neglected interdisciplinary discipline. In the dialogue, we move away from top-down approaches that reproduce modernism's fetish for science as paradigmatic knowledge and method to look more toward its intertextual and metaphoric possibilities. At a time when ecological policy making requires information about species, habitats, and human impacts, we see it as counterproductive to exclude science (premodern, modern, or postmodern) from emerging discourses.

Frederic Jameson's (1984) version of "Postmodernism, or the cultural logic of Late Capitalism," as a "new depthlessness," (p. 58) has emerged as a seminal source for social theorists. His article's nomination of capitalism in the title, coupled with its site of publication in the socialist journal *New Left Review,* politicized debates from the outset. The article itself firmly rejected neutrality: "Every position on postmodernism in culture—whether apologia

or stigmatization—is also at one and the same time, and necessarily, an implicitly or explicitly political stance on the nature of
multinational capitalism today" (1984, p. 55). Despite, or perhaps
because of, its demand for political alignment, Jameson's piece
germinated into a huge crop of postmodernism publications
distinguished by two common features: ongoing argument about
the politics, or more frequently the lack of politics, of postmodernism and a parochial neglect of science. Whereas the former—
particularly in the form of whether postmodernism is complicit
with, or oppositional to, capitalism—bears on almost everything
written within cultural studies and sociology, it has little visibility
in the much sparser field of postmodern sciences. Conversely, the
neglect of science by social theorists mirrors the scientists' limited
sociocultural and political focus. Both poles are interwoven with
postmodernism's many contradictions.

One immediate contradiction, in Jameson's own partisan account of postmodernism's complicity with capitalism, is its implicit underpinning by Marxism. Of all Lyotard's discredited
metanarratives, Marxism has probably undergone the largest
single increase in incredulity since 1984. So how do polemical
critics engage with capitalism without this master discourse that,
as a normative framework for postmodernity, is now so clearly
unacceptable? The answers vary and are not without contradictions themselves, but they intervene in public understandings of
what kind of world we inhabit. In *Hiding in the Light*, for example,
Dick Hebdige (1988) abandons the high ground of the traditional
intellectual production of totalizing theory to skid along shiny
depthless surfaces. Emphasizing a more fragmentary and less
teleological aesthetics of quotations and surfaces, he takes high
theory into everyday culture. Substituting referential density for
narrative coherence, he conveys how pop video visuals and
intertextual citations can overload their genre's causal and storytelling capability. He also traces similar postmodernizations
from fashion magazines and cartoons through to Italian motor
scooters. Reworking Lyotard's (1984) subversion of the distinction between scientific and narrative knowledge, Hebdige eschews
metanarratives in favor of "a restoration of the legitimacy of first
order narratives" (1988, p. 226) at the microlevel rather than the

macrolevel. From there, as feminists quickly point out, "there is no reason why the different stories of contemporary women from diverse ethnic, racial and class backgrounds cannot be conjoined into accounts which tell complex tales" (Nicholson, 1992, p. 98).

LEARNING FROM THE POPULAR

Hebdige's own first order narrative journey culminates in a revealing analysis of a pop video, *The Road to Nowhere*, by David Byrne's (Byrne & Kurfirst, 1986) Talking Heads. Hebdige (1988) uses the lyrics, playing word games with *The Oxford Dictionary of English Etymology's* definition of *Utopia* as *No Place* (from the Greek *ou* = not + *topos* = place), and the intertextual range of images and symbols (from avant-garde homage to a globe dripping in blood), to illustrate the decline of modernism's totalizing, teleological, and Utopian project. Instead of that project, which is predicated on a belief in infinite material resources, he favors "more structural, ecological and holistic models based instead around a consciousness of limitation" (p. 229). Happily acknowledging all decentering discourses, such as feminism and ecology, his ludic language exemplifies an active participation in constructing the kind of integrated politics of desire and knowledge he advocates. Hebdige shifts, without abandoning the analysis of power relations, from semiotics to pragmatics, from static social formations to fluid processes. After all, with ultimate goals uncertain, the everyday processes themselves take on a new importance.

Hebdige (1988) engages both with those processes through which desire and information flow for profit and pleasure and the contexts in which they are organized, disorganized, and recirculated. To an extent, his approach foreshadows subsequent phenomena, such as the evolving Internet where pornographers and feminists, environmental activists and global polluters, psychologists and neurotics, all coexist within a functioning academic, business, and gossip network (see Benedikt, 1992). He certainly connects with an age of so-called infotainments and advertorials where putative pleasures, hard sells, and facts intermingle indiscriminately. Hebdige both describes and treats seriously the contemporary realm of promotional culture in which advertisements may be as consequential as scientific reports in how the mass media disseminate images of science. In this realm, advertisers, journalists, television workers, and the odd scientist, circulate ideas about ecology and society to a general public.

Through his analyses of postmodernism as it manifests in the popular cultural domain, Hebdige widens the dialogue to interest people who might never have theorized the politics or philosophy of everyday living. Donna Haraway (1991) performs a similar integration in her "Biopolitics of Postmodern Bodies" by bringing recent theory in contact with ordinary scientific textbook illustrations and scientific advertisements. She makes her project's eco-political intent very clear elsewhere:

> I want to have charge of the animal stories in the *Reader's Digest*, reaching twenty or so million people monthly in over a dozen languages. I want to write the stories about morally astute dogs, endangered people, instructive beetles, marvelous microbes and co-habitable houses of difference. (Haraway, 1992b, p. 68)

Reflecting on the role of dinosaurs in contemporary museum culture, with a more restrained populism and a different ideology, Stephen Jay Gould (1991) also relates popular interest in museum promotions to higher funding for science education. Elsewhere, in an unusual acknowledgment of the necessity of emotional involvement, Gould (1993) also passionately advocates a range of eco-strategies, postmodern in their diversity:

> We cannot win this battle to save species and environments without forging an emotional bond between ourselves and nature as well—for we will not fight to save what we do not love. . . . So let them all continue—the films, the books, the television programs, the zoos, the little half acre of ecological preserve in any community, the primary school lessons, the museum demonstrations, even (though you will never find me there) the 6:00 A.M. bird walks. (p. 40)

In engaging with how postmodernism surfaces in the everyday, all three scholars construct from the materials of commonly available cultural experiences. Their attempts offer a lead that other environmental scientists and eco-philosophers of science might profitably follow in advancing the public understanding of postformal education audiences. Outside of schools and universities, current knowledges tend to be circulated, if not actually created, by means of newspaper sensationalizations of research, advertisements, fictional film, and television. This is an unavoidable feature of the new depthlessness in the contemporary public sphere.

HYPERCOMMODIFICATION AND THE PROMOTIONAL CONDITION

Perhaps the very notion of the public sphere is reaching, to use the ubiquitous language of commodities, the end of its shelf life. Hypercommodification, with its unique penetration of every aspect of life by the commodity form, has become one of the characteristic markers of the age. Andrew Wernick (1991) has titled this the *promotional condition,* in a more complicated sense of the term, of contemporary culture. In this realm, universities themselves, never mind individual academics and scientists, struggle to maintain any distinction they may have as noncommodified regions in which production for profit is not the dominant rationale. Extending the notion far beyond critiques of commercialization and advertisements, Wernick's thesis redefines cultural space itself:

The range of cultural phenomena which, at least as one of their functions, serve to communicate a promotional message has become, today, virtually co-extensive with our produced symbolic world. . . . [P]romotional communicative organs constituted by the commercial mass media (and even, via sports sponsorships and the like, by the organs of "public broadcasting") are also transmissive vehicles for public information and discussion in general. Through that common siting, non-promotional discourses, including those surrounding the political process, have become linked (Bush in Disneyland on prime time news) to promotional ones. It is this complex of promotional media, too, which mediates the communicative activity of all secondary public institutions— aesthetic, intellectual, educational, religious, etc.—to what used to be called "the general public." Furthermore, even if not directly commercial themselves, these secondary institutions also generate their own forms of promotional discourse . . . in the case of university recruitment campaigns, because they have become indirectly commodified. (pp. 182-183)

Although still mapping some of what Cardinal Newman (as quoted in Wernick, 1991) termed the *territory of the intellect,* modern universities are far from ensuring that "there is neither encroachment nor surrender on any side" (p. 154) and invest heavily in promoting and defending their corporate images. Places as far apart as the august colleges of Oxford, which launched a professional fund raising, and Wernick's Canadian university invest heavily to play the promotional game. In Australia, both of our institutions have circulated memos restricting, and policing, the use of their professionally designed logos. Already, in international tertiary education, institutional image is fully another commodity.

Although science does not feature in Wernick's list of secondary public institutions, it is not exempt. Webster (1988) has documented the changing links between industry and public sector research science in Britain as academic departments and research centers have been increasingly required to follow commercial procedures. Crook, Pakulski, and Waters (1992) usefully summarize the revised departmental aims: to generate profits; to become "self-exploitative of its own expertise" (p. 209) under more directive and businesslike management approaches and to concentrate development on "strategic" (p. 209) highly fundable work in commercially attractive areas, such as biotechnology. Obviously in such a climate, environmental research that might reduce the rate of profit flow is not likely to gather much corporate sponsorship.

Stronger trends were evident earlier in the United States. Stanford president Donald Kennedy (1981) told a congressional hearing that, although "basic research in universities" required "more, not less relationship to industry," there was a real danger of "some contamination of the basic research enterprise in the university by a new set of values and new objectives" (p. 8). In 1975, a group gathered at the West Coast resort of Asilomar to discuss concerns surrounding recombinant DNA research. It included practicing scientists and members of the nonscientific community and was open to selected members of the press (see Dickson, 1988). By contrast, a second group, which met at the resort of Pajaro Dunes, involved university administrators and business people from genetic engineering and pharmaceutical companies in a closed meeting organized by Donald Kennedy and cohosted by four other top research universities whose presidents attended. In such sensitive and potentially highly profitable DNA research, the composition of the Pajaro Dunes gathering would predispose it toward bridging, or papering over, possible conflicts of interest between commerce and education. As early as 1982, one immunology professor pithily identified that as a binary divide between the values of a corporate world, whose "business is to make money" (Woofsy, quoted in Dickson, 1988, p. 60) and whose "mode is secrecy, a proprietary control of information and the fruits of research" and the universities whose "motive force" is "the pursuit of knowledge" and whose "mode is open exchange of ideas and the unrestricted publication of results and research" (Woofsy, quoted in Dickson, 1988, p. 61).

We readily acknowledge this as idealistic and often contradicted by the competitive and sometimes secretive behavior of actual academics, but it is nonetheless a crucial piece of ideology that can help protect the relative autonomy of universities from a far less principled global capitalism. Such ideologies, even when more honored in the breach than the observance, can still have useful material consequences.

Hebdige's commitment to honoring first-order narratives without ignoring asymmetrical power relationships makes sense in the context of Asilomar versus Pajaro Dunes. The more open meeting constructed its story from a much weaker power base than the closed one. The university presidents' narratives of science policy are backed by a scale of institutional resources unavailable to less powerfully situated storytellers. Nevertheless, both sets of stories remain in circulation; their coexistence fosters doubt about statements by the spokespeople of prestigious institutions. Public concern may yet force a more open policy. In presenting his annual report, the president of the National Academy of the Sciences, Frank Press (as quoted in Dickson, 1988), viewed the "new mood in the country" as an optimistic one that looked "to science and technology for economic progress and national security to an extent that may be unprecedented" (p. 11). Like postmodernism itself, neither these concerns nor the trends they represent are new. Nevertheless, as the use of the word *unprecedented* indicates, they have reached enough critical mass to achieve a qualitative difference in line with Huyssen's (1984) formulation that what appears as "the latest fad, advertising pitch and hollow spectacle is part of a slowly emerging cultural transformation in Western societies" that marks "a noticeable shift" from "that of a preceding period" (p. 8).

POSTMODERNISM (C): PLOTTING TEMPORAL COORDINATES AND CONJUNCTURES

We approach postmodernism (c), the so-called condition of postmodernity, as a historical period[3] rather than as a given set of themes and cultural practices. Not surprisingly, this identification of it as a changing cultural and social formation does not go uncontested. Perry Anderson (1988) must rank among its most trenchant critics:

The futility of the term "modernism," and its attendant ideology, can be seen all too clearly from current attempts to cling to its wreckage and yet swim with the tide still further beyond it, in the coinage "postmodernism"—one void chasing another, in a serial regression of self-congratulatory chronology. (p. 332)

Strangely, given the force of his double dismissal, Anderson substantially addresses "the need for periodization" and identifies "the sociopolitical conjuncture" (p. 323) by providing a methodology and analysis of modernism. He argues convincingly for a differential development scheme, whereby different parts of the world modernized at different times so that modernity arrived much earlier in Europe than South America. As far as actual dating is concerned, we accept an equivalent uneven development across time and place for postmodernism. In broad terms, we locate somewhere around 1945, with the testing of the atomic bomb and the end of the Second World War, as the watershed for the beginning of the postmodern period. More important, for our arguments, we want to redeploy Anderson's plotting of "'modernism' . . . as a cultural force field 'triangulated' by three decisive coordinates" (p. 324) to set up a comparable triangulated grid for postmodernism and to posit relations between that map and postwar science.

Anderson (1988) selects his first modern coordinate as

the codification of a highly formalized academicism in the visual and other arts, which itself was institutionalized within official regimes of states and society still massively pervaded, often dominated, by aristocratic or landowning classes that were in one sense economically "superseded," no doubt, but in others were still setting the political and cultural tone in country after country of pre-First World War Europe. (p. 324)

We read off the equivalent postmodern coordinate as the growth of officially or commercially (or both) sanctioned diversity (including aspects of gender, race, and class). Politically, it would encompass a transnational postcolonialism common to many continents and specific national developments, such as the Australian government's replacement of the racist "White Australia" immigration policy by one of formal multiculturalism. This is far from claiming the end of ethnocentrism, either in Australia or elsewhere, but it illustrates, in one national paradigm shift, a widespread phenomenon with numerous counterparts from Africa to Europe. Culturally, it would encompass the widespread abolition of high culture-low culture boundaries and the expansion of varied kinds of public and corporate patronage. Again, this is not to claim that classical forms, such as opera, do not persist, nor continue to attract higher state subsidies and status (see Bourdieu, 1986), but that they are part of less hierarchical cultural arrangements where famous tenors also coexist as pop stars and publicists for international sporting events.

Similar trends are observable elsewhere. In science, for example, we perceive the growth of officially/commercially sanctioned diversity in a pronounced breakdown into diverse sciences (plural) or, "science's ongoing, continual, process of growth through fragmentation" (Forman, 1994). His term *fragmentation* we would supplement with *segmentation*, in the sense of managed decision making, occasionally by specific scientists (or groups of scientists) but more routinely by university administrations, powerful corporations, and government military establishments. With this reservation, postmodern pluralism applies with a vengeance to the multiplicity of new fields and the different relationships between them. Massive sales of popular science, especially the Stephen Hawking (1988) bestseller phenomenon, James Gleick's (1987) romanticization of Chaos theorists and, subsequently, his *Genius: Richard Feynman and Modern Physics* (1992), demonstrate new scientific celebrityhoods rather than the elevated recognition of preceding periods.

Currently, at a lower level of fame than Hawking, Nobel prizewinner Murray Gell-Mann (1994) presents the scrapping of the "superconducting supercollider" by the U.S. House of Representatives as "a conspicuous setback for human civilization" (p. 125). In this, he is unquestionably sincere but, as the star of two popularizations of Complexity Theory (Lewin, 1993a; Waldrop, 1993), he is also contributing to the public promotion of comparable-future big science ventures. Who knows what an extended time on the bestseller lists for his own book, allied to the accompanying promotional spiral of media appearances, might allow

Gell-Mann to accomplish? At least one earlier physics Nobelist, Einstein, has become a star, with all the attendant paraphernalia of calendars and T-shirt photographs appropriate to a Hollywood icon. If he were alive today, such popularity would probably have to be factored into political decisions for science funding.

Anderson (1988) takes his second coordinate as "the still incipient, hence essentially novel, emergence within these societies of the key technologies or inventions of the second industrial revolution; that is, telephone, radio, automobile, aircraft, and so on" (p. 324). He places that coordinate as prior to the implantation into Europe of the mass consumption industries based on those new technologies. The postmodern equivalent would be the increasingly common access, in the overdeveloped world, of mass produced goods, services, and energy from the third industrial revolution; that is, computers, microelectronic communications technology, bioengineering, nuclear fission, and so on. In addition to its imbrication in personality publicity, science becomes part of hypercommodification through its large-scale fusion with technology into the phenomenon Turnbull (1991) terms *technoscience*. Technoscience forms an increasingly integral part of business competitiveness in national and international trade as well as the full range of government military arrangements. Technoscientific knowledge impacts socially, too, from the third world's "green revolution" to the computerization of everyday advanced industrial lifestyles. Turnbull's strategies for resisting its negative aspects turn on typically postmodern tropes. In the struggle against its "totalizing and homogenizing effects" (p. 53), he recommends the recognition of "local site-specific practices" and the maintenance of "diversity and difference" (p. 53).

Scientists, as part of technoscience, play a huge active role in the construction of the technoscience world and what Rheingold (1992) calls its "reality-industrial complex" of fast multiplying "virtual realities" (p. 17) and virtual communities (Rheingold, 1994). Since Toulmin's (1982b) observation that in the "'postmodern' world, the pure scientist's traditional posture as . . . spectator, can no longer be maintained: we are always—and inescapably—participants and agents as well" (p. 255), the pace has accelerated. The speed of change requires continual adjustments, at both individual and institutional levels, toward the new place of scientists within industry and within universities as the knowledge-as-commodity bandwagon rolls on and further compresses the diminished public sphere. Under such circumstances, Forman's reflections on the modernist "flight from responsibility" (Forman, 1993) and on the "'Responsible' as [a] predicate of postmodern knowledge production" (Forman, 1994) assume greater urgency.

POSTMODERNITY: THE AGE OF ECOLOGY?

Forman's concerns retain equal validity for our final postmodern coordinate: the dual awareness of the potential of large-scale nuclear war or comparable eco-catastrophe (from the now familiar litany of environmental threats) on a planetary, and not just a social, scale. In the words of ecological historian Donald Worster (1985), "the Age of Ecology began on the desert outside Alamogordo, New Mexico on July 16, 1945, with a dazzling fireball of light and a swelling mushroom cloud of radioactive gases" and one "kind of fallout from the atomic bomb was the beginning of widespread, popular ecological concern around the globe" (pp. 339-340). For Rachel Carson (1962), along with the possibility of human extinction through nuclear war, the "central problem of our age" became "the contamination of man's [sic] total environment" through "substances that accumulate in the tissues of plants and animals and even penetrate the germ cells to shatter or alter the very material of heredity upon which the shape of the future depends" (p. 25).

As a parallel to Anderson's (1988) third coordinate of modernism, "the imaginative proximity of social revolution" (p. 325), the postmodern possibility of imminent eco-catastrophe raises once more the question of metanarratives. Not only does such a dual apocalyptic awareness shadow future life, but it poses stark questions for scientists still engaged in modernist projects, especially those with hugely destructive potential under military guidance (see De Landa, 1991). To envisage the positive features arising from the possibility of such eco-catastrophe requires an imaginative leap. Our own hopes lie with the environmental movements, with enlarging our own ecoculturalist area, and with creating the consciousness for a genuinely global movement with common goals—despite conflicting politics, asymmetrical North-South power axis, and differing sets of eco-problems.

Scientists continue to play a vital role in the negotiation of future orders—even if the mantle is extended to social scientists. Beyond their obvious theoretical and technical expertise, scientists can, without philosophical warrant from traditional metanarratives, construct first order narratives and accounts that tell complex tales from out of their own experiences and sympathies. As critical postmodernists, they can redraw the metropolitan maps of modernism and listen to the less privileged and powerful. They can both align with, and learn from, such neglected historical agents as the eco-feminist influenced Indian Chipko Women's Movement (see Shiva, 1993) and the Japanese Seikatsu Club consumer-producer-cooperative (see Mies, 1993) to constitute a new politics of interlinked truths. In abandoning the modernist aspiration of Western material wealth for all as unattainable, scientists need not abandon environmental goals, such as a planet capable of sustaining life for future generations.

To be "post-man" scientists though, they must be capable of steering clear of any residual modernist trajectories insensible to knowledges that are not exclusively Western, modern, male, and middle class. Science's crisis of legitimation does not simply result from intellectual destabilizing ploys such as the spread of so-called language games, which Lyotard borrowed from Wittgenstein. A plurality of significant differences have eroded foundational beliefs in its universality, objectivity, and special status. These include feminist demonstrations of its patriarchal bias, anthropological studies of how its laboratory tribes reject other cultural beliefs, sociological identifications of its kinship with lower-status craft work, ecological exposure of crucial contexts

existing beyond its experimental walls, and third world categorization of Western science as an ethnocentric "theology of violence"
(Sardar, 1988, p. 2).

Equally, a more modest postmodern science must steer away
from the extremities of relativism in wilder postmodernism itself,
"a hydra-headed decentred condition in which we get dragged
along from pillar to post across a succession of reflecting surfaces,
drawn by the call of the wild signifier" (Hebdige, 1988, p. 195). To
avoid relativizing any workable scientific projects out of existence,
there has to be some correspondence between propositions and
extratextual reality. Small-scale, language-sensitive, culture-
sensitive, and gender-sensitive narratives that respect differences fit better than teleological tall tales. For the measures he
takes to avoid spurious modernist universalizing and his corresponding adoption of decentering differences, Gilbert's (1994)
multicultural biology offers a good model. For his awareness of
how language and metaphor shape, even as they articulate,
conceptual thought and how he uses that awareness to explore
the constructed identity of the "immune self," Tauber's (1994a,
1994b) deconstructions of scientific discourses offer another.
Bolter (1986) has argued that technologies have epistemological
consequences; Tauber's discursive exposés of the outmoded
Western metanarratives powering both contemporary medicine
(Tauber, 1993) and the human genome project (Tauber & Sarkar,
1994), suggest how discredited epistemologies continue to have
large-scale economic, medical, and technological consequences.
Sociology, communication, and cultural studies are well placed
to align with, and extend, such interventions but would need to
address scientific discourses.

PERSPECTIVES FROM
POSTMODERN SCIENCE

This section picks up the earlier paradox that the neglect of
science by communication and cultural studies mirrors a relatively limited sociocultural and political focus in both science and
the philosophy of science. In her definitionally voluminous *The*

Post-Modern and the Post-Industrial: A Critical Analysis, Margaret Rose (1991) claims to provide "an historical and analytical overview of the most influential or significant uses" (pp. xi-xii) of the term *postmodern*. Despite multiple index entries to both *modern* and *postmodern science*, science, in an accurate reflection of the sociocultural field's lack of concern, gets scant attention in her book. Her significant chronology, for instance, ranges widely from the obscure 1934 *postmodernisimo* of Spanish and Latin American poetry of 1905 to 1914 to more recent sociologists, historians, and the expected roll call of Lyotard, Jameson, and so on (Rose, 1991). Totally absent are the admittedly scarce, but more valuable for that very reason, science and postmodern pieces: Griffin's (1988) collection, *The Re-Enchantment of Science: Postmodern Proposals*, whose genealogy records three earlier titles, Toulmin's *The Return to Cosmology: Postmodern Science and the Theology of Nature* (1982b), Frederic Ferré's *Shaping the Future: Resources for the Postmodern World* (1976), and Floyd W. Matson's (1964) even earlier use of the term *postmodern science* in *The Broken Image: Man, Science, and Society*. All these references are missed altogether by Rose as is the work of Katherine Hayles who has been writing on science, culture, and postmodernism since at least 1984.

We labor the point because it is symptomatic. To the best of our knowledge, none of these authors appear anywhere, with one exception,[4] among our own list of postmodern-shaping critics: Jameson (1984, 1991), Lyotard (1984), Appignanesi and Lawson (1989), Hutcheon (1988, 1989), Collins (1992), Hebdige (1988), Wernick (1991), and Anderson (1988).[5] In part, such a neglect reflects the chasm of ignorance separating Snow's (1964) "two cultures" divide, but it continues to retard intelligent evaluations. If postmodernism is to earn status as more than a passing style, it has to engage with the sciences. It cannot hope to deal with the persistent realism of an ecological crisis by exorcising a guilty party from the text. The sciences can be contested, subverted, transgressed, and transformed but not ignored.

Postmodernism has to see if its temporal coordinates fit with that field's history and developments. It has to find out if, and where, comparable movements exist, and it has to interrelate differences. In general, the sciences have to return the treatment if they hope to understand their relationship to the intellectual, political, and social conditions of the time and to intervene reflexively in them. For ecological interventions in particular, the stakes are even higher, and they will require further and more widespread dialogues. We also advocate searching out ecological equivalents to such suggestive formulations as Katherine Hayles's (1991) on Chaos as a new science:

> The postmodern context catalyzed the formation of the new science by providing a cultural and technological milieu in which the component parts came together and mutually reinforced each other until they were no longer isolated events but an emergent awareness. . . . The science of chaos is new not in the sense of having no antecedents in the scientific tradition, but of having only recently coalesced sufficiently to articulate a vision of the world. It is no accident that this vision has deep affinities with other articulations that have emerged from the postmodern context. (p. 5)

By fostering linkages rather than promoting a unified science and a separate scientific culture, postmodernists open a space where an ecology of connections can be forged. For a greener paradigm, sociology, communication, and cultural studies need to explore Hayles's deep affinities—particularly in relation to the corresponding shallow reaches of hypercommodified societies, the increasingly depthless public sphere, and the diminishing planetary future.

NOTES

1. Later, we try to make a distinction between *postmodernism* and *postmodernity*, but they are too interwoven in academic and popular discourse to be maintained consistently without a tedious verbal policing or the loss of a level of useful vagueness (or both) in attempting to apprehend the sometimes intangible phenomena of the contemporary.

2. Although many of these theorists are consistently nominated in the postmodern debates, we are conscious of marginalizing and excluding a whole corpus of writings by many significant others, such as Baudrillard, Deleuze, and

Guattari, as well as those such as Poster, Patton, and Morris, whose own writings, introductions, and translations have interpreted and developed that corpus.

3. In practice, as with postmodernism, the idea of a distinct postmodernity has tended to attract social scientists rather later than communication and cultural theorists (see Rosenau, 1992), although a varied body of work on both is now available (Bauman, 1992; Best & Kellner, 1991; Harvey, 1989; Kumar, 1995; Lash, 1990; Milner, 1991).

4. Hutcheon (1988), although she doesn't index science or his book, is alone in referencing a Stephen Toulmin (1982a) article.

5. We're conscious of the high proportion of men, six out of eight, in this list of definers and of the feminist critique of male writers on postmodernism for not quoting women on the subject. As a corrective, we draw your attention to Nicholson's (1990) collection, Finn's (1993) article on *Why Are There No Great Women Postmodernists?* and especially, Morris's bibliography of 182 items that contains "only works signed or cosigned as written by women" (1988, p. 17).

4

Changing Paradigms

The Greening of Social Movements

Social movements have played a crucial role in the development of a changing world and a greener society and culture. We place social movements within the frameworks of postmodernity and postmodernism yet hold reservations about the future of the ecology in these new social and cultural formations. Postmodernism has not delivered us a greener world because it is predominately a pre-ecological discourse about changing culture—just as *postmodernity*, the more embracing term, is a name for the changing conditions of a globalizing social life and not a green critique. Green maps and new paradigms have had their origins in this changing world, but they have not come from the reflexive, relativizing social theory of postmodernism or from the reflections of sociologists on globalization, new communications technology, and risk society. The green ideas we are exploring here have come mainly from the cultures of social movements.

Since the 1960s, social movement cultures have been influenced by the rising tide of popular concern about the environment. Central in this greening process are the cultures of environmentalism. Like other post-1960s social movements, environmentalism is not a single-issue movement nor is it a homogeneous entity. There are many different cultures in environmentalism, and in Australia, as elsewhere, there is a long history of difference between ecological subcultures. Conservationists, naturalists, aboriginal people, and farmers, for example, express different kinds of relationships with nature and the environment. These different groups have different practices, values, and beliefs and bring different cultural traditions into environmentalism.

Environmentalists, therefore, span the spectrum of ideology from deep ecological positions, incorporating many of the religious beliefs of indigenous cultures, to a drier green analysis relying on scientific solutions and the more standard left analysis, to the paler green managerialism of conservationism. That is, environmentalism is not an exclusively radical process. Jonathon Porritt, one of Britain's leading activists, has characterized British environmental groups as being largely co-opted "by the growthist obsessions of our industrial culture" (Porritt & Winner, 1988, p. 22). Despite this philosophical and political diversity, which creates various levels of compromise with industry and development, there are a number of deeper radical trends drawing many activists and theorists together.

In this chapter, we address a body of green theory that has emerged to challenge many entrenched assumptions about the nature of social change and that is developing into what could be called *a culture of the environment*. We see this emerging green culture as an articulation of a new paradigm because of its shift away from patriarchal, European, human centered analysis. Environmentalism has achieved this through grassroots activism and through developing new theory that enables critical analysis of hegemonic agendas. Environmentalists, however, have benefited from the emergence of more diffuse post-1960s social movement cultures. Through their involvement with these new social movements, many people have seen the dissolution of old social truths and gained an ability to understand more clearly the interests of those who have been marginalized and disempowered. We contend that a more dispersed yet increasingly mainstreamed activism is part of the condition of postmodernity, a condition that is suspicious of centralized bureaucracies and the monopolization of activism and political agency.

SOCIAL MOVEMENTS: NEW MAPPINGS

Historically, social movements have played a vital role in the breakdown and revitalization of society and culture. Social movements have always presented a challenge to the status quo by exerting pressure for a change of perspective and by encouraging new sociocultural formations to emerge. Through the mobilization of grassroots activism by various social movements, there has emerged political pressure to defend rights, contest issues, and meet the new political demands of citizens. Some of the social movements to emerge over the past 100 years have effected major shifts in the perspectives of contemporary culture—the labor movement and feminism provide good examples of the power of social movements. The achievements of social movements continue to have a profound effect on the quality of life in the West and are becoming increasingly influential in non-European cultural and social change. As mass popular culture changes over time, however, so the dynamic centers of movement activity appear to shift over time and space, moving issues from the periphery to the center. We argue that environmentalism is today shifting the agenda of all social movements; the greening of social movements is reshaping oppositional cultures.

Social movements, particularly those referred to in current literature as *new social movements*, have been central in the promotion of environmental issues in a variety of institutional sites. In particular, the cultures of new social movements contribute strongly to the shaping of discourse in the social sciences and humanities. When we turn to this varied literature on social movements and oppositional politics (a literature that is partially defined in the fields of cultural studies, communication studies, and sociology), we find sophisticated and wide-ranging analyses of the politics and radicalism of many social movements but can only note that environmentalism has historically been relatively slow to register on academic agendas. Today, there is more enthusiastic debate about the issues and methods of social change that emerge within the broad context of environmentalism and some vigorous debate about whether the new politics emerging within these movements is rendering left political analysis largely obsolete.

Rising concern for the environment in Western social and political thought provides an opportunity for new mappings of ecological discourse. Although environmental concerns have historically been marginalized by mainstream theory, these concerns have a history expressed within the context of other major social movements. Many of the campaigns of new social movements cut across a range of environmental and social justice issues. Environmental concerns have been given particular attention within the women's movement, indigenous peoples' struggles, and the peace movement before gaining a voice in their own right. Australian activists, and activists around the world, have played a role in a number of social movements, connecting into networks of supporters that become very diffuse and that have resisted institutionalization into any one political expression. This is a key feature of all new social movements (see, e.g., Habermas, 1981; Melucci, 1989; Offe, 1985; Pakulski, 1991; Touraine, 1985): "The space of action of the new movements is a space of non-institutional politics that is not provided for in the doctrines and practices of liberal democracy and the welfare state" (Offe, 1985, p. 819). It is important to understand that green concerns have emerged from Offe's broad context and are not monopolized in any single green position.

In British and Australian universities, critical analysis, especially in the social sciences and humanities, has tended to represent the dominant paradigms of the academic Left. Much of

the current literature that addresses social movements theoretically and historically remains centered on the value of human
labor, class conflict, and the goal of socialism. These Marxist,
structuralist, and socialist-feminist paradigms have been critically important in the development of a focus on inequality, but
they have also closed off much ecological discourse. In mapping
the Australian context, we need therefore to distinguish between
the historical institutionalization of the political left and new
social movements.

In the face of massive social change wrought by factors other
than a revolutionary working class, many on the left have still
continued to assert "the primacy of labor movements as agents
for social change" and would argue that "capitalist class relations
have not changed anywhere nearly as fast as the changing fashion
in theories and interpretations" (Burgmann, 1993, p. 16). Ralph
Miliband (as quoted in Burgmann, 1993), for instance, asserts
that "new social movements can achieve little without the power"
of the producing class "that alone can contest ruling class power"
(p. 16). This is symptomatic of the Left's continuing attachment
to class conflict as the theoretical bottom line. Despite the
decentering effects of student politics, feminism, poststructuralism, and postmodernism, the post-1960s academic Left remain
largely focused on dominant institutional structures and conventions and on the distribution of social power in a class society.
By contrast, new social movements, such as the women's movement, the green movement, the peace movement, and indigenous
peoples' movements, have never fully incorporated the left or right
political agenda. They have refused both the paradigms of worker-
based revolution and many of the metanarratives emanating from
the historical program of the Enlightenment (e.g., science, truth,
and progress). The mass popular connection of these metanarratives with the domination, exploitation, and pollution of nature
has, in fact, been one of the major ideological achievements of the
new social movements. For example, the greening of the media
has, as Hansen (1994) points out in his British case study, been
strongly influenced by social movement organizations, such as
Greenpeace.

THE LABOR MOVEMENT AND
THE CHALLENGE OF NEW
SOCIAL MOVEMENTS

The global struggle of working people to improve their conditions, despite the resistance of their employers, has undoubtedly been the most sustained social movement of modern industrial societies. The workers' movement is international in scope but its bureaucratic and restricted focus is problematic (Burgmann, 1993). Indeed, the labor movement has been such a globally effective social movement that its domination of the theory and practice of anticapitalism has virtually forced the development of new and different forms of protest. The international labor movement has, however, been most influential in providing a critical analysis of capitalism and in stimulating the politicization of the workforce through unionism and the cultural analysis of labor relations. In many countries, the organization of union power against the exploitation of human labor provided for major improvement in working conditions, for better rates of pay for the employed, and for social security and superannuation benefits for most workers. But it has not been fruitful in many other areas of discrimination and exploitation within the workforce or in the more general community. It has been seen as largely irrelevant to indigenous struggles and as having failed to develop insights into gender relations or assist in gay and lesbian campaigns for social justice, for example. Its marginalization of environmental issues has been a critically important motivation for the emergence of the Australian environmental movement.

Environmental concerns have a history of marginalization in the Australian labor movement. When the environment has become a public issue, concern has not come from the centralized labor organizations, with the notable exception of the New South Wales branch of Australian Builders Labourers' Federation (NSW BLF). In the early 1970s, the NSW BLF was the first labor movement to initiate industrial action over environmental issues with their famous "green bans" (Mundey, 1981). Although the

NSW BLF had the popular support of its members and much of the local community, its struggle was as much against the union movement as it was against the developers. In Australia, the trade union movement has to varying degrees supported issues concerning the environmental movement, such as wharfies' bans on loading uranium and live sheep exports, but these issues have always had other political agendas. Little sympathy has generally been given to the green cause from workers in, for example, the mining, building, and timber industries.

Most significantly, left analysis, when focused on the history of social movements or environmentalism, prioritizes an essentially traditional political analysis. Although new social movements have seen very good reason not to let go of an analysis of power and inequality, these issues have now been given a broader analytical base amid a wider range of concerns. In contrast to trade unionism, membership of many of these movements has presupposed some considerable identification with the earth, the land, and nature in ways often foreign to dominant European paradigms and often in ways that are cosmological rather than political in conventional terms. Identification with nature that takes a spiritual or cosmological orientation may involve individuals with both premodern and postmodern worldviews.

The fact that many greens have a spiritual relationship with the land and its nonhuman inhabitants is, of course, a retrograde event in any conventional political economy or other materialist analysis. Since Marx's original damning critiques of religion, the Left has generally been fiercely atheistic, always fearing any descent into idealism as a manifestation of false consciousness. Although hostility to religion is historically well-founded, there is a distinction between spirituality and religion that the Left has refused to make but that is fundamental in the theory of many greens. The spiritual orientation of many greens to the land and also to a range of premodern cosmologies (such as Buddhism, Hinduism, shamanism, and various indigenous cultures) is generally not religious in the conventional sense, but it does locate power outside an exclusively human domain. This power is of a different order to social power, which it subsumes in a larger set of power relations. An extended sense of power opens a space for power in nature, a consideration particularly interesting to deep ecology and eco-philosophy. Earth-centered cosmologies are also attractive to many because they enable the development of an extended sense of self with a more organic connection to the biosphere.

INDIGENOUS FREEDOM

Although unions have endorsed the desirability of material development and scientific progress, they have had relatively little to say about indigenous peoples' desire for cultural autonomy or their desire for continuing mythological connections. In Australia, indigenous people have been historically absent from labor movement concerns. As expressed in *Koorier* in June 1990, "There is a strong feeling among Aborigines that unions had done nothing for Koories" (Burgmann, 1993, p. 62) and that only by activist campaigns focused on natural rights have indigenous people achieved some measure of political recognition: "Aboriginal politicians have for generations passionately pursued the rights of their peoples to land, to cultural continuity, to heritage" (McNamara, 1990, p. 95). But they have also resisted attempts by the Left to swallow their concern for cultural heritage into an analysis of capitalism. The theoretical absorption of indigenous people into a pool of labor power that drives capitalism does no justice to the history of their difference. Arguments about the evils of capitalism have not attracted the loyalties of indigenous peoples in the struggles for cultural survival (cf. Alexander, 1992). They have seen the failure of both capitalists and socialists to value and protect indigenous cultural structures and associations. They have seen the resource-based nature of their political exploitation.

The anthropocenteric nature of orthodox Western ideology is one of the biggest difficulties to emerge from the European clash with indigenous cultures. Indigenous peoples have maintained a commitment to their ecocenteric cosmologies. Aboriginal Australian writer Wandjuk Marika again gives voice to the cultural position of many indigenous peoples when he says of Australia's white colonists:

They don't know about the tree, *who* is the tree,
what the tree *is*.
They don't know *what* the grass *is*,
who is the grass or *what* is in the earth
and what *in* the mountain,
what *in* the trees.
Tree is tree, yes,
but we have individual names.
What is my tree and what is my mother's?
Which river is my grandmother or which mountain is
also my mother . . . and my grandmother?
Which food is a close relative to us Yolnu.
We know which is which,
who owns the land
and how *far.*
                              —Wandjuk Marika (1995, p. 14. Used with permission.)

Indigenous peoples have often united in their reactions against the ambitions of industrial states to exploit traditional lands. Rather than work through the labor movement, however, they have formed their own international alliances in their attempt to retain their cultural association with the land (e.g., Shiva, 1988). In many cases, indigenous struggles have involved opposition from developers and workers (e.g., Brazilian gold miners). Indigenous peoples' struggles have been about racism and colonialism as well as labor relations. With the rise of black power in the 1970s, the struggle of Australian aboriginal people to define their own agenda entailed a rejection of white interference, which was seen largely as a hijacking of genuine black aspirations: "Whites became unhappy with black rejection of black-white cooperation under white leadership to achieve civil rights in favour of an autonomous black movement emphasising indigenous rights" (Burgmann, 1993, p. 34). This dialectic has been played out in the United States, New Zealand, and all countries with significant European-indigenous social relations.

Indigenous peoples' struggle for land rights in Australia has led to the legal recognition of equity rights and the return of some traditionally owned land. But these aims are not significantly articulated in terms of class or capital. They are expressed in terms of cultural heritage and a desire to continue in the traditional ways of the dreamtime. That these mythological dimensions are articulated culturally and given form in political agendas has been largely ignored by left cultural analysis. The counterculture of the 1960s was well ahead of the Left in articulating aboriginal cultural concerns and giving recognition to the continuing relevance of aboriginal cultural traditions. It has been the New Age movement, the green movement and the women's movement that have welcomed an increasing awareness of the rights and cultural values of indigenous peoples. The New Left have found themselves restricted to adopting causes because they involve labor relations or social justice issues, and in Australia only belatedly joined the counterculture in supporting Aboriginal desire for cultural equality.

Indigenous peoples' struggle for cultural autonomy and their continuing refusal to adopt exploitive land use or to give up their spiritual connection with the earth has placed them in conflict with industrially based notions of progress. The Australian aboriginal activist Burnam Burnam explains as follows:

> We see ourselves as descendants of the longest conservation campaign in the history of man, because we opted to become part of the environment itself. We did not mind Australia for 50,000 years to see it destroyed in 200 years of "progress." (Burnam, 1992, p. 94)

THE WOMEN'S MOVEMENT

But it was left to the women's movement to provide a more thorough analysis of how power and hegemonic attitudes were expressed within cultures themselves. Following the successes of its struggle to give women the vote, the women's movement has evolved as a critique of male hegemony. The women's movement has questioned status quo assumptions about the natural position of males with its analysis of male power and domination in both public and private spheres. It has also provided an analysis of the way text and history are gendered—male histories have bracketed out women in various ways.

With the successful introduction of equal opportunity legislation and the demand for changing attitudes to domestic violence, women have overthrown established notions of women's place in society. They have challenged prevailing attitudes by increasing the participation of women in education and in the labor market and changed social attitudes toward the value of female labor. The evolution of the women's movement has provided a broad spectrum of analysis of human relations and the role gender plays in determining our attitudes to nature and the natural world. It has heralded the fall of the old world order by exposing the excesses and contradictions of male hegemonic authority. The fall of male supremacy and the patriarchal order (at least, theoretically) has allowed us to further question hierarchy and domination in human society (e.g., Bookchin, 1982; Plumwood, 1993).

Like environmentalism, the women's movement is not singular or unified on all fronts. Nor is it adequately characterized by the successes of women in public office, business, and education. Many of the struggles and achievements of women have not been in the public domain. They have occurred in the home, at the coal face, often in tense relationships with alienated and hostile men who have not always found feminism a comfortable ally. Women have struggled individually to retain their dignity and common-law rights, but their successes owe much to the growing momentum of an international alliance of women groups. The movement has changed public life and working conditions and introduced new images and stereotypes into popular culture. For example, women have even entered the gym, and powerful women are now more appreciated than feared or ridiculed. Women's musculature, after many centuries, is again able to be developed; women can now have square shoulders without being scorned as masculine.

In its diversity, the women's movement has developed extensive links with other social movements—often through the agency of women who have multiple allegiances and identities. In particular, the women's movement has developed in a close relationship with the peace movement. Following feminism's analysis of gender, the peace movement has also challenged the natural rights of men to inflict violence and has developed issues-based campaigns to mount major opposition to war and the "might is right" ideology. The early peace movement galvanized women in an attempt to oppose conscription of youth. It enlisted wide popular support in its challenge of state power and male culture. The resumption of French nuclear tests in the Pacific have shown that peace activists are still able to mobilize at a moment's notice. Big bombs that cause mass destruction and genetic pollution still stimulate mass concerns for the environment. It is widely understood that war and militarism are a violation of ecologies as well as human society.

Peak environmental and peace organizations, such as Greenpeace and Amnesty International, have their roots in the nonviolent antinuclear protests of the late 1960s and have continued to deploy the moral pressure exerted by the peace movement in its struggle against war—and particularly, against nuclear war. The agenda of the peace movement is only partially about patriarchy and the state—the historical concerns of the peace movement with antinuclear campaigns also have an environmental focus. Today, the peace movement's concerns have become central in environmentalism (which itself has always been antiwar) and in feminism. Some writers (e.g., Crook & Pakulski, 1995) refer to an *ecopax* movement as synonymous with the green movement. Ecopax would perhaps be just as synonymous with the women's movement. In any case, we think it important that environmentalism is perceived as distinct from the women's movement and the peace movement.

THE GREEN MOVEMENT: FROM CONSERVATION TO ENVIRONMENTALISM

Whereas other new social movements have been diversely concerned with ecological issues, the environmental movement has developed its own institutional forms as part of the machinery of opposition. In Australia, these include large corporate-style organizations, such as Greenpeace and the Australian Conservation Foundation; smaller and more focused organizations, such as Wilderness Society; political parties (state and federal Green Parties); and a network of offices and groups often diversely affiliated to parent organizations. The growth of the environmental movement has been particularly rapid in Australia since the late 1980s, corresponding to a highly mediated revolution in environmental consciousness. Politically driven media campaigns have played an important part in this greening of popular culture, but there are many other factors involved.

However the popularity of social movements is gauged—by public opinion surveys, by media content analysis, by performance at elections—environmentalism has gained sufficient momentum to keep it on political agendas and in the media. There are apparent fluctuations in some of these indicators (in Australia, the rate of media attention and levels of concern varies, usually waning between elections) but, as Crook and Pakulski (1995) have shown, there is an underlying persistence and stability to environmental concern. In this study, when people were asked about their likely concerns 10 years from now, the environment still featured as a major issue. From 1993 Australian Electoral Survey data, Crook and Pakulski (1995) have determined that 10% of the sample population placed the environment as the most important issue in that extended time frame. This contrasted with a low in public concern for the environment in that year of 4%. But these figures may be highly conservative— Roy Morgan opinion polls for that year indicated that 21% of the population thought the environment to be the most important issue (Crook & Pakulski, 1995, p. 43). As these researchers show, health and unemployment are more pressing concerns—but this may also be a misleading distinction. When one considers that public health issues have become increasingly concerned with the environment (both as determining factors in health and as part of a more holistic paradigm of health and healing), it is likely that the environment will inevitably become of even more pressing concern because of its central significance in public health.

Increasing concern for the environment is not a uniquely Australian phenomenon. Environmentalism is today a global social movement, like feminism and the labor movement. Its roots are diverse, and it has grown in different cultures with highly diverse cultural expressions. Historically, conservationism precedes the environmental movement in its present form. During the 18th and 19th centuries, concern for loss of habitat because of urbanization and industrialization took many forms but was largely expressed politically through direct attempts at nature *preservation*—to protect natural areas from encroachment and exploitation. Arguments emerged about the utilitarian importance of preserving biodiversity, low-growth economics, and the necessity for recycling. Aesthetic arguments were also made for the necessity of the human spirit for communion and solace with nature (Nash, 1990; Paehlke, 1989). These concerns for conservation, preservation, and protection of the natural world were developing, albeit submerged in an overarching human secularism, as part of the political theory of Western democracies throughout the world.

As it happens, much of the conservation movement's pioneering philosophy has its roots in the English liberal tradition. The history of natural rights goes back in European history to the Magna Carta in 1215. This charter established natural rights as belonging to beings by virtue of their existence (Nash, 1990, p. 13). Principles set down then have been instrumental in the evolution of Western democratic states. Natural rights philosophy and the concept of democratic liberty were also rights foundational to the formation of the United States Constitution (Nash, 1990, p. 109). Libertarian concerns with human rights and freedoms have always been part of the green agenda and prioritized in conservationism's concern to preserve and manage nature for human ends. Many environmentalists today, however, argue for the extension of natural rights to the nonhuman world. This is not an altogether radical move because "the inclusion of nature in the ethical community can be seen as an extension of liberalism in an ecological direction. . . . It speaks in a typically liberal language of rights and obligations" (Martell, 1994, p. 141). The idea that nonhuman species and ecologies have rights and that humans have obligations toward them is still, however, highly radical because it profoundly challenges our conventional notions of community and social contract. Does an ant have a sense of moral duty toward humans? Do other species attempt to communicate with humans? In what sense can we really speak of an extended community involving other species, perhaps even plants and inorganic matter?

Nonetheless, the right of humans for a clean, nontoxic, and renewable habitat became a fundamental part of environmentalism's critique of industrialism and the limits to material growth. Because of the work of earlier conservationists, the instrumental nature of industrialism came under increasing criticism. Today, ecological sustainability has developed as a central critique for greens in addressing problems of industrialization and growth. "Sustainability" could be said to be a broad-ranging attempt at social planning. It attempts to provide a model for a future in which technology and social organization are such that resource use is nondepleting and nondestructive of natural ecosystems. The idea developed from discourse about resource depletion, industrial pollution, and population growth where it has been argued that with good management techniques involving recycling and nonpolluting technologies, societies could sustain an environment pleasurable for human existence. Although there is no consensus amongst environmentalists about precise detail, Hare (1992) suggests a number of commonly agreed principles, including conservation of biodiversity, limits to growth, community participation, social equity, and a global perspective. The idea of sustainability raises many paradigm dilemmas—particularly for economists, some of whom are keen to pioneer a new field: ecological economics (e.g., Jansson et al., 1994; Norton, 1995).

As we have argued, the environmental movement needs to be understood in the full context of environmental concern. In Australia as in many other Western countries, contemporary environmentalism is part of a loose alliance of new social movements. In the development of the movement, conservationists have been challenged by green radicalism, a radicalism that would install a new paradigm and a new culture of environmentalism. In prioritizing environmentalism as a new social movement, we are arguing that the concerns of environmentalists have evolved in the context of other key contemporary issues in politics and social theory. Environmentalism and ecological issues can- not, however, be dissolved into the texts and organizations of other movements. An alliance of differences cannot be reduced to centralized organizations or dominant ideologies, and if it is, the result is only further division and discord. This was particu- larly evident in the demise of the Nuclear Disarmament Party in Australia (1984-1987) where branch stacking by Trotskyites was a major destabilizing influence (cf. Burgmann, 1993; Papadakis, 1993). In the wake of the subsequent collapse of the Communist Party (Australia), the New Left Party, and the decline of the Democratic Socialist Party, the same determination by anomic radical left activists to determine the agenda of the Australian Green Party is still a disturbing influence.

The constraints of left politics are particularly important to understand if environmentalism is to develop as a democratic alliance. We have major reservations about the ability of post- Marxism to begin to contemplate the radical alternative of so much that occurs in the environmental movement. Because of the genetic coding of progressivism, science, and reason in the ideological genes of post-Marxism, the ecstatic discord of the counterculture has been ignored in left analysis of social move- ments and social change. This is a critically important absence, as we reveal in our discussion of the counterculture that follows.

In summary, new social movements have had a profound effect in the evolution of social and cultural change. They have assisted in the breakdown of metanarratives and hegemonic cultural assumptions and also continued many of the concerns of the old social movements. One of their central achievements has been in the decentering and deconstruction of hegemonic paternalism (in its capitalist, Marxist, and religious guises) and a reevaluation of the fields of nature. The women's movement particularly has challenged the taken-for-granted assumptions of things natural in social roles and obligations. There has also been a strong gay and lesbian challenge of gender stereotypes and processes of cultural exclusion. Indigenous peoples' challenges to the univer- sality of Western cultural superiority and hegemonic attitudes have demanded we recognize the natural rights of marginalized

human cultures. Most fundamentally, indigenous peoples' movements and the Greens have confronted our long-held cultural
assumptions of anthropocentrism, insisting we extend our notions of self into our ecologies and give natural rights to our
habitat.

THE COUNTERCULTURE

Academic analysis of social movements has significant exclusion zones. The wilder nomadic and romantic cultures of the
counterculture and their premodern precursors have been marginalized and repressed by the dominant materialism of left
analysis. This is paradigmatic and politically motivated and
corresponds to a long-standing antagonism between radical left
politics and all other forms of dissent. To be sure, the antago-
nisms have often been mutual, as expressed by Jay Stevens
(1989) in *Storming Heaven: LSD and the American Dream:*

> On October 7, 1966, the day after the California bill criminalising
> LSD took effect, a delegation of hippies arrived at San Francisco's
> City Hall. They carried an offering of morning glory seeds and
> storebought mushrooms, which they hoped to use, they told a
> bemused press corps, to expand the consciousness of Mayor
> Shelly. They were in the midst of this presentation, which was half
> loony theatre, half polemic, when a group of antiwar activists, led
> by Jerry Rubin, arrived to hold their own press conference. It was
> a Sixties Rorschach: on one side of the hall stood the activists, in
> work boots and jeans, while across from them were these golden-
> robed hippies. And between them . . . in between them the an-
> tagonism was palpable. (p. 393)

The origins of contemporary radical green ideas are, however,
strongly rooted in 1960s radical culture and particularly in the
development of the alternative lifestyle movement—which in Australia saw the pioneering of an ecologically based lifestyle movement strongly influenced by hippy culture but by no means
exclusively so. As Metcalf and Vanclay (1987) have pointed out,

There are many misconceptions about participants in the alternative lifestyle movement. Some myths are created by the media
in an attempt to sensationalise the alternative lifestyles movement. The proverbial Sunday paper's page three photo of naked
hippies swimming in the creek is the archetype of this form of
media representation and exploitation. (p. 3)

In our explorations of academic social movement literature, we
were unable to locate many signs of these strong countercultural
roots; we suggest they are an absence in the literature of sociology
and communications and cultural studies.

Broadly defined, the counterculture includes a variety of movements, such as the alternative lifestyle movement, pagans, hippies, artists, poets, potters, and now New Age practitioners—although this latter group is not necessarily countercultural in any
strict sense. This definition covers the full spectrum of "the
Aquarian frontier" defined by Theodore Roszak (1975). This cannot be a closely defined field or location because opposition to
dominant paradigms takes many forms and often involves the
multiple identities of individuals exploring new cultures and
practices. In contrast, Michael Zimmerman (1994) has recently
periodized the counterculture into three movements corresponding to the decades of the 1960s, the 1970s, and the 1980s. This
is analytically useful, allowing us to separate the civil rights
movement of the 1960s, the New Age movement of the 1970s, and
the new paradigm movement of the 1980s, but in so doing, he
loses sense of the organic and interconnected nature of all these
streams. Zimmerman's account is refreshingly upbeat and postmodern in orientation but still betrays the standard academic
knee-jerk reaction to hippies, occultism, and wildness.

The exclusions of the broad range of countercultural experience from social movement literature and from our disciplinary
fields signals a need for the counterculture to be reassessed as a
social movement and as a significant source of spiritual renewal.
Analysis of these exclusions and fields of difference may be
important in casting light on the slowness of green parties to
institutionalize successfully as part of mainstream political processes and may also explain the declining appeal of the Left (new

and old) to contemporary youth. The counterculture has always specifically addressed the pleasure principle, nonviolence, peace, and love. It has done so with a spirit of fun, inclusion, and personal freedom that is not often found in the academic Left or in the labor movement. The marginalization of countercultural ideas (largely by a conservative left agenda) also indicates something about the general repression of the psyche and ecstatic processes in contemporary academic analysis.

In short, the forgetting of the counterculture in academic analysis of social movements is interesting because it exposes a number of biases across the political spectrum—including a bias against youth cultures, subcultures, premodern cultures, and a more pagan and tribalized postmodernism. Academic documentation of the green movement tends to exclude countercultural voices that go back at least to the hippies and to the beats and bohemians before them. This loose coalition can be traced back through the avant garde and alternative communal movements broadly: back to romanticism, utopianism, and anarchism (see, e.g., Mercer, 1984; Munro-Clark, 1986; Roszak, 1969; Zablocki, 1971, 1980). These roots are particularly problematic for materialist and poststructural analysis because they celebrate nature in a wildly eclectic fashion.

It is, however, to the 1960s that we must turn to understand the recent roots of the antinaturalism that marks much of official academic social theory and that defines a common academic left position. From the early 1960s, the hippies and counterculturalists were widely held to be eccentric, self-absorbed, and perhaps drug crazed and quickly attracted the scorn of the proletariat and its theorists and the continuing derision of conservative social commentators (e.g., Bell, 1976; Berman, 1982; Lasch, 1980; Schur, 1976). Yet many of the early traditions of the counterculture that engaged the feelings, emotions, the body, spirituality, healing, and alternative technology were ahead of their time. Hippies, although pariahs in most accounts, were, in fact, often pioneers of self-sufficiency and participatory and egalitarian natural philosophy. Their voices often sought alliance with the tribal cultures of indigenous people and their earth-centered views.

The fundamental opposition erected between historical materialism and philosophies of personal growth was inevitable. There is a kind of Cartesian-Newtonian orthodoxy behind much of the Left's troubles with the counterculture. Marxists may take drugs, but they do not talk to the fairies at the bottom of the garden. Hegel is on his head, after all. Thoughts do not travel, spirits do not abide, planets do not influence, and crystals have no power to heal. Among the ranks of the true believers on the Left, these countercultural traditions were, and still are, mysticism, idealism, or Hegelianism: something to be resisted to the end. Even the more progressive critical school, which Merchant (1994) reviews so sympathetically, remained wedded to the domination of high culture and rational analysis and was hardly sympathetic to hippies, pagans, and psychedelia. Anna Bramwell's (1989) book is typical in its heavy-handed treatment:

> Green theory today ranges from CND [Campaign for Nuclear Disarmament] to the European *Nouvelle Droite*. It incorporates the new pagans, such as the nomadic bands of witches, who visit Stonehenge for the solstice and follow the astral plane across Britain's sacred land, the matriarchal witches who worship at exactly the same standing stone in Germany as did the pagan Nazis. (p. 231)

In one sweep, Bramwell links pagans to the New Right and Nazism, effectively closing the door on any positive valuation of the counterculture's self-exploration and worshipping of nature.

There is a kind of ideological subterfuge at play here in the linking of counterculturalism and fascism. We know of no concerted effort by hippies or greens to use systematic violence against the state or their opponents. We do not think that, in the defense of ecology, the burning of bulldozers or the spiking of trees amount to fascism or terrorism. The same cannot be said of the Maoists and other radical left factions who supported the terrorism of the Baader Meinhoff group, or the Red Brigade, or indeed of Western Communist Parties that have supported the totalitarianism of Soviet, Chinese, and Cambodian state apparatuses, even despite considerable evidence of their atrocities.

Today, revolutionaries such as Lenin, Stalin, and Mao have been cast in a less than progressive light. Even the heroes of the intellectual Left, such as Sartre, Althusser, Foucault, Barthes, and many others, have all at times condoned the violence and repression of communist state apparatuses, and that of the Left generally, in their struggles with capitalism. To worry about the fascistic tendencies of hippies or tree-hugging deep ecologists might appear disingenuous to say the least. Perhaps in this very spotty history, there are good psychological reasons for the dying priests of the left to oppose postmodernism and slur the legacy of post-1960s students of the *Tibetan Book of the Dead.*

Marxist and neo-Marxist analysis is not sympathetically disposed to genuinely cross-cultural analysis. Typically, it has shown an intolerance to the possibilities of sharing multiple realities such that we might speak seriously about the rainbow serpent, Mother Earth, and other spiritual and mythological themes and values. Cultures inclusive of religion, mysticism, intuitive processes, personal development work, or enlightenment seeking do not excite the Left. Nevertheless, these exclusions are, in fact, at the heart of many social movements that have either broken away from Marxism (e.g., eco-feminism and postmodern feminism) or were always at odds with it—the counterculture, indigenous peoples' movements, the peace movement, and avant-garde art and literature.

From cultural studies, Andrew Ross's (1991) critique of the New Age movement in *Strange Weather* is a good example of the instinctive rationalizations of the Left. In the chapter titled "New Age—A Kinder, Gentler Science?" he gives us a thumbnail sketch of New Age belief systems represented at a British trade fair. Here, Ross is the rational interlocutor in a journalistic account of a commercialized new social movement that hasn't quite got it right. Ross, as he admits, is hardly an ethnographer or anthropologist in this book and is always going to reject the irrationalism of premodern cultures and the metaphysical. His main concern is with the politics of the movement—to show that New Age philosophy is marketed and sutured into capitalism. However, whereas the New Age movement is significant in itself, it does need to be placed in the broader context of the counterculture.

The movement that Ross observes is really the market end of a very loose network of individuals, groups, and organizations who would see themselves as spiritually alternative to mainstream religions and often continuing traditional philosophies and healing practices. Historically, it was the eclecticism of the 1960s's alternative lifestyle and hippy movement that provided the spiritual and ecological launching pad for the birth of the New Age. Ross (1992) acknowledges this in his later essay, "New Age Technoculture"—"most of the transformational rhetoric of New Age comes from the 1960s counterculture" (p. 554).

Ross's accounts of the New Age movement are pathbreaking in cultural studies. He has very acutely perceived the significance of the New Age and countercultural movements to key issues and themes in cultural studies and social theory, but as Jennifer Slack has pointed out, he is not a fan (as cited in Grossberg, Nelson, & Treichler, 1992, p. 553). Ross's own view is that a lack of ethnographic orientation enables him to retain a greater political objectivity: "We often cede too much ground in submerging our own voices, ground that will be occupied by other less sympathetic voices" (Grossberg et al., 1992, p. 553). This does not score well for methodology. Nonetheless, Ross's account is politically incisive and usefully supplements Zimmerman's more sympathetic analysis. Ross is certainly accurate about the tensions between New Age, deep ecology, and social ecology:

> Above all, New Age consciousness, whose activist roots lie in a deep, mythical affinity with nature, has played an important role in shaping the social and cultural activism of the ecology movement, increasingly divided between the philosophies of the deep ecology movement and social ecology. Neither side, however, seems to want to claim New Age as an official ally. Deep ecologists denigrate New Age's evolutionary devotion to growth as a technocratic strategy for using the earth as an expendable resource, citing the image of Spaceship Earth as an example of New Ager's technocratic contempt for a planet, which, once exhausted, will be left behind (Devall & Sessions, 1985). Social ecologists, on the other hand, equate New Age influence with the mystic nature cults, wiccan goddesses, and so forth, that have saturated the

eco-feminist with an atavistic taste for supernaturalism (Book-chin, 1990). From this perspective, New Age thought is seen as a dangerously antisocial element, exhausting the rationalist re-serves needed to reconstruct a free society living in nondominating balance with the natural world. (1992, p. 546)

ENVIRONMENTALISM'S DISILLUSION WITH THE LEFT

The idea that there are two different philosophical sides in the ecology movement is an abstraction from a much broader proc-ess. The environmental movement incorporates deep ecology and social ecology as distinct perspectives, but in mobilizing against logging, or promoting land care, or radicalizing dietary practices, environmentalism is a process of mobilization of many differences toward common ends. Social movements are goal oriented and create alliances between individuals and groups who might oth-erwise be at odds. These alliances provide the numbers and the collective will necessary to push green critiques through institu-tional and ideological constraints and opposition.

This is one of the reasons we have drawn attention to the oppositional categories of Ross's and Zimmerman's accounts—the indication of different analytical positions does not guarantee a balanced representation of the range of experiences and multi-ple positions that environmentalists may have. New Age, deep ecology, social ecology, hippydom, and so on certainly draw committed identification from individuals, but the practices and cultures of new social movements and postmodernity are not simply intellectual debates between differing positions. In prac-tice, individuals are often not so concerned to locate themselves for the convenience of academic analysis. Positions define ex-tremes and go on to create them. Most people simply move between extremes.

Nonetheless, there is a concerted effort by some left activists and theorists, such as Ross, to show the relevance of materialist perspectives to environmental and ecological debate. There is much common ground in this concern: opposition to the ideology and practice of multinationals, right-wing governments, consumerism, overexploitation of natural resources, and so on. Despite this ecumenism in theory, there are, however, still significant differences that define fault lines in the environmental movement—and provide potential for new syntheses. Although the concerns of the environmental movement and the Left may now be to some extent crosscutting, the intellectual and political roots of the labor movement and its orientation toward socialism and the redistribution of wealth and resources are not synonymous with those of environmentalism. Indeed, as Robert Paehlke (1989) points out in *Environmentalism and the Future of Progressive Politics*, "a socialist-environmentalist synthesis would require a revision of socialism as fundamental as the revisions sustained by liberalism in the late nineteenth and early twentieth century in the face of the socialist challenge" (p. 198). Toward that end, the play of differences between the Left (old and new) and the environmental movement has been critical in the major decentering of the Left itself and its movement toward greater ecological sensitivity.

As Paehlke (1989) emphasizes, socialist theory springs from the upheaval wrought by the industrial revolution. It is anchored in the creation of an oppressed and exploited working class during the 19th century. It was the misery and oppression of workers that Marxists felt would guarantee a revolutionary change. Founded in ideas of scientific materialism, revolution, and redistribution, socialist concern lay with the need for industrialization to provide increasingly improved living standards (material wealth) for its workers. It was not concerned to provide an ecological critique. Nature was still a limitless resource. But heavy industry and the mass production of goods continues to be regularly punctuated by ecological issues. Problems (some say disasters) arising from industrial growth are seen by many to be just as bad (some say worse) when in the hands of the vast centralized bureaucracies of a socialist state. Today, Marxists and post-Marxists alike have had to acknowledge the fact that environmental degradation is not just a problem of the exploitation of the working class. Ecological decline is the outcome of ideologies that encourage polluting technologies, pressure on scarce resources, and mounting globalized exploitation (cf. Cotgrove, 1982; Martell, 1994; Paehlke, 1989). This acknowledgment of the complexity of ecological crisis is perhaps the first step toward the greening of the Left and critical social theory. In Australia, the early motivations for this greening developed from confrontation between environmentalists and the industrialized and unionized sectors of the workforce (i.e., timber workers and miners). These early, and mostly bitter, confrontations with the old Left by environmental activists have encouraged the development of a coherent and persuasive challenge to socialist theory and its prioritization of the value of human labor among other ecological values.

Labor movement and left attachment to economic growth has been a major problem for Greens. From the beginning, the labor movement was seen by environmentalists to quickly find common ground with its old enemies, the capitalist industrialists and developers. Both Marxism and liberal economics agree that over time, capitalist enterprises grow in size—economies of scale encourage and allow the centralization of key productive and administrative functions. From the point of view of unit output, this may indeed be a solution, but as Schumacher and others (including progressive left critics such as Murray Bookchin) have argued, small is beautiful and rational. As Paelhke (1989) points out, the rejection of the inevitability and desirability of economic growth is "an essential element in an environmental revision of socialism" (p. 199). Under prevailing economic conditions, growth and ecology are on a collision course. The development of an ecologically sustainable economy calls for a complete reappraisal of prevailing economic models. At the least, the value of ecologies has to be reassessed and included as part of the calculus of development and its critical appraisal.

Neither ecological aesthetics nor pragmatics have had much impact on industrial societies. Historically, there has been a shared interest from the Left and the Right in the survival of the industrial system of exploitation of natural resources; both sides share a dependence on economic growth and industrial technology. They both assumed that economic, social, and ecological problems could be solved with new technology. Socialism even legitimated this technological determinism theoretically by emphasizing the determining effect of social relations in the functioning of technological systems. Generally, socialist theory assumed that industrial technology could be safe, efficient, and nonpolluting in a socialist world (Paehlke, 1989). The idea that technology was only unsafe because it was in the hands of capitalists solved none of the main green concerns. Recent history has demonstrated that capitalists and socialists have both been environmentally reckless, investing massively in industries that are highly polluting and in the continued rampant exploitation of natural resources. In practice, however, under both capitalism and socialism, the health and safety of workers has been sacrificed to the gods of progress, growth, and profit. This is the ugly face of industrial imperialism.

Environmentalists have widely rejected the confidence of Marxists in centrally organized structures and the revolutionary potential of the working class. The centralization of state power in particular runs counter to green analysis of power relations and the importance of regionalism. There are many sources for this antiauthoritarianism and concern for decentralization—the counterculture, for example, has from the beginning expressed a strong distrust of authority and institutionalized forms of power and knowledge. The post-1960s turn-on, tune-in, drop-out generation continued perennial traditions of nonconformism and rebellion that work their way through all new social movements. As we have argued, the counterculture, and later the Greens, expressed core values of self-sufficiency and local participatory democracy rather than the collectivist and centralist notions of socialist organization. These competing values spin around many axes and now include the relativism of postmodernism and the deconstructionism of poststructuralism.

Paehlke (1989) has usefully summarized some of the major disputes along the path of the greening of the Left. He sees the main contradictions between environmentalism and left analysis as arising out of the issues of economic growth, technology, the distribution of power, exploitation of the environment, and the integrity of personal autonomy. In short,

- Few Marxists see the need for the end of economic growth.
- Technology is seen as an essential means of generating social wealth.
- Left analysis advances distributive rather than ecological values.
- It promotes the centralization of political power.
- It disputes the central importance of personal autonomy. (Paehlke, 1989, p. 197)

GREENING OF THE LEFT

The development of green politics in Australia has involved a historical tension between what have been labeled *green green* and *red green* positions. Many, especially the young, have failed to see the political relevance of much of the left agenda, and like many orthodoxies after the 1960s, left organizations have seen their numbers fall sharply. New Left green organizations have not been successful in their attempts at conversion:

> They have not been very successful at attracting the angry, disillusioned, and cynical, apart from those who have long been engaged in left-wing politics. They would dearly like to attract new social movement activists, but these blue denim incorruptibles evince deep-seated distrust of the red-green organizations for their connections with the "old politics" of socialism and the labor movement. (Burgmann, 1993, pp. 215-216)

Over the past few years, we have seen chameleonlike communist and socialist organizations greening their agendas. For example, the Australian Communist Party, which closed shop in 1989, reopened its doors as The New Left Party with environmental issues incorporated in a social justice agenda. Left organizations now publish under such titles as the *Green Left Weekly* and the *Green Left Review*. Unable to give up the central ideas of socialism, they are instead "recognising that socialism cannot be built on rubbish heaps, that ecological problems cannot wait until the revolution" (Burgmann, 1993, p. 213). Left organizations have adopted a red-green political agenda. As Burgmann goes on to say, "Marx's writings have been pillaged anew in a search for confirmation of the inevitability of capitalist failures towards the environment" (p. 214). For more inclusion in the green paradigm, however, the Left has to go a deeper green. It is not enough to simply change the color of shirts and socks; green is more than an issue of color:

> Many greens call for quite radical change in economic priorities, political structures, social lifestyles and cultural value systems. There are also strong elements of democracy and egalitarianism in radical green thinking which are at odds with conservative emphases on authority and hierarchy. (Martell, 1994, p. 140)

THE GREEN AGENDA

Greening is about the establishment of a green moral imperative and is not restricted to any one political viewpoint. As we have argued, environmental and ecological analyses have come from a variety of institutional locations and from across the left-right political spectrum. The green movement is an instance of the vitality of cultural diversity. Just as the women's movement and the gay and lesbian movement have been able to problematize gender and deconstruct the male-female, masculine-feminine dichotomy, the green movement has achieved much through a similar deconstructing process. Pioneering green politicians Petra Kelly (1984), Jonathon Porritt (1984), Drew Hutton (1987), and many others have indicated that the ecological crisis has to be seen as related to varied causes, that whole modes of life and worldviews are involved. According to the Australian historian and green politician Drew Hutton (1987),

> Significant sections of the population in modern industrial societies—perhaps as many as 10 percent—see reality in a whole new way; they have a different system of ethics from mainstream society, and they organise themselves on principles which are different from what is usually held up as the norm. (p. 15)

Although green philosophy has been the recipient of many of the achievements of other social movements, its main focus defines a radical new position. Having absorbed and developed many of the issues on contemporary social agendas, Greens have emerged with a wide-ranging challenge to the various accounts of the so-called dominant paradigm. Green theorists have extended the arguments of feminism and implicated anthropocenterism and Eurocenterism, as well as patriarchy, in the current decline of habitat (e.g., Devall, 1990; Martell, 1994; Merchant, 1994; Plumwood, 1993; Redclift & Benton, 1994). They have raised ecocenterism as a human rights problem enmeshed in unsustainable technological development as well as raising moral issues regarding the rights of nonhumans and ecosystems. Their emphasis on connection and the mutual interest of all species positions humanity as part of a system. Some form of species egalitarianism, or at least species recognition, is at the basis of green philosophy and politics.

Green theory is politically and thematically diverse, containing many fault lines, tensions, and conflicts. Within this diversity and difference, there is, however, an emergent worldview or new paradigm that is able to contain the radical differences of eco-feminism, deep ecology, scientific ecology, and all the other stake holders in green and environmental institutional locations. Framing this emergent green paradigm, a loose global systems theory runs through all green theory from the deep ecology of Naess, Devall, Sessions, and Capra to the materialist eco-feminism of Plumwood and Janet Biehle (1991). The idea that the planet is a large number of interconnected systems with humanity being but one component is a common position. In this view, humans are seen as connected to an increasingly fragile ecological network like all other life forms. The coemergence of secular essentialist and spiritual feminist positions in eco-feminism (e.g., Daly, 1978; Gablik, 1991; LaChapelle, 1985; Salleh, 1984) further develops this idea that the planet is a large number of interconnected systems.

Eco-feminism is particularly important in the articulation of green politics. For many environmentalists, their location as women has influenced their environmental views. Women's identification of patriarchy as a dominant institution of oppression has enabled environmentalism to develop a more thoroughly pluralist movement. But again, in this pluralism, it is worth emphasizing the views in common that define environmentalism as a coherent difference; in particular, the idea of a global system is fundamental. Like deep ecology, eco-feminism encourages us to think of ourselves as simultaneously living different sorts of connections, all of which we can effect in some way. In this emerging global systems theory, ideas such as James Lovelock's (1979) Gaia hypothesis, in which the planet is conceived as a living, self-regulating superorganism, are becoming more popular because of their ability to define this globalism in empirical ecological terms. Gaian theory is also more optimistic than mechanistic science in suggesting that ecologies can be self-healing. At the heart of this globalizing, there remains a basic contradiction between the interests of humans and the interests of other species and "wild" places. In green theory and philosophy, we are now seeing the development of models that are more biologically and ecologically based than presently available in social theory. We are seeing ideas that suggest organic connection through all systems—ideas that relate to an interconnected biosphere that functions as a global entity and is perhaps even alive in some way. With the development of these themes comes a rethinking of our favored position on the top branch of the tree of life.

SUMMARY AND CONSIDERATIONS

The historical outcomes of social movements in Australia have been considerable in terms of new laws and social justice, dollars to the needy, and trees saved. These outcomes are a reminder of the continuing presence of broadly based social protest and activism in Australia today. This is true on an international basis: The labor movement, the peace movement, the women's movement, indigenous peoples' movements, and the environmental movement have had global impacts. All of these movements have attacked social inequalities and campaigned for social justice and equity in various ways. The political campaigns waged by individuals, groups, and organizations within social movements have strongly influenced daily life and the political agendas of dominant institutions. They have strongly influenced the development of environmentalism.

The roots of ecological resistance need to be traced back through the centuries—back through the rise to dominance of science, technology, and Christianity and the exclusion and marginalization of earlier more eco-centered cosmologies (see Chapter 1, particularly). From this rich history, green perspectives have emerged as an increasingly coherent and articulated analysis of hierarchy, exploitation, exclusion, and technological expediency. Today, this greening is a sociocultural movement that has emerged organically from grassroots constituencies and has involved widespread shifts in culture and identity. Academic histories of this greening tend to exclude its partial character as romantic rebellion, ecstatic religion, mythos, spirituality, sex, drugs, and rock and roll. From its early beginnings in post-1960s social movements, the green movement has been a mass movement drawing in popular and esoteric cultures and changing academic themes. The exclusion of the counterculture from the annals of social movement literature in sociology, communication, and cultural studies is indicative of a rift between red-green and green-green positions. It is perhaps in the development of a broader theoretical discussion that many other of the significant differences among environmentalists can be given a stronger voice. As we might expect, some of these differences deliver exciting new possibilities.

We develop a more focused theoretical analysis in the next chapter, arguing that space is needed for the development of an ecoculturalist theory of self. Starting from an interactionist perspective on self, we propose a greener theory of the self: Through the self, we connect with our ecologies and act as individuals with rights, duties, obligations, and expectations. Through the self we are also able to identify with different positions and withdraw from others. Ignored by many theorists and idealized by others, self is a controversial subject that casts new light on the identity changes occurring in new social movements.

CHAPTER

5

Living in the Biosphere

Eco-Selves and Decentered Identities

They sought it with thimbles, they sought it with care;
They pursued it with forks and hope;
They threatened its life with a rail-way share;
They charmed it with smiles and soap.

—Lewis Carroll (1967, p. 89)

In this chapter, we want to explore the exclusion of self-concepts from social theory and how this might be addressed through a convergence of perspectives—from a postmodernized interactionism, through deep ecology, to the coming of the cyborgs. We are particularly concerned to show how a postmodernized interactionism can contribute to an understanding of processes of ecological identification. Our starting point is the observation that the critical importance of ecological location in the conceptualization of self and identity has not been addressed in social, cultural, and communication theory.

The recent work of Stuart Hall (1994) is, we think, typical of the failure of Marxism, structuralism, and theorists of the post to seriously address the issue of ecological crisis and its impacts on social theory. Hall, one of cultural studies' foremost architects, continues to regard nature-environment as other to human subjectivity. In "The Question of Cultural Identity," he lists "five great advances" (p. 20) in social theory and human sciences that define modern identity as fragmented. According to Hall, Marxism, psychoanalysis, structural linguistics, Foucault, and feminism have all had decentering effects on the conceptualization of the subject and identity and, following Raymond Williams, Hall notes the passing of a subject that is "singular, distinctive, unique, (Williams, quoted in Hall, 1994, p. 119) and individualistic. He writes of shifts, ruptures, and decenterings that have occurred in social theory and "the human sciences," all of which have had "a great impact on thought in the period of late modernity," and whose effect, he argues, has been "the final decentring of the Cartesian subject" (p. 120). This is not, however, the final decentering of the Cartesian subject. Hall's conceptualization of late modernity is pre-ecological. Hall does not regard ecological crisis as significant in its decentering potential and therefore fails to address the radical impact of ecological crisis on social theory and on our understanding of subjectivity and identity. Hence, Hall's posthumanism continues an anthropocentric left tradition.

We argue that the individual in society, his or her subjectivity, sense of selfhood, and experience of a life world, all have an ecological dimension. We all experience our selves as being in a relationship with an ecology, and we all express our selves in a conversation with this web of connection. We orient ourselves to nonhuman others as well as human others and reference groups. We are all essentially grounded in, and bonded to, a nonhuman world. We experience this connectedness in various ways—from the enjoyment of a good view to the use of high technology; but our experiences and the activities that generate them always depend on shared resources. Life and meaning are fundamentally ecological. This has radical implications for the way we theorize society, culture, communication, and the self: As we argue throughout this book, there is an ecological dimension in all theory.

Environmentalism and green politics fill out this dimension. The continuing successes of green politics demonstrates that there are many who will defend the environment against human encroachment. In this defense and promotion of natural interests, individuals identify with ecological others and articulate ecological selves—a move that has not been lost on politicians. This greening produces changes in identity and the way individuals feel about their relationship to others. Greening entails a greater identification with nature and the development of an extended self—an eco-self. The theory of self in an ecological context is today a problem of postmodern dimensions. The self is articulated in multiple contexts; it is globalized, vectorized, and deconstructed. Yet despite these decentering flows and fragmentations, the basic phenomena of the self identified by interactionists in the early 20th century continue—only now, in the context of postmodernity, ecological crisis, and the general context of new social movements. Internal dialogue, significant others, social reference groups, networks, and the noisy bustle of the symbolic interaction of society, culture, and ecology continue to provide coherent identities and personal boundaries, contested and multiple as these may be in contemporary society.

The marginalization and exclusion of ecological considerations from discourse about self has strong parallels with the struggle gender awareness has waged in modern patriarchal texts. As discussed in earlier chapters, this is a similar problematic to that encountered by feminists attempting to work within patriarchal frameworks. Progress for women, though, has depended on much more than textual reform in education and reasoned argument or changing media propaganda. Women (and men) have also sought to change their attitudes and even language itself—feminists have long emphasized the need for new discourses and new language in their efforts to secure new identities and practices. These shifts have allowed us to think new thoughts and to question taken-for-granted assumptions such as the natural status of just two categories for gender. An ecocentric shift also encourages new transgressive thoughts—such as the idea that identity and self-awareness are ecological in essence. Self can now be seen as socially constructed and sustained in community with an enormous number of interconnected others along with their ecologies and habitats. As soon as community is extended beyond the human sphere, a number of significant barriers are crossed: The dualisms of nature-culture, reason-emotion, mind-matter, male-female are, in practice, all transgressed by life and nature itself.

One of the basic philosophical and theoretical problems that concerns us here is the question of who or what we think we are. Specifically, if theory and common sense locate our humanness outside of, or transcendent to, ecological fields and considerations, we will continue to reproduce alienation and problematic cultural dualisms. Running counter to this ecological alienation, greening is a reaction against many of the alienating paradigms of modernity. For deeper green theorists, the development of new discourse involves paradigm shifts and decenterings across non-human spheres. Ecological vision locates humanity in an extended community of other life forces and their ecologies. In working toward the preservation of ecologies and the cultivation of ecological awareness, dichotomies are transgressed, identities shifted, and the self becomes extended and inclusive. This expanded sense of self is a practical achievement that is possible because of the intrinsic ecological potentials of all selves. In this chapter, we argue that social theory needs to specifically address these potentials.

THE WAY OF THE SELF

But can we continue to talk about the *self* as a meaningful category? Is the self just an outmoded, bourgeois abstraction? Or if there ever was a self, has it not become fragmented in postmodernity? We address these questions from a (loosely) postmodern interactionist perspective. Self, we believe, is still a key concept in the phenomenology of the life world. Self is the paramount modality of the awareness the individual has of its place in the life world. Self is the awareness the individual organism has of its membership in a society and is the fundamental means by which an individual experiences identity and location. If personal awareness extends to allow bonding with other life forms and the nurturance of the nonhuman, then the nonhuman others that populate our individual life worlds form part of the dialogue with the self. Clearly, even without the stimulus of new social movements, the symbolic interaction that occurs between self and other often involves nonhuman life forms and their ecologies. Yet we have still to develop the theoretical tools that will allow an ecological self to be adequately expressed in social theory and general philosophy.

The idea of an ecological self is manifestly not simply a problem for deep ecologists and New Age philosophers. The whole modernist paradigm of self-perception—its glorification in individualisms that cut across gender, class, and ethnic sensibilities—is challenged by any broadening and recentering of the self across nonhuman territories. Furthermore, the reintroduction of the self onto theoretical agendas allows the political program of individual and species rights to proceed on a basis that is more informed by phenomenology and the subjective insights of poststructuralism and postmodernism. This is important if critical theory is to remain in postpositivist cultural formations.

This is an issue for all theorists of postmodern identities. With the enthusiasm of poststructuralism to deconstruct authorship and bourgeois individualism, the reflexive subject has lost its theoretical voice. In postmodernism, the proposed multiplicity and fragmentation of the subject remains depersonalized and ultimately incoherent without some theoretical account of self. If self is excluded from the texts of communication and cultural studies and social theory, we are left with the abstract projections of a universalized politics and an insufficiently grounded authoritarian text about the subject. Self, or personal consciousness, is the enduring vehicle and process that mediates all perception and individual understanding. Self is formed in the social matrix of local culture and ecology. It reflects and expresses a certain worldview as well as the idiosyncratic and sometimes chaotic imperatives of a single organism. Self is the primary locus of individual experience. There is something ephemeral, private, and nonobjective about the self, and it is partly for these reasons that it has been avoided as a continuing subject of major interest in social theory. The self, however, like nature and the universe, is a category that is never exhausted of meaning.

As discussed in Chapter 4, the avoidance of self in contemporary academic theory stems from the dominance of left analysis. This dominance has been continued in the paradigm shifts of poststructuralism and postmodernism. Despite the historical success of sociology in overcoming the foundational opposition of positivism to the very idea of a social science, left analysis has strongly favored the public sphere over the private sphere and resisted phenomenological or interactionist insights in its reflex desire to find scientific truths. Broadly speaking, the antihumanism of modern left analysis has been a deliberate effort to avoid the traps of individualism and any prioritization of individual subjectivity. In this widespread bracketing of individual experience, there is therefore no provision for theoretical feedback about the experience of ecological connection. Nor has the greater sophistication of poststructural analysis transcended the ecological dilemmas of traditional left analysis. In the final analysis, neither materialist dialectics nor poststructural textual analysis are ecological theory—they are resolutely human centered. Ecology, however, has not been the only exclusion in the preoccupation of socialism and the labor movement with the struggle between labor and capital. Microsociological concerns, with the recognition of subjectivity and interaction, generally have been marginalized as have macrosociological concerns of connection between non-European myth, identity, and culture.

Clearly, there are a number of sound philosophical reasons for revaluing the self as an important site for theoretical analysis. In this chapter, we particularly draw on interactionism, phenomenology, and deep ecology to develop an ecoculturalist and postmodern outline of the self. In this account, the self remains as an enduring vehicle and process. Self is a perennial framework for perception and experience, always mediating daily life and the worlds we create.

The search for self is, for us, a path with theoretical heart. There is, we can safely say, a self to which we all return even if it might have changed when we weren't there, when we weren't reflexively aware. This self is the individual's sense of continuity and location and incorporates the construction of identities, roles, and personal histories. Selves can be centered or decentered—we can feel together or all over the place, we can be in a fuzzy spot of tension, or we may be a self in a process of discursive construction-deconstruction-reconstruction. We may be dispersed across a 1,000 texts, or we may be no self at all: just an articulation of structures and differences in discursive processes. Undoubtedly, all these things are happening continuously. There is probably no end to the ways basic paradoxes are expressed through the self. The self is simultaneously a point of return and departure, a paradox of continuity and change, of multiplicity and unity.

The ecological self we are pursuing is postmodern in the sense we developed in Chapter 3. It is reflexive, relativistic, and anchored in multiple realities. Our postmodern formulation is also consistent with the principles of symbolic interactionism, a model of the self originating in the insights of the pioneering North American sociologist George Hergert Mead (1863-1931). Mead (1934) talks of the self as arising out of social relations (or interaction) and being developed and sustained in interaction and communication. From this basic relational insight, the self is open to different theoretical possibilities and the incorporation of ecological considerations. The idea of the self we develop is a starting point for further analysis and play in many traditions; questions about who and what we think we are remain perennially interesting.

THEORIZING *SELF*

Nonetheless, self, and self-experience, remain highly problematic for the social sciences and humanities, whose recent preoccupations have been very much against introspective theorizing. Not since the heyday of positivism and the philosophy of the

Vienna Circle have we seen such a concerted effort to separate knowledge and method from the subjectivity of individual percep- tion and the life world. The legacy of poststructural and postmod- ern theorizing would seem to be a deconstructed subjectivity in which self and subjectivity are exposed as a socially constructed fiction. Concepts such as *death of the author* and *death of the subject* signify a turn away from the celebration of individual worlds and subjectivities and from personal power for the sake of a better appreciation of the nature of social power and the structures of domination, exploitation, repression, and the text (cf. Game, 1991).

The success of this post-Marxist project has meant that, broadly speaking, social theory has turned away from the concept of self and its phenomenological domains of self-experience and introspective methodologies, such as dream analysis or the ex- ploration of fantasy or ecstasy. This means a turning away from the more introspectively grounded insights of critical theory, phenomenological sociology, post-Meadian interactionism, intro- spective synthesizers such as R. D. Laing and Peter Berger, and pre-poststructuralists such as Georges Bataille. There are many other writers and perspectives that can be positioned within these zones of rejected subjectivisms. Karl Marx's original admonitions against bourgeois individualism have influenced generations of critical social theorists to the point where theory becomes ab- sorbed by the social and subjectivity is limited to its textuality. The self then disappears as an unstated subjectivity—a personal indulgence from which we need to escape to find history and some kind of truth. This great escape occurs between the extremes of the reflexive amnesia we find in Marxism and poststructural deconstruction, which dissolves the self in textual analysis. These extremes both travel the road to total institutionalization (cf. Goffman, 1961).

To save the self from total deconstruction, we look now at how the self takes meaning as private experience and public perform- ance. Picking up Erving Goffman's (1959) analogy with the thea- ter, we might consider self as a way of making daily life meaningful through fictional (i.e., textual) processes. Our memories become meaningful as we recall and reconstruct the past; our projects take meaning against our priorities, desires, and strategies. In our storytelling, we develop narratives of the self. In our role play, we explore stereotyped expectations about behavior and the boundaries of the self. All these interactive processes are flows of meaning we construct with a degree of art and agency.

We commonly understand ourselves in narrative terms. We position ourselves in unfolding narratives. Our storytelling, photo albums, diaries, and even memories place us as the subject of events, adventures, sagas, dramas, and so forth. These narratives of the self are, however, not the same as self per se. Self has a reflexivity and creative presence that always holds some opportunity for escape from the tyranny of texts and oppressive social situations. Self is an enduring site of innovation, creativity, passion. Self, we think, has a phenomenology, ontology, and methodology; it is capable of being encountered, experienced, charted, and mapped as well as invented, constructed, and deconstructed. Self is, however, a particularly resistant kind of fiction that is routinely committed to its own permanence.

There are interesting parallels between theoretical moves toward deconstruction and work in personal development, mysticism, shamanism, Western occult traditions, and ascetic religious traditions. The stripping away of self is a fairly universal therapy and avenue to personal empowerment. The self has been widely described as an obstacle to be overcome, worked through, or transcended (e.g., Krishnamurti, 1969; Metzner, 1971; Suzuki, 1956; Watts, 1973). There is, in other words, at least one interest held in common between the puritanism and self-avoidance of much of the institutional Left and religious mysticism. Both want to get away from the self. As phenomenologists and interactionists insist, however, the self is something to which we always return in the routine experience of daily life; in the here and now of the life world (Schutz & Luckmann, 1974).

OTHER RETURNS . . .

Post-Marxist approaches, such as social ecology (e.g., Biehl, 1991; Bookchin, 1982; Gorz, 1980; Plumwood, 1993) are, as we have suggested in earlier chapters, trapped by the logic of dualism and have an aversion to deep ecology and postmodernism. Not for them the global ecology of Gaia, the mysticism and cosmology of the counterculture, or the reflexive mobility of the self. Social ecology, like managerialist shallow ecology, is not a particularly reflexive, introspective, or deeply philosophical discourse. Here, the postmodern ecological baby is thrown out with the modern bath water of political puritanism. If, however, we recognize that the self is a constant framework for routine social experience, we can address postmodernity without sacrificing the individual's agency, location in social structure, or experience of social conflict. This is evident, for example, in the postmodern interactionism of Norman Denzin's (1992) *Symbolic Interactionism and Cultural Studies*. But whereas we are in accord with Denzin's interactionism, and his incorporation of media texts, his analysis is still pre-ecological—as we show later. Like Denzin, we want to engage postmodernism in our interactionism, but we have one additional fundamental concern: ecology.

In engaging postmodernism as an ecological project, we seek to emphasize that nature, ecology, and environment, like self, are discursive projects that are realized and experienced in material and symbolic ways. All these constructs are in the space of simulation and the other prior phases of the image that Baudrillard (1983) identifies in *Simulations*. This heterogeneous formulation enables us to retain an ecological realism as we slide into postmodernism. The real and the hyperreal coexist, along with the imaginary, the fake, and the authentic. We can find dualisms and dichotomies in all these cultural formations, fields of experience, and multiplicities of the self. This cultural mapping takes us well beyond the poststructuralism of cultural studies and sociology and may help make better sense of the chaos of shifting paradigms and multiple identities registered in postmodernity.

ON WITH INTERACTIONISM

Our earlier description of self theorization, as marginalized by the modernist materialism of left analytical perspectives, helps explain why common knowledge in our academies has privileged materialism and textualism and routinely assumed that individualism, essentialism, and idealism lie down the pathways of introspective methodologies. It also helps explain the otherwise puzzling neglect of the interactionist tradition in European and Australian disciplines and the continuing mistaken assumption that interactionism is merely a consensus model of society with no potential for the analysis of conflict or the political economic processes at the core of society (e.g., Cuff, Sharrock, & Francis, 1992; Haralambos & Holborn, 1990; Layder, 1994). The interactionist tradition has had fairly bad press from these political sociologists who have argued that interactionism does not adequately address questions of power and conflict and that it does not have a theory of society.

True as these complaints may be, it is nonetheless the case that the theoretical conjunctions of feminism, poststructuralism, postmodernism, and interactionism are potentially symbiotic. Denzin's (1992) *Symbolic Interactionism and Cultural Studies* clearly demonstrates this possibility. He argues that interactionism needs more input from the fields of communication and cultural studies, that politics and the text need more foregrounding. Denzin demonstrates that the basic interactionist model of self in society remains a valid starting point for a critical account of the routine structures and processes of subjective experience in modernity and postmodernity. In its theoretical opposition to solipsism and individualism (Burkitt, 1991), interactionism is spiritually at one with Marxism. But in its ability to accommodate multiple selves, interactionism is more aligned with postmodernism. In practice, we remain more or less centered in the processes of negotiating who we are, even when situating ourselves in the "arcs and gaps" (Collins, 1992, p. 349) offered by the noncoalescing subject positions of postmodernity. Despite the decentering effects of postmodernity on the self, individual life worlds remain oriented toward the production and maintenance of social selves. Self is the paramount reality in individual experience. The globalizing effects of postmodernity make self-production a more mediated and complex undertaking, but as long as social interaction remains the source of primary group loyalties (e.g., the family, the tribe, the peer group, the subculture, the club), the social production of self will continue, as outlined by interactionists. The formation and maintenance of selves are central processes in social life and key processes in a capitalist social order. Advertisers, politicians, parents, and teachers are all in the business of constructing and reconstructing individual selves.

In short, the production of self is a phenomenon that remains at the heart of social life in a globalizing postmodernity. The scope and centerings of the self are, however, variable. Postmodern selves confront a variety of competing reference groups, texts, and discourses. In Australia, University Open Learning programs now compete with B films for late night programming and other off-peak viewing locations. Through advertising in particular, psychoanalysis, art, film, and literature have been stitched into popular culture. Television has brought many high cultural genres into the psyche, and the signs and symbols of the unconscious are part of the symbolic exchange of daily life. In postmodernity, the everyday is merely the surface of the many fields of consciousness compassed by the individual. The psychic underworlds of social life routinely break through in art, literature, film, and advertising—we are all exposed to the symbolic worlds of dream and fantasy. The routine and the taken-for-granted are now thoroughly intertextual. This is one of the liberating effects of multiculturalism—there's always some other legitimate perspective out there. There is always at least one line of flight available.

Interactionism, or any other theory of self, does, however, need to register ecology as a new context of self-production. This move could have a major impact on fields that depend on a theory of self to underpin their positions. For instance, an ecologically oriented interactionist theory of self is particularly important in the context of social movement theory because it provides a middle way between eco-feminism and deep ecology. The positioning of these two perspectives as mutually exclusive has been deeply divisive for environmentalists. The tensions between the deep ecologies of Fox (1990) and Devall (1990) and the eco-feminisms of Plumwood (1993) and Salleh (1984), for instance, are no longer productive for the political or theoretical projects of environmentalism. Arguably, these positions can both be seen to presuppose a social self that is born and sustained in social relations, communication, and culture. Eco-feminism and deep ecology still bifurcate from this point, however. Eco-feminism works toward the rights of women in an ecology, whereas deep ecology works more toward the subversion of anthropocentrism. These different directions are not quite antithetical, despite their deep polarization. As Freya Mathews (1994) has written,

> Ecofeminism and Deep Ecology, with their complementary inter-
> pretations of the interconnectedness thesis, each capture an
> important aspect of our metaphysical and ethical relationships
> with nature. For if it does consist in a web of relations, then . . .
> it may be seen as both a whole and as a manifold of individuals.
> (p. 243)

An interactionist theory of self that locates us in an ecology can potentially provide a common ground from which the sought-after "dialectical reconciliation of these two views" (Mathews, 1994, p. 236) can be achieved. The assumption of a multiperspectival self is, in fact, implicit in Mathews's statement about the complemen-tarity of eco-feminism and deep ecology. It is, after all, precisely the multiperspectival abilities of our selves that allow us to contemplate contradictions and dilemmas. Self is the process in which philosophical difference can be held in tension and trans-gressed. The reflexivity of the self is constituted of multiple tensions—this is part of the condition of postmodernity and not simply the alienation of modernism's tormented individualism.

Although following Mathews's (1994) lead in distinguishing parts from the whole, we do not agree with Mathews that she should abandon "the ethical conclusions to which Deep Ecology is normally assumed to lead" (p. 236). "The insistence of deep ecologists that we are one with a nature which best knows how to look after itself" (p. 239) is not really the logical dilemma Mathews feels it to be. What deep ecology needs is a theory of self that is not trapped by the stasis of a moment of identification with broader nature. *Identification* needs to be understood as involving more than passive absorption into an undifferentiated whole. A theory of self that allows the ecological dimensions of communi-cation, identification, and interdependency to be expressed can accommodate this apparent contradiction between part and whole. In a greener interactionism, self is always a conversation between a part and a whole—the individual and society, the individual and its ecology, society and ecology. A theory of self needs to capture that dynamic. An ecological theory needs to locate the dynamic of self in an ecology. Toward that end neither eco-feminism, deep ecology, nor classical interactionism is suffi-cient in itself.

REAPPRAISING MEAD AND
THE INTERACTIONIST TRADITION

In the interactionist tradition, society and self are copresent realities. G. H. Mead's (1934) foundational notion of self as a conversation, or dialectic, between an *I* and a *me* represents the ongoing construction of self in a social space. Self is in society, and society is in the self. This insight is still a useful starting point from which to explore the theoretical possibilities of self in a changing world—a world that, since Mead's time, is increasingly mediated by technology of various kinds and now challenged by ecological crisis. The increased mediation of the self and its broader ecological identifications does not negate the fundamen-tally social nature of self that interactionism identifies, but the meanings of *self, society,* and *social* may be more ambiguous. This is now a world in which there are a multiplicity of discourses that provide multiple horizons of meaning and the possibility of more heterogeneous processes of identity formation.

Individuals are today being socialized in the contexts of globali-zation, multiculturalism, and the decline in significance of the nation state. Identity with, and loyalty to, a nation now sound strangely outdated, modern ideas. Postmodernity is a condition in which many things may contest for priority in the formation of identity and loyalty. The continuing compression of space and time and the disembedding of society and individuals that now occurs constitute new conditions for the life world (Giddens,

1991). This challenges both the coherence and meaning of individual worlds, but it also challenges modern interactionism, whose bias has been to the functional and routine rather than the new and changing. Postmodernism's permissiveness now allows us to more easily contemplate the transgressions of dualisms and stereotypes that occur with multiple identities and selves: core selves, male selves, female selves, dream selves, transcendent selves, ecological selves, and so on, are all part of the self. This heterogeneity points beyond interactionism's traditional sociological positioning and introduces a more expanded and dynamic sense of self.

Nonetheless, the emphasis of interactionism on social relations as a key to consciousness, self, and society has an obvious parallel with Marx's thought, as does the problematization of boundaries between individual and society. This, we might suppose, is a high point of modernity: a convergence of theorizing that takes us out of the so-called monadology of early philosophers, such as Descartes, Leibniz, and Kant, and toward the recognition that individuals and societies are somehow constructed. This takes us out of the so-called essentialism of isolated individuals and social atoms and potentially resolves the individual-society dichotomy through the idea of a self formed and sustained in continuous response to society. This is perhaps the major contribution of G. H. Mead to contemporary social theory.

The articulation of the individual as a self is an important resolution of the problematic dichotomy between individual and society that occurs in classical social theory (see Burkitt, 1991; Cuff et al., 1992; Layder, 1994). The great advance of interactionism over Marxism in the theorization of daily life, however, is the idea that the self (and *mind*, the more general matrix of conscious awareness) is mediated by language and other symbolic behavior, such as our orientation to others—for example, significant others, generalized others, and reference groups. The individual is active in the construction and reception of society that it internalizes into personal space and reproduces through social interaction. As Berger and Luckmann (1972) argued in *The Social Construction of Reality*, this is a dialectic process mediated by the self. Self is simply a part of everyday experience. In this approach, the individual is not negated or bracketed out of our understanding of communication, culture, and society in favor of history, destiny, or a depersonalized subjectivity. Mind, consciousness, and reality are in the realm of the social and always mediated by language and the self.

Most generally, the radical insight of Mead and interactionists is that the individual's self-awareness is always sustained in social relations—self is always involved in processes of interaction and communication with others who are themselves all bearers of culture and society. Self is a reflexive process in which the ability to see oneself from the position of the other is the culmination of a process of childhood development where the infant progressively models a universe of experience. Self, here, is a series of positionings with respect to the various others that orient thought and behavior. From a greener perspective, our attitudes to nature and nonhuman life are also negotiated and constructed by significant others and reference groups, many of which may be nonhuman.

GREENING INTERACTIONISM

Despite Mead's apparent consensus orientation, his narrow view of the cultural value of other species, his uncritical assumption of the nature-culture dichotomy, and his probable sexism, there is no a priori reason to exclude ecological considerations from the field of the self in post-Meadian theory. With a broader understanding of the social construction and identifications of the self, we can allow ecological others to be significant points of orientation in decision making and other routine activities, such as the stories we tell to sustain our identities. Ecology is, however, only one of the exclusions that post-Meadian theory needs to address. Closer reading of Mead's (1934) texts reveals a self that is relatively tension free and untroubled by psychological underworlds or the tensions of multiple identities in modernity and postmodernity. These limitations largely arise because classical interactionism has been too respectful of disciplinarity—the constraints of empiricism and sociology have tended to limit its incorporation of media texts, psychology, and semiotics. The theoretical worlds of the post are not so constrained. In a more interdisciplinary epoch, new possibilities arise—today, the discourses of the self as recorded in psychoanalysis, mythology, and ethnography are even more relevant to the project of interactionism. Self is not simply a category of social psychology or interactionist sociology. Our ideas about the self are broadening and even extend to ecology. As we argue, the theorization of an expanded self needs to involve cross-disciplinary mapping.

For these reasons, the arrival of a postmodern interactionism in Denzin's *Symbolic Interactionism and Cultural Studies* is an important event. One of the shortcomings of his project, however, is that like Hall, Denzin is seduced by the human centered materialism of left analysis. This provides serious obstacles to the development of ecologically oriented theory. Denzin's identification of a material self, for instance, is definitely pre-ecological, deriving from William James's turn-of-the-century conceptualization. As early as 1890, William James (as quoted in Naess, 1985) had referred to those material things with which we identify (after our social identifications) as our material self:

> The body is the innermost part of the material self in each of us; and certain parts of the body seem more intimately ours than the rest. The clothes come next . . . . Next, our immediate family is part of ourselves. Our father and mother, our wife and babies, are part of our bone and flesh of our flesh . . . . Our home comes next. (p. 257)

Denzin (1992), 100 years later, has reasserted a similar onion theory of the self and its spheres of identification, but the onion now includes an ideological self that overlays the material self:

> The self of persons connected in part to their identities, is a multilayered phenomenon and comes in several forms. The *phenomenological self* describes the inner stream of consciousness of a person in the social situation. The *interactional self* refers to the self that is presented and displayed to another in a concrete

sequence of action (e.g., as a customer). Self is also a linguistic, emotional, and symbolic process. The *linguistic self* refers to the person filling in the empty personal pronouns (I, me) with personal, biographical, and emotional meanings. The self also involves material possessions. The *material self,* or the self as a material object, consists of all the person calls his or hers at a particular moment in time (Denzin, 1989). The material self is also commodified in the exchange relations that the person enters into. The *ideological self* is given in the broader cultural and historical meanings that surround the definition of the individual in a particular group or social situation (e.g., tourist, husband, wife). (p. 26)

It is certainly necessary to develop a vocabulary that allows us to distinguish among the different activities that constitute the self. In speaking of different selves, we need to define not so much different identities but different modes of experience and different levels of engagement with culture. Like Hall, Denzin does not develop an ecological self, but he usefully reminds us that there are distinctions to be made between the experience of an inner stream of consciousness, interaction, language, and ideology. Our relationship with nature and the material world is, however, more than an inventory of all those objects we call our own; it is more than our individual articulation of ideology and culture. The *ecological self* is a recognition of interconnection and involves our identification and symbiosis with nonhuman worlds—a recognition that out "there" is in "here"; the material world forms part of our extended body. But there is no reason to stop our materiality with commodities and material objects. What about the other life forms and ecologies that sustain us? Clearly, people do care for, and closely identify with, a nonhuman environment. Ecological objects, subjects, and experiences are now, for many, easier to identify with than the inanimate objects and commodities of any pre-ecological phenomenology or interactionism. The chair, the table, and the pen have many essences. Their chains of association stretch from steel mills to rain forests, through the semiosphere, and back to the historical investment of human labor.

The self mediates all these chains of association. In daily life, our understandings of, and participation in, the flows of matter, information, and labor that constitute our ecologies are mediated by the self and its spheres of interest. Through our textual contemplation of connection, the internal dialogue goes on, as often as there are readers and thinkers and others. Reference groups, structures of relevance, and zones of identification may change, but the self goes on. Indeed, if we allow the possibility of identification with a nonhuman world to be a legitimate part of the repertoire of self, many benefits follow. Apart from a richer field of identification in socialization, our mythological heritage may become more accessible, particularly those premodern ecstatic roots that go back to earlier tribal conditions.

Self has always been understood to be extended in the interactionist tradition. As we have seen in William James and Norman Denzin, it extends conceptually into a material sphere. But there is a wilder side to the self: one in which dichotomies and dualisms are transgressed and human centeredness made problematic—or at least, this is what we have in mind with the postulation of postmodern eco-selves. Denzin's theorization of the self is important, nonetheless, for the way he shows that the articulation of differences about gender and race, for instance, can proceed in terms of location and position without abandoning many basic social psychological insights and without essentializing a unified self. But Denzin does not go far enough. As we have argued, nature and ecology are fundamentally implicated in the interactive processes of the self. Because the self is sustained symbolically in a semiosphere, it can also be read for the ecological inclusions and exclusions that structure all texts. We can read the self as structured by the dualisms we have already raised as problematic: nature-culture, male-female, mind-matter-spirit, and so on. But we can also understand the symbolic interaction of self as ecological and part of much broader spheres of identification.

We might note that under the spell of postmodernism, this is a time when the repressed returns, and binary categories are transgressed and bifurcate in chaotic ways. We can now write of a biosphere and a semiosphere as having many potentials and many impacts. But in writing of postmodern ecological selves, we are not attempting to resurrect an essentalized, individualistic, idealist, or bourgeois construct—even though we may walk a thin line, at times. Self, as we present the idea, is a dynamic, multiple, and largely social construct. Self is about location and agency, but it is also about narrative and myth. Selves seek identity and tell stories. This seeking and telling is both personal and public and always involves the negotiation and contestation of social and cultural conversations, roles, norms, values, and language. All these social formations are institutionalized and always present in the dialectics of self.

SELF AND SOCIETY: FROM IDENTITY LOGIC TO IDENTITY POLITICS

As we have seen in earlier chapters, the negotiation of these contested dualisms is part of the identity politics of new social movements and now also part of popular culture. This personalized identity politics is part of the ground of all social life, but it takes a particularly coherent form in the development of new social movements. Here, identities are formed in a more overtly collective way and in deliberate opposition to particular views, practices, institutions, and organizations.

The politicization of the self in new social movements and identity politics represents a new phase in the theorization of the self. This broadening of the field of self calls for its theorization to move along from identity logic (where the unity of the self is normative and part of the logic of bourgeois individualism) to identity politics where difference can be contested and new selves emerge. This places another challenge in the interactionist camp: Like all modernist social sciences, interactionism is bound by a level of normative commitment to the ideal of value freedom; this raises perennial problems for theory that sees itself as reflexively involved in the constitution of its theoretical objects. Thus, in classical interactionism, we see theory that does not set out to contest the cultural context of daily life—people's beliefs and worlds merely provide data from which the structures and process of social interaction eventually emerge in the contemplations of sociologists. This is despite the fundamentally dynamic and interactive orientation of interactionism's basic concepts and methodologies. There is, however, no a priori reason why the phenomenology of interactionism, or what simply amounts to its participatory reflexivity (which is its basic methodological commitment), cannot be extended into a world of contested subjectivities and contested texts of the world and into an ecology. As soon as culture is deconstructed, a semiotic dimension of interaction emerges to enrich our worldview and understanding of difference. As Denzin's work indicates, the understanding that socialization is today thoroughly mediated opens up an avenue for interactionism to emerge into postmodernity. But in its classical form, it does not prioritize political expression—in this, it is definitely pre-postmodern.

The roots of this pre-postmodernism are interesting to trace. In a passage titled "Theories about Identity," the interactionist sociologists Peter Berger and Thomas Luckmann (1972) simply advise us that "identity is a phenomenon that arises from the dialectic between individual and society" (pp. 152, 195). Elsewhere, they further remark that identity "is objectively defined as location in a certain world and can be subjectively approached only along with that world" (p. 195). Identities, in this interactionist-inspired account, are simply threads in a bigger process. Identity, here, is routinely created in processes of mutual recognition and is more or less defined in the institutional contexts of roles, work, leisure, politics, recurring patterns of sociotechnological life, and potentially also in our geographical and ecological senses of place.

Despite the breadth of this empirical field, identity in interactionist and phenomenological sociology is not, as we have already indicated, a primarily political concept or a concept defined in the context of contested differences; it does not address the politics of social movements, the marginalization or exclusion of minorities, or the routine pathology of self. It is interesting to note that it took an antipsychiatrist, R. D. Laing (1967), to introduce a serious note of conflict to the phenomenology of daily life, with his classic essay, "The Politics of Experience." As Laing pointed out, others see us as other: The social field cannot be considered as essentially benign. The self is always in potential conflict. Conflict is always a potential of communication and the definition of the situation. Laing's success in exposing the family as a site where madness arises in interpersonal relations radically reconfirms the power and centrality of communication in the making and breaking of selves. Laing's work, like Goffman's, remains to be incorporated into a more conflict-oriented interactionism.

It is surprising that communication per se is not a central issue in interactionism. Communication, like the air and the biosphere, becomes a global background. Denzin (1992) points out that interactionists have generally not paid sufficient attention to communication: "A neglected term connects the word 'symbolic' and 'interaction'. That term is 'communication'. . . . Interactionists have neglected the symbolic side of their theory choosing instead to build theories of interaction" (p. 95). This provides some explanation of why Denzin should try to marry symbolic interactionism with cultural studies. Symbolic interactionism also needs to be revitalized in the context of the centrality of communication to poststructuralism and postmodernism; all fields would benefit.

Fundamentally, Mead's (1934) notion of self as a socially mediated dialectic between an *I* and a *me* does not adequately explain the formation of identity either at an individual or a collective level. It lacks a sense of the self as a narrative. Norman Denzin (1992) thinks this is where cultural studies and the literary turn make a significant contribution to interactionism and sociology. The stories people tell are important; subjects are narrative texts (p. 90). But Denzin does not develop this point as a critique of Mead. The British sociologist Anthony Giddens (1991) is more direct in that respect. To emphasize the narrative quality of the self, Giddens prefers the term *self-identity*, which is "the self as reflexively understood by the person in terms of her of his biography" (p. 58): "A person's identity is not to be found in behavior, nor—important though this is—in the reactions of others, but in the capacity to keep a particular narrative going" (p. 54). Self-identity emphasizes reflexive awareness and the ongoing routine creation of the self. Giddens is critical of Mead's reliance on the internal dynamics of language to account for identity formation:

> The I/me (and I/me/you) relation is one internal to language, not one connecting the unsocialized part of the individual (the I) to this social self. *I* is a linguistic shifter, which gets its meaning from the networks of forms whereby a discursive system of subjectivity is acquired. The ability to use *I*, and other associated forms of subjectivity, is a condition for the emergence of self awareness but does not as such define it. (pp. 52-53)

ENTER THE CYBORGS

The recovery of narrative as a source of creative reconstruction of the self allows a space where all the texts of the world have purchase on identity formation. This also opens up the question of identity to all disciplines, movements, and cosmologies: from communication and cultural studies to psychoanalysis, and from deep ecology, the counterculture, and New Age, eastern religion, and shamanism, to feminism and the various cultures of new social movements. There are many stakeholders in the theorization of identity. The theorization of self and identity and their practical negotiation in social life are today all part of popular culture.

In this postmodern space of multiple potentials and transformation, we take directions from our dreams and fantasies and may even seek to surgically change the shape of our bodies to play out these ideals more fully. The horizons of meaning, structures of relevance, and subuniverses that the phenomenological sociologist Alfred Schutz defined are now in cyberspace. The era of the cyborg has arrived. The interface between mind and matter has been transfigured (yet again) by new communication technology—this time, in league with the microsurgeons.

The question of self and identity becomes increasingly complex as new technologies continue to reshape our worlds and ourselves. The increased mediation of the self that has occurred with

the rise of mass media, and now cyberspace, foreshadows radically changed notions of the self. Any suggestion of ecological
selves needs today to be situated among the technological imperatives that shape postmodern selves. New technologies shape
selves and ecologies: They are sutured in for better or worse.

In an age of miracle prosthetic devices, it is inevitable that
cyborgs should arrive. From Donna Haraway to Arnold Schwarzenegger, the naturalness of the human mind and body have been
supplanted by a technologized heterogeneity. Biology, machinery,
and consciousness itself are now being sutured together. This
could be seen as the fulfillment of a number of collective fantasies
or archetypal myths. With the ecstatic union of communication
technology comes the blurring of the distinction between biology
and technology. As with Christianity and related technologies of
self imposed by church-state formations, however, the black hole
at the center—the godhead—is not fully on earth or in heaven. It
is located somewhere far more intrusive, somewhere in-between,
somewhere where you can't get your being around the control
processes—a place where information wants to be free: cyberspace and its quickly gestating embryo, the Internet.

It is now obvious that the self is textual and cultural in worlds
that are highly mediated by new communication technologies. All
the sites of our multiple identities—whether in diverse subcultures, in audiences, in work, in play, or in ecologies—are increasingly saturated with texts and codes. Our worlds have never been
so visually and textually rich. A communication and information
revolution has irrevocably changed the reality of daily life. It is
now a smaller world in the sense that information flows faster
and in far greater volume through globalized communication
networks, and by direct proportion, the territorial scope of the
self increases. There are now many more others out there just
waiting to become part of our worlds. The screen and network are
fully a technology of self-production commanding a vibrant subculture that is in some danger of mutating into a new human
nature: a bionic reality with a bionic ecology. Until that point of
cyber-gnostic transcendence, however, the articulation of self in
an ecology remains a highly material process, involving our

bodies and our homes, what we eat and what we consume (in the broadest sense), and now, what we tune in to. We have roots and aerials (cf. Wark, 1994a).

THE GHOST OF SELF

We might expect the self-constructs of poststructuralism and postmodernity to be far too feisty for interactionism. These are worlds of decentered selves, worlds without a sacred canopy, codified mythos, or unified worldview. These are worlds of sliding signifiers, networks, screens, and simulations. As Baudrillard (1987) has observed, the enchantment of the "interior" and "scene" has been supplanted by the screen and network. The self is now mediated by screens and many texts. And, to cope with it all, the self has multiple identities—this can either be interpreted poststructurally to mean multiple locations in social space structured by gender, ethnicity, and class, or in terms of role theory, alternating locations, or both. Presumably, as long as the phenomenological *I* remains, we will not become fragmented into a chaotic series of past (or future) *me's*. The conversations of the self will continue. And conversation is ubiquitous. In every way, we are a conversation, a continuing symbolic relationship that occurs across public and private spaces (cf. Carey, 1989). And if we expand this model to take in the psychoanalytic models of Freud, Jung, and Lacan, even in sleep there is no easy escape from society, for in sleep we dream.

It is at this point that the project of interactionism appears anemic. Mead's self is an abstraction from a very big field of communication, not all of which is fully conscious. Just where, in a social and ecological field, we draw boundaries around communication between the *I* and the *me*, and between *self* and *other* is theoretically negotiable. The mapping of these boundaries is becoming an increasingly important issue in a world of expanding connection and symbolic exchange. In this mapping, the paradigmatic exclusions are interesting to contemplate. Once again, we see that it is the unconscious, the transpersonal, and the ecological realms of communication that most threaten the ordered worlds of disciplinary specialists, from interactionists to structural Marxists and feminists alike.

The articulation of ourselves as ecological has the potential to extend the self beyond the present limitations of the silicon chip and fiber optic cord. Perhaps in cyberspace the postmodern premodernism of new tribal cultures will participate in the reformation of ecological vision, along with the modernism and postmodernism of contemporary science. Deep ecology might well be a radicalizing cultural influence.

INSIGHTS FROM DEEP ECOLOGY

One of the attractions of deep ecology is the idea that there might be something about our individuality and experience of self that is not culturally constructed, such as a possibly presymbolic dark space where inchoate impulses stir and thoughts struggle into consciousness, or a postsymbolic ecstasy. Whatever their semiotic nature, these are spaces where meditation and dreaming become technologies of the self (devoted to diverse purposes). This takes us toward the concerns of mystics, shamans, witches, priests, and psychoanalysts. The rearticulation of these often premodern concerns are today connecting many to the wonder and urgency of nature and its vastness and fragility. And with the intrusion of Chaos theory, we are now advised of nature's, and our own, unpredictability. Such speculations raise age-old dualisms and dichotomies: order and chaos, the heavens and the earth, the Gods of the sky and the gods of the earth, culture and nature. In a sense, we have seen it all before; mythologies have an uncanny way of returning.

This reanimated nature text holds many potentials, but it may not be able to easily articulate certain kinds of experience that occur at the boundaries of self and communication—such as interaction with other species. This has certainly not been a mainstream concern. There are, nonetheless, many subcultural and premodern texts that deal with the subject—as may be found in the countercultural and New Age discourses discussed in the last chapter. The subject of our interaction with nature and other intelligences is perennially fascinating but invariably marginalized in Cartesian-Newtonian frameworks. A communications revolution has, however, guaranteed that there are a number of ecocentric discourses available today. In the discourses of philosophers, poets, pagans, premodernists, and postmodernists we can choose from a wide range of types of experience. We can choose from different genres and different knowledge traditions.

There is a wider experimental pluralism to be found in deep ecology in comparison with social ecology, eco-feminism, communication and cultural studies, or sociology. As its philosophers advise us, deep ecology is experientially based and directed toward the cultivation of an expanded sense of self. As Zen masters, mystics, yogis, and occultists tell us, however, there are many paths toward that end. Nonetheless, preferences are declared in the discourses of deep ecology: The Eastern philosophical traditions of Hinduism and Buddhism have been very influential, along with the more ecocentric philosophies of indigenous cultures. Naess (1985), Devall and Sessions (1985), and Fox (1990), for instance, all draw inspiration from these sources.

Many of these ancient traditions offer what are essentially technologies of the self. These technologies are all centered on meditation of some sort. As Don Juan demonstrated to Carlos Castaneda (1971), meditation is aimed at shifting the assemblage point—more as a practical achievement than a theoretical activity. Meditation generally involves sitting still, relaxing, and, through the manipulation of the mind and body, cultivating altered states of awareness. In these states, the perceived boundaries of the self are challenged. Identity logic changes: Subjects may, over time, find unexpected affinities in the universe and potentially identify with all manner of other sentient beings—from gurus to kangaroos.

One of the key sought-after effects of meditation is effectively the deconstruction of the self. Different traditions offer different possibilities for the reconstruction, but always, the emphasis is on the achievement of less ego-centered, extended awareness. This is very different from an awareness that is simply refocused.

Meditation is a form of play with the internal dialogue that dominates everyday awareness. In other words, Mead's *I* and *me* are directly in the line of attack. This mundane self needs to be bracketed out to enable new experiences and new worlds to emerge. One may seek to identify with everything, or nothing, or many things in between—but the normal processes of thought are generally perceived to be an obstacle to awareness. In meditation, reason becomes problematic. Thought is used against itself.

This expanded self has an obvious ecological potential. As deep ecology asserts, the cultivation of deep ecological awareness involves identification with other living things and their ecologies. There is a duty of care that emerges in this process. At this point, discourses cross, and deep ecologists and eco-feminists hold hands.

SUMMARY:
TAKE IT PERSONALLY,
THE NATURAL IS POLITICAL

It is important to look at ideas we hold about the self in a changing world because our notions of self and the symbols we deploy will be of direct relevance to the worlds we build in the future. The way we refashion our ecosystems will emerge fundamentally from the structurally constrained use of our symbols of self-expression. The breadth and diversity of all that we identify as self and subjectivity will clearly determine our ability to deal with difference, otherness, and multiplicity. In this chapter, we have contrasted post-Marxist and poststructural subjectivities with the idea of a postmodern ecological self grounded in interactionist theory.

The theoretical traditions that bear historically on discourse about self and subjectivity are vast. In our mappings, we have placed interactionist and phenomenological notions of self and identity in the context of poststructuralism and postmodernism. Superficially, there is a contradiction. The former postulate decentered, fragmented, and multiple selves and subjectivities; the latter seem to return to an identity logic that historically has privileged a white, patriarchal, Western view. But there is a theoretical common ground: Interactionism develops a process model of the self in which communication is a major axis. These processes of the self are, furthermore, not a priori anathema to social structure, difference, conflict, or ecology—and indeed, it is with these directions that interactionists and cultural theorists may find themselves increasingly concerned.

If there is one clear message from post-Marxist poststructuralists, such as Stuart Hall, it is that subjectivity is positional. Our experiences are structured by our social, cultural, and historical locations. The way that we conceptualize self-identity or subjectivity is always mediated by these considerations. For these post-Marxist projects, the death of the subject and the death of the author signal a refusal to re-create bourgeois individualism and essentialized subjects. This allows projects of emancipation and cultural contestation to proceed without the distraction of nomadic subjects or the full span of subjectivity.

Self and *identity* are still key concepts in constant need of clarification, even if they are from time to time occluded by the dialectics of history, power, and personal politics. Despite all this work on subjectivity, there can be no easy resolution to the paradox of the self. The reflexivity of the self guarantees its ability to always be capable of transcending the last definition. Or as Lewis Carroll (1967) concluded,

> In the midst of the word he was trying to say, in the
> midst of his laughter and glee, he had softly and suddenly
> vanished away—for the Snark was a Boojum, you see.
> (p. 96)

Alternatively, as a postmodernist might say, because self is reflexive, the question of location is always subject to a basic indeterminacy. To rephrase Heisenberg's Uncertainty Principle: we may know where we are, but we may not know who we are—and the more we know who we are, the less we know where we are—perhaps this is what happens when the nonecological self disappears into the particle accelerator of contemporary culture.

6

Greening Media Studies

*Natural Histories and CS
(Communication Studies)
Theory Zones*

S ketching out ideas about what a greener cur-
riculum of media texts might entail, this chapter analyzes specific texts and genres as sites where social
theories and controlling imagery vie for public acceptance. As part
of our greening process, we contrast diverse factual and fictional
material with the more ecocentric timescale and generous biopolitics of natural histories. Developing that contrast further, we
argue that media critics and communication, cultural, and social
theorists might all dismantle some of their existing disciplinary
boundaries to similarly extend their scope. In addition, we propose expanding the existing idea matrix of our fields to accommodate previously discredited, non-Western knowledges.

LOADING A MORE
ECO-FRIENDLY CANON

We begin by addressing the existing canon of texts and genres, which form part of media studies curricula and their methodological matrix. Consideration of the canon involves examples of what might need to be dropped, what might need to amended, and what might need to be added. But the idea of the canon is not only central, it is, as many puns on *exploding* it in papers and at conferences indicate (see Ferguson et al., 1990), highly problematic. From our teaching experiences in Australia and Britain and our knowledge of North American curricula and literature, the canons (for they certainly are plural) of media studies (both as a distinct degree in its own right and as part of sociology, communication, and cultural studies programs) diverge radically. They are heavily weighted by such diverse factors as nationality (British media studies look at different texts than North American media studies), institution (some universities include journalism as a key component, others do not; some favor extensive hands-on components, such as video making and photography, others do not) and history (some Australian courses feature multicultural foci distinct from U.S. postcolonial foci). To keep in touch with fast-shifting popular fashions and vanishing television texts, media studies' canons also tend to change more frequently than other canons, such as literary studies. Nevertheless, we believe that certain aspects commonly recur and can serve as examples to indicate specific and general directions for "greening."

Content analysis of print and television news has remained a fairly consistent, if variably weighted, feature of media teaching. Chomsky and Herman's (1988) famous study, *Manufacturing Consent: The Political Economy of the Mass Media*, for example, plotted the coordinates of media coverage as a propaganda map that was best understood as mobilizing "support for the special interests that dominate the state and private activity" (p. xi). Their critical cartography laid out vast variations in international reporting. They contrasted extensive U.S. press coverage of Cambodia with the virtual absence of East Timor coverage by measuring column inches over a comparable time and event span. In other parts of the globe, they found similar loadings biased in favor of reporting European deaths over South American deaths. As an empirical approach, their study retains methodological relevance, and it can easily be adapted to analyze differential (geographic, ethnic, and economic) coverage of ecological concerns.

Over the past few years, their study has become prominent again through the *Manufacturing Consent: Noam Chomsky and the Media* (Achbar, Symansky, & Wintonick, 1992) film and Chomsky's high public profile. Partly as a result of the study's increased media profile, it has been possible to make the media's systematically biased coverage itself a mainstream media, as well as an academic, issue. Chomsky and Herman (1988) established clear links between political power and media mappings of the world by their academic tracking of geopolitical, and sometimes race-based, distortions of contours of international coverage. Their kind of broad-ranging political-economic critique has considerable potential to be adapted to the issue of environmental racism. At present, however, existing research, which points to consistent ethnic bias in the geographical positioning of environmentally unfriendly industries and pollution dumps, occupies space in relatively specialist areas, such as social ecology, rather than in media and media studies.

In Britain, comparable content analysis work at the national level by the Glasgow University Media Group (1976, 1980, 1982) plotted the class bias of television news reporting of industrial disputes through logging coverage times and analyzing language and image deployment. In both Britain and the United States, these interventions led to extensive media exposure and confirmed how communication research, in moving from the university to the public arena, can affect publics and media workers nationally and internationally. In addition, the Glasgow University Group's news categories already have an environmental entry and only require minor adjustments to make them more ecologically relevant. Adaptations along these lines could identify the priorities assigned to environmental matters and expose how media texts construct biospheric information.

MEDIA ECO-CRITICISM
AND CULTURAL RESOURCES

Anders Hansen's (1994) collection of critical work, *The Mass Media and Environmental Issues*, follows some of these directions. In his chapter, "Mediating the Environment," for instance, Simon Cottle (1994) divides the environmental concerns of television news into nine main categories: pollution (air, water, and land), animal habitat-animal exploitation, land conservation-cultural heritage, urban squalor-congestion-development, natural disaster, environmental party politics, radiation-nuclear, nutrition-food, and mineral exploration. His research into the environmental presence of these categories for 2 sample weeks of news both verified existing criticisms and suggested fresh directions for research. He confirmed the expected event orientation, which foregrounded natural disasters as almost 50% of the environmental coverage of mainstream news, with an accompanying absence of slow-moving change and less clearly visible social and material processes. Earlier studies have identified this bias across areas as diverse as coverage of crime (Chibnall, 1977) and the Iranian Revolution (Walker, 1982).

Such systematic event orientation by media workers poses a particular challenge to concerns with apparently uneventful eco-degradation that may be invisible (in the case of radiation) or slow (in the case of rising temperatures and rising sea levels). In these cases, significant trends may not be demonstrable until they become virtually irreversible. Just as feminists have consistently done in relation to the media invisibility of women, media critics and environmental activists can at least draw attention to the significance of the absences.

On a more positive note, Cottle (1994) found, as did Hansen (1994) in his piece on Greenpeace, that activists in Britain were able to win news time for certain slower-moving processes by dramatizing them. One small-scale cyclist demonstration led by a costumed "King Canute" gained exposure for the seemingly uneventful, because gradual, growing tide of traffic and its pollution. In this case, the protesters made the processes newsworthy through their dramatic visualization of the idea to inflate the news value of the small event of a traffic jam. On animal habitats and exploitation, which made up the second highest logged category of television news's concerns, Cottle (1994), less predictably in terms of media research findings, found greater and more diverse environmental coverage in the so-called softer news of early morning and midday. That positive program coverage he put down to good photo opportunities and the chance "to indulge engrained cultural sentiments and nostalgic feelings for the loss of a natural order and way of life in which man [sic] and nature are thought to have enjoined in a less complicated, if often vitalistic, relationship" (p. 116). Cottle's emphasis on the significance of feelings restores emotions to the critical stocktake. This is important because the mediation of the environment can be complex affectively and involve emotional links with content, representation, and scheduling.

Media draw from different sources and different sets of cultural resources in constructing their versions of what is real and what can be realistically achieved in social and ecological terms. Accordingly, analysts need to be aware of the danger of "media centrism" (Schlesinger, 1990), whereby they give media too much agenda-setting power in relation to "the importance of cultural resources in the privileging of some issues rather than others" (Hansen, 1991, p. 444). The Glasgow University Media Group's (1980) configurations offer the analytic strength of explicitly comparing and contrasting how different resources present different versions of reality. Over the same period of time, for example, the Glasgow Group set official government statistics of industrial disputes alongside television content statistics of industrial disputes. That kind of detailed comparison can check on how governments, through their rhetoric and public relations wings, can influence media stories and present as green but still actively pollute and implement environmentally unfriendly policies. One positive consequence of Margaret Thatcher's (in)famous "green" speech was that it led to greater press coverage that scrutinized record, rhetoric, and the distance between them with more specialist expertise (see Hansen, 1991).

All of the above studies focus on information-oriented media, or what Corner (1991) usefully terms "the *public knowledge* project" (p. 268). Because this project contributes substantially to the setting of political agendas, both press and television news would need to be retained as part of ecologically revised canons. So would current affairs because, as the traditional whistleblowers of government and commercial corruption, the genre already has enough environmental exposés to its credit to earn a position in any ecologically revised canons. Less conventionally, however, in line with Chapter 1's emphasis on the semiosphere and Chapter 3's blurring of the traditional demarcation of television fact and fiction, we contend that a canonic hierarchy founded on placing fact over fiction obstructs as well as informs. It is prone to overlook important shifts in cultural resources, especially in terms of the emotions and pleasures more commonly available in entertainment media or, to use Corner's (1991) matching term, "the *popular culture* project" (p. 268).

At a time when regimes of truth often result from a relation of correspondences between propositions, representations, and extralinguistic factors rather than any direct access to so-called objective reality, popular entertainment forms can also extend ecological awareness. This can happen not only in general public consciousness but in specific academic fora. Some popular forms already engage with temporal perceptual shifts and the greater inclusiveness that such an increased awareness might entail. Social theorists might learn from these forms. In the communication, culture, and social studies fields, our stories need not be restricted to histories and (her)stories but might include other (earth)stories with different time frames.

TELLING OTHER STORIES: UNNATURAL HISTORIES, NATURAL HISTORIES, AND BIOPOLITICS

Media stories divide into genres that order temporal representations of the private, social, and nonhuman world; most are so immersed in anthropocentrism that they usually exclude, or marginalize, all other ecological factors. For ecologically revised canons, we propose one of the notable exceptions: television natural history genres. In the way their extended time frames go beyond human-dominated perspectives and in the way they typically foreground the nonhuman, these genres encourage a broader biopolitics of representation. Natural history genres serve to critique the unnatural exclusion of the nonhuman in screen stories and screen histories. Later in the chapter, in line with postmodernism's three Rs, we will also analyze the potential of a comic "unnatural" history of a third kind to foster other eco-friendly generic and disciplinary cross-fertilizations.

The Australian Broadcasting Corporation's *Nature of Australia* (Vandenbeld, 1988) offers an excellent example of what natural history genres can do. It covers the island continent's emergence from a shared landmass with Antarctica prior to human inhabitation through to the industrial nation of the 1980s. It thus temporally relegates the human contribution to a much smaller role than conventional histories. Extending comparable coverage to the whole planet, the British Broadcasting Corporation's *Two Seconds to Midnight* (Appleby, 1993) begins far farther back to tell "the story of the earth from 4.6 billion years ago to 50 years in the future" so that if "the earth's history were 1 day, humans would appear at 2 seconds to midnight." By compressing earth's history to a day, the program relegates all human interventions to only a couple of seconds of that time. Carl Sagan's 13-part *Cosmos* television series (1980-1981) offers an even more massive time-space extension, which puts a different perspective on human activities.

To a large extent, these program divisions find parallels in disciplinary divides. This is not simply to endorse the kind of claim made by Trimble (1989), that "natural history writers speak for the earth" (p. 1). Nevertheless, historians (in a less anthropocentric use of the term) dealing with the prehuman years of our biosphere's development tend to cluster in natural history and associated scientific disciplines, whereas their generic screen equivalents occupy low-status television criticism areas. The material focus of these disciplines and genres usefully supplements evangelical-style eco-histories, such as Ponting's (1991) *A Green History of the World*, which tend to romanticize past organic relations between land and people. Their different disciplinary bases also encourage perspectival relativism. In looking at the Mediterranean as *The First Eden*, David Attenborough (1987) asks that his audiences consider reserving stretches of beach for animal birthing rather than income from tourism. With an even longer-term timescale and similar opposition to human overdevelopment, *Nature of Australia* logically contemplates the abandonment of conventional sheep and cattle farming in the interior in favor of maintaining the unique flora and fauna as better long-term earners from international tourism (see McKie, 1992).

Neither media nor history has substantially addressed such biopolitics or what a Jeremy Rifkin (1991) book titles *Biosphere Politics*. After observing how the peace and antinuclear movements have directed modern war history attention from military casualties toward the increasing mortality rate of civilian populations (especially in the nuclear age), his book records how ecologists during the Gulf War declared it, and all wars, to be wars on the environment (p. 143). This discursive deployment of biosphere contains subversive possibilities in subtly undermining nationalist, and other human, claims to territory. Its usage implies allegiance less "to the special interests of a few" than to "the planetary concerns of the many" and "not just other races but also other species" (Sagan, 1991, p. 21). By promoting different controlling imagery than domination and separation, even Dorian Sagan's scientific optimism invokes an enlarged collective view of humans as part of an interconnected natural world.

The institutionally entrenched neglect of the biosphere in war representations is evident in one of the most screened histories of recent times: the Vietnam War. Applied retrospectively, a more biopolitical perspective would suggest that, once detached from national interests, no history of Vietnam would be able to ignore ecological devastation. Vietnamese land will still hold bombs, land mines, and toxicity (including Agent Orange) for generations of postwar flora, fauna, and people. Yet in almost every cinema and televisual representation—although Oliver Stone's cinematography in the 1993 film *Heaven and Earth* does picture a romanticized lost Eden (see Singer, 1993)—such perspectives surface, if at all, incidentally. Ecological devastations become peripheral casualties of war rather than central discursive and political issues. Screen histories split the human and animal continuum along genre lines with natural history programs favoring deep time and non-anthropocentric attitudes against almost all other genres' preferences for shorter time spans and little earth, or other species, awareness.

Some natural history television series do offer other takes on the process through special photography that, using time-lapse techniques, reveals the previously secret life of plants, insects, and other minute or slow-moving organic forms. Radically different possibilities could be created by melding that newly mappable territory with an ecocenteric perspective akin to those found in some science fiction writers. A combination of natural history, high-tech photography, and science fiction would allow a re-imagining of the biosphere's history by situating humankind alongside parallel stories about all others who inhabit it and even the planet itself. This imagining would enable embodied perspectives from the silent, nonhuman, and nonsentient, "spoiled" of the land to be seen alongside the better charted human centered history of its spoilers. The resulting combination might also help to cultivate what Bolton (1981) calls "that state of mind present in the wisdom of so many older cultures: the habit of viewing the . . . earth as their mother" (p. 174).

COSMOLOGICAL SCIENCE STORIES AND OTHER INTRODUCED SPECIES

Although the sciences remain profoundly sexist, they sometimes challenge anthropocentrist attitudes in other disciplines, including our own. A recent undergraduate cosmology textbook happily begins by acknowledging that the "history of ideas on the structure and origin of the Universe shows that mankind [sic] has always put itself at the centre of Creation" but that as "astronomical evidence has accumulated, these anthropocentric convictions have had to be abandoned one by one" (Roos, 1994, p. 1). Relatively early in the postmodern debates, *The Re-Enchantment of Science: Postmodern Proposals* (Griffin, 1988) attempted to draw together science narratives and other cultural tales. Most consciously of all its contributors, Brian Swimme (1988) proposed that "we tell the many stories that comprise the great cosmic story" and "that this activity of cosmic storytelling is the central political and economic act of our time" (p. 47).

Swimme's (1988) chapter sees late 20th-century scientific cosmology's story of the universe as "a supreme human achievement" having "a status equal to that of the great religious revelations of the past" (p. 51). He concludes with the tale of an imaginary future storyteller starting, "at the beginning of the Earth, the whole planet was a boiling sea of molten rock" (p. 54). Swimme's futuristic narrator uses an extended temporal consideration of the kind familiar in natural history with an associated increase in respect for the nonsentient: "We revere rocks because everything has come from them—not just the continents and the mountains, but the trees, the oceans and your bodies" (p. 54). Like natural history, such a relativizing perspective invites imaginative identification via a far longer time frame than is normal in a social world organized around short-term profits.

Another less temporally extended film text offers a more bizarre critique of the same commercial mind set. *Cane Toads: An Unnatural History* (Lewis, 1987) is postmodern in its self-reflexive mix of fact, fiction, information, and entertainment. It debunks the natural history genre, in a different sense than our usage of unnatural, as excluding the nonhuman and it makes telling environmental points. It does this, as its video sleeve notes indicate, by comically positioning ecological information alongside critiques of scientific rationality:

Australia is being rapidly taken over by a fat slimy ugly creature who sees its sole purpose in life as being the pursuit of sexual gratification. *Bufo Marinus*—the cane toad was imported into Queensland from Hawaii in 1935 for a specific reason—to combat the grey-back beetle that was destroying the sugar crop. The mission failed: the beetle could fly and the Cane Toad couldn't. Oblivious of its failure the cane toad adapted to its new surroundings and proceeded to breed so rapidly that it has now become a pest of plague proportions . . . . Could it be that the total conquest of Australia is just a hop, step and a jump away? (Lewis, 1987)

Continuing to interweave "comedy, environmental tragedy and scientific history," the documentary announces that "on 22nd June, 1935, 102 cane toads arrived" in Australia with a "mission: to control the cane grub" and protect sugar farmers' profits. In tracking the failure of this pest control measure, the film blends surreal shots from an amphibian's point of view with standard generic sequences of university lecturers in studies, ecologists in fields, and zoologists in laboratories—although the mix of actors and real people makes it difficult to be confident about these representations.

The uncertainty proves usefully unsettling. *Cane Toads* accentuates it with surreal lighting and obviously contrived camera angles, including one unforgettable toad's eye view of passing road traffic. The soundtrack is equally obtrusive with stereotypical national music in the worst travelogue tradition accompanying every different overseas location and a children's choir version of the hymn "All Things Bright and Beautiful" counterpointing amphibian faces in ugly close-ups. Through these subversive techniques, *Cane Toads* foregrounds the extremely strange and self-contradictory behavior of the human species, which ranges from love to unrestricted violence, toward the toads. It clearly conveys the instability of the humans, and later their metaphors, for governing ecosystem management. Initially deployed by humans as militant allies on their mission impossible, the toads soon exemplify what one ostensibly scientific speaker calls "classic human disasters of a monoculture" as "gradually" their "single introduced species" replaces "many many natural species . . . with repercussions all the way up the food chain." By the film's end, cane toads become an invasion machine described as posing as big a danger to contemporary Australians as did the enemy armies of World War II. Representationally, *Cane Toads* uses positive postmodern effects without sacrificing either a critical biopolitics or a humorous sense of perspective.

Cane Toads also fits well with recent media studies work on status and genre. Stressing their link to narrative, Bill Nichols (1991) sees documentaries as resembling "fictions with plots, characters, situations, and events" as well as referencing "a 'reality' that is a construct, the product of signifying systems" that "must be scrutinized and debated as part of the domain of signification and ideology" (p. 107). To apply Nichols's formulation to screen histories, they, too, are undoubtedly fictions "(un)like any other" in directing us toward a world "where not only information circulates but matter and energy" whose "physical forces can be unleashed for or against us by discourse, linguistics, or even more directly, by nature" (p. 110).

More self-reflexive, eco-sensitive screen history canons could profitably adapt Nichols's double frame of simultaneous resemblance to, and difference from, fiction. They could also engage with postmodern documentary practices and debates about referentiality and representation that, in cutting across genres, make space for the nonhuman. So, too, could academia. Screen genres have counterparts in university disciplinary divisions. In the face of urgent environmental issues, communication theorists, historians, sociologists, and media critics alike might dismantle some existing disciplinary boundaries and expand the spatiotemporal dimensions of the stories they routinely consider telling. By aligning less-hierarchical combinations of nonrealist story and factually informed material with the more generous temporal biopolitics of natural histories, they could better relate nature's animal, human, and physical forces.

HOLES IN THE CS THEORY ZONE: ECOLOGY, GAIA, AND OTHER WISDOM TRADITIONS

To reformat communication and cultural studies' idea matrix along these lines entails reevaluating other previously discredited knowledges and underused cultural resources. Ethnocentrically implicated in TWIT, psychologist Robert Ornstein's (1986) dismissive acronym for the Western intellectual tradition, our fields consign certain other knowledges, such as shamanism, Sufism, and Zen Buddhism, to virtual oblivion. By omitting these traditionally valued layers of wisdom ozone, the fields risk overexposure to ultra-Euroamerican discourses. Current idioms of identity that express subjectivity as nothing but a site of conflict and nature as nothing but a human construct represent a particular danger. By emitting theoretical CFCs destructive to ideas of the self as also an ecologically embodied agent of change, our current knowledge configurations disempower individual actions and retard the sustainable development of ecocentric approaches in our fields.

It follows that our current preferences for Western perspectives, such as mind over body, are simply preferences and not necessarily any expression of superiority. These kinds of preferences in communication and cultural studies normally relegate other valuable traditions of knowing to oblivion. Such preferences emerge logically from our (i.e., as modern Western social theorists, as distinct from some eco-feminists and deep ecologists) implication in TWIT and, especially, that mega-ethnocentric discourse, *the* Enlightenment, singular. Its legacy includes the modernity project but excludes millennia of other, lower-case and plural, enlightening movements and enlightenment traditions. As Peter Hamilton's (1992) retrospective summary puts it, "in its simplest sense the Enlightenment was the creation of a new framework of ideas about man [sic], society and nature, which challenged existing conceptions rooted in a traditional world-view, dominated by Christianity" (p. 23).

Condensing the 18th-century world to one single paradigm dominated by Christianity, Hamilton's breathtaking condescension betrays its intellectual parochialism. In aligning with notorious 19th-century dismissals of non-Western civilizations as barbarians whom the West rescued from "the idiocy of rural life" (Marx & Engels, 1888/1967, p. 84), Hamilton similarly wipes out the "traditional world-views" of over half the globe. In its own intellectual practice, the Enlightenment did little to live up to its famous Kantian motto of "dare to know." In its search for knowledge, for example, the Enlightenment did not chance descending very far down the European social ladder—Peter Gay's (1973) massive two-volume summary concludes, "the lower orders" were "the great unexamined political question of the Enlightenment" (p. 517). Nor did it risk challenging gender apartheid or considering more ecocentric perspectives. On the positive side, subsequent social theorists have attempted to fill the Enlightenment lacunae with regard to race, class, and gender; on the negative side, few have engaged much with the absent environmental dimension. As major educational and geopolitical beneficiaries, we have failed to redress significant omissions from the legacy. In particular, we continue to ignore the potential of these absent non-Euro-enlightenment perspectives to revitalize ideas of subjectivity and nature for contemporary eco-conditions.

In restoring a pre-Enlightenment emphasis on the relationships between human activity and the condition of the biosphere, our approach in *Eco-Impacts* conflicts with a growing movement that would position the key contemporary divide as being between urban and nonurban. David Harvey (1993) is just one prominent figure who conceives the "distinction between built environments of cities and the humanly-modified environments of rural and even remote regions" as "arbitrary except as a particular manifestation of a rather long-standing ideological distinction between the country and the city" (p. 3). At one level, he is right. At another, what he dismissively labels "a persuasive antiurban bias in much ecological rhetoric" (p. 3) we see as a much needed reconfiguration of the anthropocentrism dominant among social theorists. Conceptualizing the major conflict as between city and country people, Harvey can overlook nonhuman and nonsentient nature. In the light of species extinction rates and planetary destruction, his categorizing of them as separate spheres might yet prove to be a more disabling division. In effect, he supports a well-established divide between scientific considerations of ecosystems, which *include* everything but people, and social theoretic considerations of communities, which *exclude* everything but people (see Slack & Whitt, 1994).

Disregarding the species divide for comic effect, Andrew Ross (1994) proposes an ironic hierarchy in which "humans rank low," whereas "endangered species can be mustered according to a celebrity scale of size: the gnat-catcher, the snail darter, the spotted owl, the panda, the African elephant, the dolphin, the whale" (p. 6). Although Ross's sarcasm undercuts a tendency in popular sympathy, that tendency has yet to make significant inroads into overall animal conservation. Like Harvey, he aims to separate endangered species from endangered peoples and is not mindful of the fact that, outside of cities, the biggest threat to both comes from habitat destruction: "It is a terrible irony that as our resource consumption reaches farther into rain forests and deserts, it destroys the only remaining cultures that know how to live in balance with the environment" (Davidson, 1993, p. 3). Nor does Ross's sarcasm accurately reflect the agendas of sociology, communication, and cultural studies, which consistently focus on people to the exclusion of all else on earth. With the growth of more ecocentric perspectives, nonhuman issues might begin to get more attention, but to present them as pushing human issues to the bottom of the scale is absurd. It is particularly absurd in Ross's own view of cultural studies when "after twenty years of the modern ecology movement we have little that can properly be called a green cultural criticism" (Ross, 1991, p. 6).

A TALE OF TWO PATS AND AN ABSENT EQUATION

In 1992, we attended a conference at the University of Melbourne titled "Cultural Studies: Pluralism and Theory" or, in initials, "CS: PAT." Overall, in terms of ecological issues, we found it to be just that, cultural studies PAT, in the sense of smug and secure. Some of the best known Australian and North American names in the field spoke at length but, apart from Ross himself, made virtually no attempt to respond to his earlier call to "explain some of the desired connections between social life, natural life, and economic life" (Ross, 1991, p. 13).

Afterward, on reading Anne and Paul Ehrlichs's (1991) book, *Healing the Planet,* we discovered, through a PAT of a different nature, one key absent equation. The Ehrlichs measure the environmental impact of any group or nation (I) by equating it with PAT, or "the product of its population size (P) multiplied by per-capita affluence (A) as measured by consumption, in turn multiplied by the technologies (T) employed in supplying each unit of that consumption" (p. 7). They go on to show how the I = PAT equation "shows immediately that, all else being equal, doubling a population's size will double its impact on the environment" and even if "individual impact (A × T) is halved while the population doubles, the total impact will remain the same" (p. 7). The PAT equation "underlines the perils of continually pressing for more of today's sort of economic growth, especially in rich nations" (p. 9). In these ecological mathematics, the environment is perceived as a global problem with unequal contributors—a formulation that allows for differential impact and common cause.

The Ehrlichs (1991) preface their book with a similarly inclined epigraph from Ed McGaa's, *Mother Earth Spirituality:*

> Mother Earth cannot heal herself alone. She needs our help. We two-leggeds must all come together and form a commonality of realization, a realization of potentially fatal calamities. Most of our remedies will be to cease, or drastically curtail, what we have been doing.

McGaa's work as an Eagle Man would be the contemporary equivalent of one of those thought traditions Marx and Engles associated with rural idiocy. Nevertheless, McGaa's shamanic wisdom, contemporary ecology, and much environmental science converge on "the essential strategy for saving biodiversity and ourselves . . . reduce the scale of the human enterprise" (Ehrlich & Ehrlich, 1991, p. 37). It would be interesting to see their modest proposal of a tithe, "to dedicate at least 10 percent of your time" (p. xv) to healing the planet, taken up within our own fields. How quickly would social theory alter through the simple tactic of positive discrimination in favor of a minimum 10% quota on books, conference papers, and journal articles addressing ecological issues? At present, it is not only the Ehrlichs, McGaa, and similar environmental thinkers and activists who struggle to find air in the hothouse CS atmosphere; Gaia herself struggles for breathing space.

THREE FACES OF GAIA: THE SCIENCES, THE PROJECTS, AND THE GODDESS

Lovelock's (1979) first Gaia book, *Gaia: A New Look at Life on Earth*, states its origins and scientific hypothesis simply and clearly:

> Journeys into space did more than present the Earth in a new perspective. They also sent back information about its atmosphere and its surface which provided a new insight into the interactions between the living and the inorganic parts of the planet. From this has arisen the hypothesis, the model, in which the Earth's living matter, air, oceans, and land surface form a complex system which can be seen as a single organism and which has the capacity to keep our planet a fit place for life. (pp. ix-x)

In his 1992 book, *Gaia: The Practical Science of Planetary Medicine* 13 years later, Lovelock (1992) has little to retract scientifically despite over a decade of dissent. This is not to say he does not still have detractors: The Ehrlichs follow Stephen Schneider (1990), from the National Center for Atmospheric Research, in their flat rejection, "that the earth itself is 'alive' is indisputably wrong" (Ehrlich & Ehrlich, 1991, p. 20). However, given the debates about what constitutes human life and death, we remain convinced that conceptual factors play the largest role in such questions. Moreover, even as strong a scientific detractor as Schneider himself has "come to realize the absurdity of the situation in which an interesting and controversial idea like the Gaia hypothesis was being debated largely in nonscientific forums" (Schneider & Boston, 1991, p. xiii). Accordingly, he and Boston coconvened a scientific conference and coedited the proceedings in a book, *Scientists on Gaia*. We labor this point for two reasons. The first is to remind many social critics that Lovelock's thesis has validity as a scientific hypothesis that generates experiments, is open to verification through standard scientific protocols, and has generated provisional results in the form of environmental evidence (see Schneider & Boston, 1991). The second is that Lovelock's words, "a new insight into the interactions between the living and the inorganic parts of the planet," touch on one of the most controversial aspects of ecological challenges.

Given the Gaia hypothesis's standing as scientific and public discourse, its relative absence in sociology, communication, and cultural studies remains somewhat puzzling. Compounding this is the further neglect of some associated projects, particularly the Gaia atlas series, which makes ambitious attempts to come to terms with past, present, and future environmental questions. Demonstrating considerable sensitivity to class, race, and gender issues, the series tries to make its information, discourses, and activist resources attractive and accessible to a wide public. Yet *The Gaia Atlas of First Peoples: A Future for the Indigenous World* by the joint authorship of "Julian Burger with campaigning groups and native peoples worldwide," was published in 1990 without any reviews in the communication and cultural studies journals and has rarely been referenced since. Similarly, *The Gaia Atlas of Future Worlds: Challenge and Opportunity in an Age of Change* (Myers, 1990) passed almost silently through our fields and, despite a plethora of books, journals, and journal issues involving cartography, remains an underconsulted set of maps.

Turning to Gaia's more controversial second face, the question of the Goddess, we quote Jean Shinoda Bolen, who claims that as "archetypal images, Goddesses have the potential to be experienced inwardly to begin with" in a manner that connects with other inward-looking knowledge traditions. In appealing to different styles of knowing, Bolen (1990) rejects the dualistic mind-body, contemplation-action, and inner-outer splits that still undergird much social theory and its associated practices because even "when feminine qualities are deified and abstracted as life-giving or life-sustaining they are still embodied" and when "the planet Earth is revered as Gaia, for example, this not just an idea or just a spirit, but the presence of the Goddess in living matter" (p. xiv). Hallie Inglehart Austen (1990) testifies to the associated danger in losing this kind of speaking voice and bodily wisdom:

> Many people are awaking to something primal peoples have always known, which is that we cannot drain Gaia's resources without destroying ourselves and other forms of life. Significantly, a key element in the Earth's survival, the Amazon rainforest, is named after Mediterranean women warriors who were the last holdouts against the patriarchal Indo-European culture. . . . At this point Gaia and the Amazon, and thus all life on our planet, are threatened. (p. xxi)

Many other Western-educated people continue to give credence to these kinds of narratives and connections. They certainly align with personal and environmental empowerment in ways that post-wall social theoretical narratives have not convincingly achieved.

DON'T SHOOT THE MESSAGES:
ANCIENT WISDOMS AND
MODERN POPULARIZATIONS

Visible evidence of their social currency is the number of popular book titles that promulgate ideas deriving from a range of perennial wisdoms and indigenous peoples. From the pomposity of David Maybury-Lewis's narration of the 1992 10-part television series, *Millennium: Tribal Wisdom and the Modern World*, through James Cowan's (1993) grandiosely titled *Messengers of the Gods: Tribal Elders Reveal the Ancient Wisdom of the Earth*, to Knudtson and Suzuki's (1992) more modest, *Wisdom of the Elders*, popularizations abound. This alone should provide incentive for social theorists to broaden their curricula. We ask for communication and cultural studies to at least consider some of their ideas in the spirit of say, cyborgs, that more currently acceptable way (see Chapter 9) of expanding a narrow idea matrix. Moreover, unlike many present knowledge configurations, which seem to be retarding the sustainable development of ecocentric approaches, their ecological frameworks support a power-sensitive idea pluralism. This emerges from what Freya Mathews (1993) calls

> a certain background assumption, namely that the world is an interconnected whole, and that we, as individuals and as groups, are dependent on it and each other. This—ecological—assumption encourages the proliferation of diversity—in epistemological and political as in biotic domains—but only to the extent that diversity promotes the integrity of the system as a whole. (p. 227)

From that perspective, we might look to tribal, and other, traditional wisdoms as endangered idea species without compromising the field's discouragement of dominatory knowledges and knowledge forms. Environmental discourse draws considerable inspiration from connections with premodern and indigenous cultures. New sciences, and other disciplines, also engage with the various notions of wise practice in these previously discredited traditions. The Harvard Mind Science symposium, for example, featured participants as diverse as psychologist Howard Gardner and the Dalai Lama. Another of its participants, Robert Thurman (1991), addressed such questions as "why does modern, Western, cognitive science need the old-fashioned mind science of Tibet?" and "if the Indo-Tibetan tradition does have something to contribute, what is it?" (p. 54). Similarly, Hecht and Cockburn's (1990) historical-scientific account of the Amazon has no hesitation in hailing native peoples of South America as "accomplished environmental scientists" (p. 36) and, in *Blackfoot Physics: A Journey Into the Native American Universe*, theoretical physicist David Peat (1995) examines that Native American tribe's knowledge system as a recognizable relative of modern Western science.

A comparable openness to the value of other traditional ideas, particularly those from the Native American shamanic tradition, enlivens the television series, *Northern Exposure* (Brand & Falsey, 1991). In exploring some illustrative extracts, we suggest that exposure to other learning traditions might educate communication and cultural studies along similar lines to the way the show's fictional Alaska educates that exemplar of Western rationalism, Jewish medical doctor Joel Fleishman. In the episode culminating in the exiled New York doctor's vision quest, he undergoes the Native American ritual of the Giveaway (which involves him giving away all his material possessions). This might almost be an extenuated parallel of the environmentally necessary reduction in consumption required by most modern Westerners. In his own words, Fleishman is chastened enough by the experience to consider different ways of perceiving himself, his society, and his subjectivity. Typically, too, the episode surrounds him with stunning natural imagery, to which he remains oblivious. This allows for a visual link with the natural world as a counterpoint to the script of his nonstop neurotic verbosity. *Northern Exposure* offers a kind of television equivalent to the reassurance given by natural rhythms of change: "The recurring cycles of the year are not simply entertaining phenomena, . . . but signs that the cosmos is still intact, that we remain in something larger and more reliable than our own short-lived enthusiasms" (Ford, quoted in McKibben, 1990, p. 94).

Whereas the philosophy of *Northern Exposure* holds "that Alaska is not a just a state, it is a state of mind" (Kutzera, 1992, p. 74), we would add that it is also a place in nature—albeit a place in Washington state rather than the far frozen north. The persistent shots of the full moon that mark off segment endings and beginnings, for example, visually contrast with Joel's mind-dominated comprehensions. In a gently humorous manner, they also imply that perspective's limitations. On a larger scale, they invite viewers to contemplate human subjectivity as interconnected with nonhuman aspects of the planet in ways that align with belief systems as diverse as those of Australian Aborigines and Zen monks.

To shift for a moment from the desert and cave settings of so-called primitive thought to the more familiar great Hall of cultural studies, Stuart Hall (1991a), we find him exclaiming, "The universe is coming!" (p. 13). However, his discussion of the imminent arrival chooses to restrict the identity impact of an "ecological understanding of the world" to denying "the notion that the nation-state and the boundaries of sovereignty will keep things stable because they won't" (p. 14). Hall's pre-ecological views fall short of Freya Mathews's more thoroughgoing, and less anthropocentric, subjectivity. In *The Ecological Self*, Mathews (1991) uses Spinoza's philosophy to justify nondualistic conceptions of the world common to many traditional peoples. Whether it is Rick reincarnating as a still-fickle dog, Maggie picnicking with her other grouchy dead lovers, the whole of Cicely in thrall to seasonal change, or Ed and his fellow Native Americans talking to a spirit guide invisible to most of the township's white population, *Northern Exposure* acts as though an interlinked universe has already come and has fun playing with these kinds of ideas.

EASTERN, AND OTHER, EXPOSURES

Northern Exposure doesn't only relay ancient knowings, its inhabitants enact fresh rituals that suggest how modern Westerners, especially men, might regain touch with "the rhythm of this Life/Death/Life cycle" (Estés, 1992, p. 112). When, after the Alaskan winter, Cicely's ice finally cracks, the town's males celebrate the coming of Spring with neo-pagan spirit by running naked through the town in the freezing cold. In her book, *Women Who Run with the Wolves*, Clarissa Pinkola Estés likewise commends inner responsiveness to cyclical patterns:

> The Life/Death/Life Goddess is always also a creator Goddess. She makes, fashions, breathes life into . . . . Nature does not ask permission. Blossom and birth whenever you feel like it. As adults we need little permission but rather more engendering, much more encouraging of the wild cycles. (1992, p. 114)

Even more than *Northern Exposure, Women Who Run With the Wolves* gives power back to enabling, nonexclusive stories. Estés's book draws from her work as a Jungian therapist—a therapeutic tradition much more receptive than the Freudian tradition to non-Western wisdom. The book practices what she calls "a sort of wolf Buddhism" (Estés, 1992, p. 103) empathetic with both the animal world and traditional knowledges. From the beginning of her magnificent retelling, contextualizing, and interpreting of folk tales, she pulls together the inner and outer connections of overintellectualism, social prejudices, and environmental danger: "It's not by accident that the pristine wilderness of our planet disappears as the understanding of our own inner wild natures fades" (p. 3).

If, in its eco-politics, *Northern Exposure* is less explicit, it is innovative and allows for audience ambivalence. The show raises a range of ecological issues through the character of Mike Munro, a character "allergic" to 20th-century pollutants. In the script, Munro is compared to the canary in the cage whose greater sensitivity to atmospheric pollution traditionally warned miners of the approach of deadly gas. Munro is also portrayed as a neurotic. This leaves space for a measure of doubt and creates opportunities for comedy without disallowing some environmental points. He exits the show as a heroic eco-warrior engaged in a Greenpeace-like direct action to save whales. Film and soundtrack of his actions is presented seriously and constructed as admirable by the Cicely community who gather together to watch. It remains a rare prime-time endorsement of environmental activism as heroic and life transforming. One significant eco-political omission in *Northern Exposure* is the key Alaskan environmental issue of oil and mineral exploitation (from which individual Alaskans gain an allowance). The struggle between environmentalists and oil companies over how much oil should be taken has continued in the U.S. Congress but has been absent in the television series.

As is usual with most successful prime-time television, *Northern Exposure* had a special Christmas show. Unusually, the episode relativized different religious approaches, from the Catholic, the Jewish, the atheist, through the North American

materialist to the Korean Buddhist, to celebrating, or not celebrating, the season. Nevertheless, one tradition drew the diverse
audience happily together without denying their own distinctive
beliefs and celebrations. In the show's culmination, a modernized
Native American ceremony unites the community. The audience
is shown, by facial close-up shots, as experiencing awe at the
retelling, around the time of the winter solstice, of the story of
how Raven (mythical-trickster of Native American lore) brought
light/the sun to humans.

As part of a culture that is transforming the very source of life
into carcinogenic rays, we argue for abandoning Enlightenment
ideas of automatic superiority and for interactive learning with
the knowledge traditions of non-TWIT peoples. Their complex
understanding of how we might go on living as a species without
recklessly destroying other species might well exceed our own;
their capacity to find meaning in life without increasing material
and energy-expensive prosperity might also prove invaluable.
Again, we stress that this advocates neither a simple return to
static traditional values nor a wholesale reinstatement of indigenous worldviews but a plural exchange with mutual respect. At
what they term the *techno-cultural interface,* Tafler and d'Agostino
(1993) see indigenous storytelling as recuperating "technological
advances that have distanced human societies from the rigors of
their environment" (p. 51). In transcending generational, spatial,
and temporal constraints, this storytelling acts as "the harbinger
of more advanced telecommunications" (p. 52). This is not just
futuristic. Outside the world of television, networked Native
American nations already merge familiar identities into their
version of cyberspace systems: "a runner crossing snow-capped
mountain tops, a messenger flying across the land of the Crow
on the back of a big-beaked bird . . . bringing ancient messages
into the future" (Hedlund, 1992, p. 32).

Much further back in time, Buddhism, too, transformed with
its move from China to Japan; as we write, the Dalai Lama travels
the globe speaking to the media of how exile influences Tibetan
Buddhism. Many current followers of Buddhism, and other Eastern meditative traditions, are themselves Westerners. In this time
of posts, a post-perennial wisdom aligned with Western ideas of

democracy is not inconceivable. Future eco-impacts might en-hance the prospect by bringing forward both a lower standard of economic living for the majority of the world's people and an emotional encounter with the increasing proximity of the death of nature (and humankind). These kinds of changes will not be painless, and Anthony Giddens's (1992) controversial attempt to mainstream therapeutic discourse in sociology may yet turn out to be another way forward. Without doubt, the West continues to threaten the whole ecosystem with our population's dispropor-tionate share of affluence, disproportionate consumption of re-sources, and disproportionate possession of technologies. To pun on the Ehrlich and Ehrlich's (1991) planetary equation, our communal *I*, as Western social theorists, might equal an unsus-tainably "PAT" ideology and threaten our own survival.

7

Aligning Media

Debatable Divides
and Boundary Crossings

As well as occupying a key intersection of the popular and the academic, media texts and how they are studied help erect, maintain, and shift parameters of understanding across a number of important divides and borders. This chapter looks at media eco-advocacy and some of its discontents. In moving toward a more ecocentric approach, we link various media eco-criticisms with diverse eco-texts to blur, or cross, 10 symbolic or practical boundaries (or both) and explore their less bipolar borderlands.

BOUNDARIES (I):
NOT REINVENTING WHEELS

Once again, trails blazed by the women's movement provide directions for disciplinary change. They also indicate some ways of linking the environmental dimension to other relations of subordination. Feminist screen theorists have already, as part of their own project, worked through theoretical issues still to be confronted by a more ecocentric study of the media. Therefore, to avoid reinventing methodological-political wheels, we suggest that media eco-critics reassess their uniqueness. Even at this late stage, critics might openly draw ideas and inspiration from earlier work by women.[1] Indeed, the boundary-crossing strategy of this chapter owes a debt to *Crossing Boundaries: Feminisms and the Critique of Knowledges* (Caine, de Lepervanche, & Grosz, 1988), and we borrow from media work such as Ann Kaplan's (1983, 1984) and Annette Kuhn's (1982) convenient reviews of feminist film theory. In sometimes bracketing gender concerns with nonhuman aspects, however, we do not imply that women are actually closer to nature. Instead, as we argue elsewhere in the book, the exclusion and marginalization of the interests of women in the texts of patriarchal Cartesian-Newtonian discourse provide guidelines and precedents for our understanding of the way nature, other species, ecologies, and the biosphere are also marginalized and excluded. Our aim is to build on feminist approaches through extending their pertinence. In addressing the representation of environmental issues, we adapt the following six questions in the context of broader media issues:

1. How are women (or nonhuman aspects of the planet) represented visually (and across different media discourses)?
2. What functions does a woman character (or nonhuman aspect of the planet) perform within film (and other media) narratives?
3. Are certain fixed images of women (or nonhuman aspects of the planet) being consistently appealed to?
4. How do women (or nonhuman aspects of the planet) not function; how are they not represented in film (and other media)?
5. What absences, disjunctions, ruptures, and inconsistencies, at image or narrative level, or both, exist?
6. In what ways do women (or nonhuman aspects of the planet) function as signifier or structure, inform, or relate to those absences?

In applying our adaptations, we start with the eco-friendly genre of a cartoon film designed mainly for children. *FernGully: The Last Rainforest* (Younger, Faiman, & Kroyer, 1992), like much fantasy and science fiction (see Kuhn, 1990), operates on the other side of realism and so can more easily adopt a less anthropocentric perspective. *FernGully's* sustained breaking of the species barrier between humans and other animals usefully contrasts with ecological exclusions in mainstream movies. The two connect because the opening part of our first adapted question, about how nonhuman aspects of the planet are represented visually, depends heavily on its second part concerning the representation across different media discourses. The link foregrounds associated questions of generic and textual status. As Chapter 3's contrast of television news and comedy argued, factual genres usually have more status (and, therefore, in many television cases, more resources) than fictional ones. In this specific case, *FernGully's* low ranking is further confirmed because it is aimed at the children's market. It remains to be seen whether the boundary-breaking *Babe* (Miller, Miller, Mitchell, & Noonan, 1995), in terms of audience, budget, and politics, with its creative reworking of *Animal Farm* through Joseph Campbell, will undermine these assumptions and attract more serious critical attention. It is interesting that in cross-generational terms, George Miller said in an interview that his favorite review of the film said: "Kids, all you need to know you'll find in *Babe*. Take your folks" (as quoted in Murray, 1995, p. 54).

BOUNDARIES (2): CROSS-GENERATIONAL AND STATUS BARRIERS

In these films, perhaps because they are aimed at a younger generation of audiences and belong to relatively discredited genres, radical views of planetary ecology flourish. *FernGully* is a magic place in a rain forest inhabited by fantastic life forms: a young fairy called Crysta; her elf friend Pips; Batty Korda, a brain-fried bat (voiced in manic fashion by Robin Williams); Zak, a human boy who is shrunk to fairy size, and the keeper of the Old Powers, Magi Lune, who dies in the course of the narrative. All of them join together to fight Hexxus, the ancient enemy of the forest, freed by a nightmarishly depicted "Leveller" machine driven by humans "clearing" the rain forest for development. In sharp sensual contrast, *FernGully* accommodates fairy flight with a dazzling illustration of animated Australian rain forest biodiversity from flame trees with bright red flowers to rainbow-colored lorikeets and wompoo pigeons. As the visuals gradually integrate the human boy, Zak, into this web of life, they imply more similarities with, rather than differences from, the nonhuman.

Question 2—what functions do nonhuman aspects of the planet perform within the narrative?—also emphasizes interconnectedness. In the final showdown at the eco-OK Corral, Crysta, in the manner of classic western genre heroes, defeats the evil Hexxus. One key difference is that Crysta's weapon is not a six-gun but a simple glowing seed, that connects her with "the magic she shared with all of life" (Young, 1991, p. 122). Crysta flies the seed into Hexxus's mouth to trap her within the growing tree that emerges from it. The conclusion doesn't require much interpretation but, narratively, makes the produce of nature share the heroic role with Crysta. In playing off classic cinema good-versus-evil narratives, *FernGully* makes a relatively conventional happy ending: The damaged creatures recover; Zak returns to the human race with a new eco-consciousness; and, in the pride of place, the rain forest regrows after its devastation. However, by positioning forest regeneration as the crowning moment, *FernGully* usefully reverses the conventional role of nature and wilderness. This male hero walks off into the sunrise of civilization determined to deter future rain forest development. Such repositioning invites a reappraisal of how nature, usually in terms of scenery, functions in more adult cinema from the western films of John Ford to their remakes in the Highlands of the 1995 film *Rob Roy* and the scenery in road movies such as 1991's *Thelma & Louise.*

These kinds of reappraisals lead into the third question: Are certain fixed images of nonhuman aspects of the planet being consistently appealed to? As a variety of Levi-Strauss-influenced structuralists (e.g., Wright, 1975) have shown, divisions between the country and the city, between rural and urban, and between nature and civilization underpin much film. Outside of children's and cartoon films, few media texts give nature an active narrative role or allow nonhuman aspects a shifting function—notable exceptions include Godfrey Reggio's 1983 nondialogue film, *Koyaanisqatsi.* The vast majority of texts and genres similarly restrict Question 4's concern with the functions and representations of nonhuman aspects. Few, however, can avoid Question 5's absences, disjunctions, ruptures, and inconsistencies at image and narrative level. Various kinds of great outdoors as threat, haven, or both occupy visual and script space from the blockbuster action of James Bond movies to the imitative 1994 Schwarzenegger vehicle *True Lies* and character dramas from the 1990 *Driving Miss Daisy* to 1994's *Blue Sky.*

BOUNDARIES (3):
BEYOND THE SPECIES BARRIER

The sixth and final amended question—in what ways do nonhuman aspects of the planet function as signifier, or structure, or inform, or relate to those absences?—can probably best be illustrated through the changing history of the natural history genre. Any canon of environmental texts would have to include examples of ecological programs that go beyond traditional natural history. These programs, and their putative genre, have a tangled genealogy. Commenting on nature and wildlife movies since 1951, Alexander Wilson (1992) sees their "discontinuous ancestry" as including "animal stories, science journalism, conservationism, ecological advocacy, social anthropology, adventure stories and tips on hunting and fishing" (p. 117).

Equally accurately, he observes that any one single program "will be a hybrid of different documentary forms and will express deeply contradictory ideas about nature and its relation to human culture" (A. Wilson, 1992, p. 117). At the forefront of Wilson's

ancestral history is the story of how Disney studios transformed
the land and its inhabitants into a kind of Disneyland by a fusion
of phototechnologies and ideologies so that,

> For all they opened up and "revealed" of life, the early Disney
> movies also came with their own constricting logic. The animal
> stories they trafficked in were among other things transparent
> allegories of progress, paeans to the official cult of exploration,
> industrial development, and an ever rising standard of living.
> Those blooming flowers in "living color"—a signature of Disney's
> film work—legitimized our metaphors about economic growth. . . .
> They were fictions of victory for the New Century of Progress.
> (A. Wilson, 1992, pp. 118-119)

As the quote demonstrates, one of Wilson's (1992) great
strengths is to restore social relations to nature. A less common
one is how he restores nature to social relations. For both tasks,
he uses a range of miniseries and movies. He commends Jean-
Jacques Annaud's 1988 *The Bear* for how it locates "the movie's
'nature' within human culture, to relate natural history to the
conventions of time" (p. 154) as well as how it shifts the point of
view "back and forth between humans and bear protagonists" to
avoid "allegories of pristine nature" (p. 154). Perceiving that
"Disney's anthropomorphism allows animals to be addressed as
social beings, and nature as a *social realm*" (p. 154), Wilson
welcomes the resulting "breach in the species barrier between
human and animal" (p. 154). Open to "the possibility of interspecies intimacy" (p. 154), Wilson argues in favor of anthropomorphism as "an historical and strategic intervention." Unfashion-
ably but in parallel with the recent revolt against too restrictive
an application of Said's orientalism (e.g., Turner, 1994), he probes
easy acceptance of what one naturalist called the inferred des-
potism of animal study and anthropomorphism. In an interesting
echo of Estés (1992), he, too, would shift the "wall between
humans and the natural world" from absolute barrier to "permeable, moving, shifting, able occasionally to be leaped over—as it
always has by hags and shamans" (Wilson, 1992, pp. 154-155).

The totem animism in the worldview of hags and shamans differs in one critical respect from Wilson's understanding of interspecies permeability: It is not simply a projection of human attitudes. In other cultures, animals and nature spirits have their own powers. As chief Letakota-Lesa of the Pawnee tribe said around 1904, "In the beginning of all things, wisdom and knowledge were with the animals. . . . and that from them, and from the stars and the moon, man should learn" (quoted in Campbell, 1984, p. 8). The ability to enter these nonhuman domains involves a deliberate shift into animal worlds and resembles a communion rather than a process of human patronage or projection. Neither Wilson nor Disney come close to those powers of hags and shamans.

BOUNDARIES (4):
TOWARD LOCAL AND GLOBAL ALLIANCES

A. Wilson's uncommon crossing of the species barrier remains uncommon. Outside of children's films, few attempts, as George Miller puts it in the equally exceptional context of *Babe,* are made "to sense what is going on beyond the membrane that separates the world of the humans and the animals" (quoted in Murray, 1995, p. 10). In ecological advocacy programs, for example, other issues dominate that genre's evolution toward more committed environmentalist genres and personnel. David Suzuki's 1987 autobiography, *Metamorphosis: Stages in a Life,* for example, recounts his gradual move from a Canadian Broadcasting Corporation (CBC) science show to the more philosophical and overt environmental advocacy of CBC's 1990 eight-part miniseries, *A Planet for the Taking.* That series was based around the thesis of a human species out of balance with the rest of nature and asks, in "The Runaway Brain" episode, if we can "begin to see ourselves not as dominant but integral, as just one part of the complex pattern of matter and life."

En route to his eco-conversion, Suzuki (1987) records political differences among wildlife filmmakers. Some believe that through "superb nature films" they chip "into the public's sensitivities" but to maintain credibility, "must avoid taking an advocacy position" (p. 263). Others, including Suzuki himself, see the problem as going beyond overt advocacy to tackle the "ooh, ah, oh dear" syndrome, whereby the audience are first invited to go "ooh" and "ah" at the wonder of nature but by the end are expected to go "oh dear" because of the explicit message saying how that wonder is threatened. Suzuki sees the next stage as moving audiences from sympathy to activism.

How that is to be done remains the big challenge for filmmakers. For a greener media studies, the challenge has a number of parts: to get the film and television text makers' ongoing attempts to do it onto the agenda; to search analytically, and through audience studies, to show how this greening might be done; and to foreground critical perspectives that move toward sustainable progress. Study of the evolving genre of environmental advocacy programs would be one essential route. Even a cursory survey of the literature reveals that anthropocentrism still distorts the focus of critical attention. One result is that critical debate tends to cluster around more anthropological series, such as the 1992 *Millennium: Tribal Wisdom and the Modern World,* rather than less human centered series. That focus still leaves the integration of the human and nonhuman, the local and the global, unresolved.

Moves to resolution are further hindered by the huge gulf that usually separates environmental discussions of the local-global nexus from sociology, communication, and cultural studies' discussions of the same nexus. Stuart Hall's (1991b) politics of the local-global, for instance, registers no awareness of local versus global activism debates among environmentalists such as the prolocal Wendell Berry (1977, 1981, 1989) whose view that planetary activism is impossible has been contested by Alan AtKisson's (1990) call for the necessity of conceiving individuals, households, and localities as embedded in the global. A significant exception is Donna Haraway's (1992b) "The Promises of Monsters." In that essay, she offers one of the most sustained refocusings, and an appraisal of indigenous media use, within a cultural studies framework. It is not, perhaps, incidental that she came to the field after having first established her credentials as a scientist and feminist.

Haraway builds on Hecht and Cockburn's (1990) *The Fate of the Forest: Developers, Destroyers, and Defenders of the Amazon,* which situates current practices within a lengthy history of exploitation. Conceptualizing the forest as the cocreation of biological and human history, they reject the myths of the Amazon as "the last remaining outpost of Eden" (Hecht & Cockburn, 1990, p. 11). As a consequence, they conclude that any "program for the Amazon begins with basic human rights. . . . Forest people seek legal recognition . . . [and] look to a redistribution of resources and power, and invoke a vision of development that uses their knowledge, their culture and their ideas" (p. 239). Picking up Hecht and Cockburn's point that the Amazonian biosphere is an irreducibly human-nonhuman collective entity as fundamental, Haraway (1992b) calls for reforms ranging from "direct control of indigenous lands by native peoples" to "an end to fiscal incentives for cattle ranchers, agribusiness, and unsustainable logging" (p. 311). Consistent with the cocreation position, she presents rain forest protection "as a necessarily joint human rights-ecological issue" with indigenous people as "part of *all* international negotiations involving their territories" (p. 311). Haraway (1992b) concludes that

All the people who care, cognitively, emotionally, and politically, must articulate their position in a field constrained by a new collective entity, made up of indigenous people and other human and unhuman actors. Commitment, and engagement, not their invalidation, in an emerging collective are the conditions of joining knowledge-producing and world-building practices. This is situated knowledge in the New World; it builds on common places, and it takes unexpected turns. So far, such knowledge has not been sponsored by the major oil corporations, banks and logging interests. That is precisely why there is so much work for North Americans, Europeans, and Japanese, among others, to do in articulation with those humans and non-humans who live in rain forests and in many other places in the semiotic space called earth. (pp. 314-315)

BOUNDARIES (5):
THE POLITICAL ECONOMY
OF PUBLIC-PRIVATE DIVIDES

In that media-informed semiosphere, resource issues matter, too (see Golding & Murdock, 1991). It is an area where the majority of eco-advocacy texts emerge from what might be called public television. That is to say, out of noncommercial channels, such as the government-funded Australian ABC, British BBC, and Canadian CBC organizations and U.S. public television, such as PBS and WGBH, or production companies supported by environmental organizations such as the National Wildlife Federation and the Audubon Society. All of these organizations produce or fund, either independently or in joint production deals (often with each other), environmentally oriented programs. Significantly, the widely circulating television system of the U.S. commercial networks generate few programs that belong in the environmental advocacy genre. Recent research confirms that a comparable scarcity is likely to emerge in Britain in the future because

> New types of environmental programme will increasingly come under threat as a result of the government's restructuring of broadcasting. If free market forces prevail, broadcasters will be forced to maximize audience ratings, and because documentaries about environmental matters tend to attract small, specialized audiences they will inevitably suffer. . . . A recent report by Oxfam for the Third World and Environment Broadcasting Project warns: "Deregulation . . . threatens to cut off the life blood for environmental and current affairs documentaries" (quoted in Lee, 1990). (Anderson, 1991, p. 473)

In a world increasingly privatized and increasingly promotional, public television systems can usefully be seen as fostering a critical idea commons as a space open to all. We see one contemporary media manifestation of the tragedy of the commons as the endangering of that public space for informing environmental citizens of their countries and the world. Environmental advocacy programs prominently feature the local and the global in close interconnection and contribute a crucial ecological dimension to the politics of information of factually oriented public knowledge formation. Any one program, or series, faces severe difficulties in encompassing all the "three political levels: the institutions and processes" (its formal channels and fora); "the substance of politics" (its issues and policies), and "the foundation of politics," the processes and concepts on which government is based (Carpini & Williams, 1994, p. 75). Indeed, even with the advantage of permanent staff resources, many expensive, better orchestrated and resourced public health campaigns from road safety to AIDS have not necessarily translated into change across these different political levels.

That same Carpini and Williams (1994) article, " 'Fictional' and 'Non-Fictional' Television Celebrates Earth Day: Or, Politics Is Comedy Plus Pretense," also involves analyses of programs on environmental pollution. As their title signals, the authors are derogatory rather than celebratory about television coverage. They start promisingly, from our point of view, by attacking the divide between fiction and nonfiction as unhelpful. They move on to make four telling criticisms about how all their chosen eco-texts—simplify scientific complexity and uncertainty to "employ a catastrophic perspective on environmental problems" (p. 93); implicate audiences, through individual "hero" narratives, in individualistic solutions rather than institutional and political change (p. 94); assume "that public opinion translates into policy solutions" (p. 88); and do not "seriously address the trade-offs between regulation and economic activity" (p. 93). Their critique applies, with some qualifications, to many eco-advocacy programs outside of those they selected for analysis. Such a sustained eco-advocacy text as *Race to Save the Planet* (Angier, 1990), therefore, can usefully be considered in the light of Carpini and Williams's criticisms to illustrate eco-text and eco-criticism interactions.

Typically for an eco-advocacy series, as its credits reveal, *Race to Save the Planet* is produced by WGBH, Boston, in association with the University Grants Commission of India-Gujarat University, the Chedd-Angier Production Company, and Film Australia, with major funding support from the Annenberg/CPB Project and the Corporation for Public Broadcasting. Shown internationally on broadcast television, sometimes with different hosts and narrators than the U.S. pair of Meryl Streep and Roy Schneider, *Race to Save the Planet* has an additional life as a video set with accompanying teachers' guides that help to situate its aims and scope. If not quite Carpini and Williams's (1994) "catastrophic perspective on environmental problems" (p. 93), the series opens and closes with urgency: Its final video is called *Now or Never,* and its initial background notes claim that

> Population growth and industrialization in the twentieth century have put immense pressure on the earth's resources. It has become clear that the impact of human activity around the globe is pushing natural systems beyond crucial environmental thresholds. . . . *Race to Save the Planet* clearly points out to its audience that the creation of a sustainable world begins with individual values and choices, yet extends to encompass every community and government around the globe.

Race to Save the Planet's 10 individual titles give a good indication of its priorities:

1. The Environmental Revolution
2. Only One Atmosphere
3. Do We Really Want to Live This Way?
4. In the Name of Progress
5. Remnants of Eden
6. More or Less
7. Save the Earth—Feed the World
8. Waste Not, Want Not
9. It Needs Political Decisions
10. Now or Never

BOUNDARIES (6):
THE ECO-LIMITS OF CITIZENSHIP,
NATION, AND GENDER

As its individual program titles, production, and funding origins suggest, *Race to Save the Planet* covers the important issues
and addresses individuals as citizens of the world as well as
citizens of individual countries. At this point, we explicitly dissociate ourselves from positions constructed entirely around individual property ownership of land and resources. Such positions
propose that the commons are ruined because they are communal and not privately owned. The works of Garrett Hardin (1968,
1974), still unfortunately influential within some strands of the
environmental movement, construct this as the real tragedy of
the commons. More recently, Hardin (1989) has asserted that
there is no global population problem but only population problems in separate nations. Adopting a lifeboat analogy underwrit-
ten by crude neo-Malthusianism, he opposes any general ethics
of sharing as rocking the precarious lifeboat of wealthy nations
who put themselves at risk by feeding poorer nations or by
allowing their citizens to immigrate. This is a divisive and manifestly absurd analogy. Derived from a view of justice so partial
that it obstructs the reality of which nations cause disproportionate environmental deterioration, Hardin's modern revolution of
the rich against the poor would put the commons of the air we
breathe and the seas that sustain us at the mercy of the very
people who have already polluted them (see Luper-Foy, 1995, for
a more sustained critique).

It is interesting that although Carpini and Williams (1994) ask
for eco-advocacy programs to point more directly to concrete
political action, they themselves remain within a nationalistic
rather than biospheric framework. As their after note to one
program analysis puts it, in a 2-hour show, rather than just ask
the viewers to check how their political representatives vote on
environmental issues, they "could have actually been informed
of the records of our Senators and Congressmen, or at least how

to find out about such things" (p. 97). As social scientists, they no doubt see the omission as crucial. They appear less sensitive to the need to entertain as well as inform and unaware of the international afterlife of U.S. programming from Australia to Zimbabwe. To ask environmental programs to address fundamental political education on top of environmental education might distract them from more specifically ecological matters by requiring that they take on board too large a cargo of local didactic content. From our perspective, that might actually inhibit the promotion of the fundamental attitude shifts in Carpini and Williams's Level 3 "foundation of politics," which we see as necessary for the establishment of a distinctive environmental agenda—especially one engaging with the human-nonhuman relationships so neglected by social theorists.

On these relationships, *Race to Save the Planet* is relatively restrained. The *Remnants of Eden* episode gives most attention to the nonhuman world. Nevertheless, throughout all 10 programs, the series does feature impacts on other species and nonsentient land alongside human issues as they arise. In considering the pollution of the Rhine, for example, the fatal impact on the seal colony at the river mouth merits attention along with the pollutants in Amsterdam's drinking water. The series also nominates speakers who frequently offer conflicting perspectives between an individual or nationalistic point of view and a more Gaian and global one. Thus, a Thai official acknowledges that whereas banning wood cutting in Thailand and buying it from Burma makes sense for his country, he concedes that it does not make the same sense for the planet. Another speaker suggests that we need to ask how big a car the planet can afford rather than how big a car we can afford.

This marks a significant extension to anthropocentric ideas of citizenship. Generally, citizenship depends on rights in four basic spheres: civil liberties, including, for example, free speech, religious freedom, and the right to possess personal property in civil society; political rights to participate in democratic public life, including, for example, voting rights and jury duties; and the third, social, and fourth, cultural, set of rights: "full membership of a social and cultural formation" with the right "to participate in existing patterns of social and cultural life and the right to challenge these configurations and develop alternative identities and forms of expression" (Murdock, 1992, p. 20).

For Murdock (1992), in line with our tragedy of the information commons argument, the maintenance of these rights through communication systems requires more than "free-markets" to "guarantee diversity of expression and open debate" (p. 21). He opposes hanging democracy on the concept of consumer choice through the current "concerted attack on public cultural institutions and a vigorous promotion of market mechanism and the pleasures of consumption" (p. 22). Instead, he argues convincingly for a concept of citizenship "based on a politics of diversity and difference" that "can provide a new justification for public communications and offer alternative definitions of empowerment to those promoted by the market" (p. 23). This necessary advance remains pre-ecological in its exclusion of the diversity and difference of the nonhuman world. Roderick Nash's (1990) chart of the expanding concept of rights follows natural rights from the Magna Carta of 1215 through the 1863 slave emancipation proclamation to the endangered species act of 1973. Imbricated in this legislative trajectory, which has moved on to protect the land itself through international world heritage laws, is a wider notion of planetary citizenship that grants the nonhuman some rights. The subject of nonhuman and ecological rights is a central component of contemporary discourses of environmentalism. This contrasts sharply with the culturally dominant paradigms of media representations that consign ecocentric texts, such as *FernGully*, to the low status of children's genres or to the relatively underwatched arena of public television.

At this point, we want to address the equivalent lack of status for eco-feminism within social theory. The majority of critics either associate it totally with the nonrational (Biehl, 1991) or virtually ignore it. This disregard occurs despite recent edited collections that raise significant sociological and philosophical issues (Diamond & Feman-Orenstein, 1990; Gaard, 1993; Warren, 1994) and that include substantial Third World material (Mies & Shiva, 1991). Two recent books on ecological thought provide good illustrations of this disregard. Peter Dickens (1992) devotes less than 2½ pages (pp. 139-141) of a 195-page book on *Society and Nature: Towards a Green Social Theory* to feminism (eco-feminism is indexed under feminism), and Tim Hayward's (1994) *Ecological Thought: An Introduction* gives even less than 2 (pp. 124-125) in a 214-page book. Significantly, both fuse feminism and eco-feminism in the context of discussing production and reproduction. More significantly, both virtually dismiss[2] eco-feminism on the strength of short quotes from different single articles by Kate Soper (1979, 1992). Surely, eco-feminist engagements merit as much consideration as yet another chapter on "The Ethics of Ecological Humanism." In a third recent book, *Natural Relations: Ecology, Animal Rights and Social Justice*, Ted Benton (1993) indexes ecologism, economism, and eco-socialism but excludes eco-feminism and the eco-feminist anthologies entirely, although he, too, references Soper three times. Benton's key question, "Why should Marxists come so belatedly and reluctantly to a recognition of the political importance of ecology?" (p. 1), would benefit from the additional one of why do social theorists move so belatedly and reluctantly to a recognition of the importance of eco-feminism? Again, it is hard not to detect familiar Eulightenment values, in a late-Marxist form, shaping the priorities of all three books.

BOUNDARIES (7):
ENCOMPASSING CONSUMERISM
AND THE COST OF COMFORT

To return to eco-advocacy programs as distinct from wildlife series, such as *Life on Earth* or *The Trials of Life*, we argue that their low priority, in terms of audiences and critical consideration, is cause for regret. Far from avoiding Carpini and Williams's (1994) trade-offs between regulation and economic activity, a program such as *Race to Save the Planet* goes into actual brand names, detailed percentage reductions of energy use, and explicit measures (including restrictions on cars) required to reduce greenhouse warming. *Race to Save the Planet* informs viewers in detail about such matters without neglecting controversy. In the "Only One Atmosphere" episode, for example, many so-called experts, who are nominated as having scientific credentials, are presented as in conflict with viewpoints from other nominated experts about the different possibilities for atmosphere change, global warming, and so on. In "Do We Really Want to Live This Way?" the series also confronts some convenience lifestyle consequences directly:

> Los Angeles is unhealthy for the trees, and the mountains, and the people below. It has reached its limit. . . . For now the polluted air around here and in many industrialized cities around the world is part of the cost of comfort.

The final program of the series sets out *Race to Save the Planet's* conclusions. It opens with a strong human angle around the words *changing the world*. That is followed by various stories: an ex-marine working to close a toxic work dump in California; a Russian woman who has organized her Moscow neighbors to fight air pollution; a dynamic professor who started a nationwide movement to restore Kenya's devastated forests; a Greek businessman who devised a way to prevent oil pollution at sea; and a diplomat's vision that resulted in a treaty protecting the Mediterranean. In its use of heroic individuals, some of whom are far from ordinary, the program frames solutions, which cluster around the standard environmental three Rs of "reduce (waste), reuse, and recycle," in individualistic discourse. Although Program 8, "It Needs Political Decisions," has advocated more sophisticated individual-government interaction (notably, Bjorn Gillberg's comment that government agencies are nothing without people chasing after them), Carpini and Williams's critique of individualist framing and solutions still fits.

In its closing minutes, the last program makes explicit the Worldwatch Institute research underpinning its construction. It moves easily from identifying the four horsepeople of the environmental apocalypse into the more Gaian perspective pioneered by *A Planet for the Taking*:

As the century closes, four challenges stand paramount. First, reduce population growth. . . . Second, slow greenhouse warming. . . . Third, reduce and recycle waste. . . . Fourth, conserve forests and wild species. . . . Although we are only a single species in nature, we have a unique ability to destroy. Of course, regardless of whether we treat it wisely, the earth will go on. It is us who need the earth. We depend on its bounty to sustain us and our children to come. It is our own future that's at stake. We are in a race to save ourselves.

A female narrator speaks this voice-over during stock images of crowded motorways, massive waste dumps, forest clearing, and black smoke billowing from factory chimneys. Apart from the Gaian positioning of humans as just another species, albeit an exceptional one, it is old-fashioned message television. The message is clear: Humanity is central, is at fault, and has the solution in its own hands. If the form and content offer little new, then it remains a message still not prevalent in communication and cultural studies unprepared to engage with, either directly or in representational terms, issues of overpopulation, air pollution, waste management, habitat conservation, and so on. It also addresses individuals as citizens of a world cohabited by other species and implicates first world human inhabitants specifically for the high environmental cost of their commitment to comfort.

BOUNDARIES (8):
MIND-BODY, INTELLECT-EMOTION,
AND ENTERTAINMENT-EDUCATION

In the political economy of television, information shows, however well done, tend, with the exception of news, to have limited mainstream circulation. After noting this, Carpini and Williams (1994) go on to reveal their traditional political outlook. We spend some time on their critique because it encapsulates many of the general strengths and weaknesses of social science approaches. They are traditional not just in terms of their unreflexive anthropocentrism and their distrust of emotion but in their disregard for the power of humor, the specificities of popular culture, and its textual and intertextual possibilities.

Carpini and Williams's (1994) limitations emerge most clearly in their analysis of a genuinely popular eco-entertainment show. Time Warner's *The Earth Day Special* (Baskin, Bernstein, Witt, & Hemion, 1990) celebrated the 20th anniversary of the first Earth Day. It "was the 16th most watched show that week" and "millions of television sets were tuned in for the consideration of an important issue high on the public agenda" (p. 88). "High on the public agenda" sets the tone for their critique, which sets out to show how the program fails to be informative enough and is shot through with contradictions. From an assumed high ground, they quote Candice Bergen-Murphy Brown's remark, "I'm not quite sure what's happening here, it's difficult to describe," and comment sarcastically, "We couldn't agree more" (p. 88). Outside of information television, however, that is not necessarily derogatory. Feminist media critics, among others, have suggested uncertainty, the space in contradictions, and the positive effect of exposing viewers to a less secure viewing position as significant values. In addition, in terms of the postmodern three Rs, Carpini and Williams's critique ignores the political usefulness of self-reflexivity, that reflexivity's potential to draw attention to the complexity of referentiality in media representations, and how little the U.S. position is relativized in relation to other nations.

Predictably, Carpini and Williams (1994) have problems around the emotional crisis that ecological decline produces. They also end up falling into the kind of contradictions they themselves criticize. After castigating *The Earth Day Special's* confusion and its lack of a structuring viewpoint, Carpini and Williams then acknowledge one clear and central guiding audience position for the whole program. They show how this is established from the precredits appearance of film and television stars Danny DeVito and Rhea Perlman as an ordinary couple, Vic and Paula, in a living-room set preparing to watch *The Earth Day Special:*

> Throughout the show, they reappear as the audience and signal to us the changing emotions we are supposed to experience at

each stage of the show (sort of an environmental version of
Kubler-Ross' stages of grief): denial of environmental problems;
shock at recognition of the severity of the problems; hopelessness
and depression; finally hope and optimism at what each of us can
do as individuals to solve the problem. (p. 99)

What Carpini and Williams (1994) seem to find demeaning—
"sort of an environmental version of Kübler-Ross's stages of
grief"—we view as an interesting representation of emotions and
emotional stages absent in their own, and most other social
theorists', work. Moreover, in identifying the celebrity couple's
linking role, the critics reveal the program makers as having both
a coherent framing strategy and an overall knowledge of what's
happening here. Continuing on the show's disorienting effect,
Carpini and Williams regret that there is no character development, which is a generic trait of dubious value to most sitcoms
(see Feuer, 1992), soaps (see Brown, 1987), and many of the other
popular forms the show vigorously cannibalizes. Carpini and
Williams assert, without argument, evidence, or logic, that "our
understanding depends on knowing that in 'real life' Perlman and
DeVito are married" (p. 89). In fact, that extratextual knowledge,
although it might add something for those who follow the stars
in other media texts, is not at all relevant to understanding their
function. As a result, Carpini and Williams downplay the clear
environmental messages filtered through the couple and their
interaction with popular television forms. In watching a quiz
show, for example, the couple argue over which is the correct
answer in relation to environmental questions about waste generation and disposal by U.S. citizens. This requires absolutely no
audience appreciation of the couple's identity. Furthermore, by
introducing ecological politics into the bland general knowledge
discourse of the quiz show, Perlman and DeVito demonstrate how
that genre might be greener.

Carpini and Williams (1994) appear equally blind to positive
interpretations elsewhere in the show. The celebrity persona of
Robin Williams who preaches, in the loud-suited attire of a
dubious salesperson, "about the virtues of mindless progress and the
transition of humans from 'hunter-gatherers to shopper-borrowers' "

(p. 90) is not theoretically informed enough for them. In the context of eco-advocacy programs and associated environmentalist emphases on the need for a more extended timescale, we think such humor can be thought provoking as well as funny. Send-ups of snake oil politicians and industrialists selling various kinds of developmental progress provide some inoculation against the still-frequent appearance of such people outside of entertainment programs.

Through the character of Bette Midler as Gaia, a Mother Earth so sick that she requires intensive care, *The Earth Day Special* introduces the ills of the planet. Rather differently from Lovelock's (1992) *Gaia: The Practical Science of Planetary Medicine*, potential courses of "treatment" are proposed by diverse practitioners who include science popularizer Carl Sagan and a variety of fictional media characters, including the teenage doctor prodigy from *Doogie Hauser, M.D.*, Nurse Colleen McMurphy from *China Beach*, and Christopher Lloyd as Dr. Emmette Brown, the time-traveling inventor from the *Back to the Future* trilogy. Carpini and Williams (1994) ask if it matters "that information is provided by 'fictional characters' as opposed to celebrity experts?" (p. 90). We think it does, and not just in their negative sense, because the fame of the fictional characters can help to increase popular awareness of environmental issues and can, sometimes, as in the case of Lloyd who comes back and says "I've seen the future, and it's not good," extend the temporal frame of consideration.

Of course, there are risks in celebrity politics, especially in a nation that made Ronald Reagan president, but some risks may be worth taking. Although *The Earth Day Special* is guilty of preferring information that "agrees with the dominant perspective of the show" (Carpini & Williams, 1994, p. 90), we welcome its public promulgation of statistics interwoven with issues and are less averse than Carpini and Williams to explicit partiality. If, unlike *Race to Save the Planet*, expert debate is absent, the general trends on global warming, land degradation, pollution, and population have attained greater scientific acceptability than Carpini and Williams allow. In the meantime, we, along with many scientists and environmentalists, believe that attempts to establish scientific consensus are not only notoriously difficult but might delay action to prevent potentially irreversible environmental consequences. At the least, television programs that increase public concern and raise environmental consciousness might stimulate action to establish more refined risk assessments. One of *The Earth Day Special's* segments, an exchange between Robin Williams as Everyman and Dustin Hoffman as Everylawyer, makes some relevant points:

WILLIAMS: Who do you represent?

HOFFMAN: People.

WILLIAMS: What people?

HOFFMAN: What do you think about what's going on around here?

WILLIAMS: Well, I'm a little concerned? To begin with the oceans are polluted.

                              •   •   •   •

HOFFMAN: No acid rain in a mall. No smog in a mall. Don't worry about atmosphere. You get all the atmosphere you want in a mall. . . . Photosynthesis can be argued both ways. The jury is still out on photosynthesis. You're living in the best country in the world. Where are you living?

WILLIAMS: America.

HOFFMAN: That's right, because you elect the people you want to represent you. What are they called?

WILLIAMS: Politicians.

HOFFMAN: What—they just passed a new clean air and water act? They spent months working on that. . . . They beat it up a little, they punched holes in it.

WILLIAMS: Sheer compromise.

HOFFMAN: They compromised it right down . . . for good reason, why?

WILLIAMS: The lobbyists.

HOFFMAN: The lobbyists work for?

WILLIAMS: Special interest groups.

HOFFMAN: Special interest groups serve?

WILLIAMS: The corporations.

HOFFMAN: And who are the corporations?

WILLIAMS: Well, executives and lawyers. People like you.

HOFFMAN: So what are you worried about?

Despite this, Carpini and Williams (1994) do have a case with their two concluding assertions: that "taken as a whole," television "does not deal with [conventional] politics in a wide variety of ways" and that television "is firmly situated within and supportive of a consumer culture hostile to any but the most modest forms of oppositional political action (p. 95). In the dominant culture, the repeated call on consumers to, in Bette Midler's concluding words, "Recycle! Reuse! Reduce! Replace!" as the major actions, remains within a very limited range of individualistic options. Nevertheless, *The Earth Day Special* repeatedly makes the point that it is a first step and an important first step, which contrasts with "the failure of collectivist thinking to account for the importance of 'private' or personal acts in people's everyday lives, and, consequently, the failure affectively to persuade people to abandon an individualist for a collectivist identity" (Ross, 1991, p. 68).

In advocating this social movement philosophy, *The Earth Day Special* begins to construct an ecological metanarrative from the roots up. It even makes space for nonhuman contributors through comic animal characters, such as Bugs Bunny and the Muppets. In one scene, set in a swamp, Kermit and his frog nephew, Robin, watch the show with an audience of other noisy amphibians:

ROBIN: This Earth Day show makes it look like things are pretty bad for the people.

KERMIT: Yeh, actually it's worse for the animals.

LIZARD: It's killing us off.

KERMIT: Yeh, you see when people mismanage the earth, they destroy our homes.

LIZARD: And next thing you see, another species extinct.

FROG CHORUS: Dead and gone! Dead and gone! Dead and gone!

. . . .

ROBIN: All of this doesn't seem to have much effect on people, there's more of them all the time.

KERMIT: True.

ROBIN: Uncle Kermit, would we become extinct?

KERMIT: Well, it's possible unless people can try to fix the damage they've caused to the earth.

FX: Absolute Silence.

ROBIN: So, it's not really up to us.

KERMIT (direct to camera): No, it's up to people.

FROG CHORUS: Up to them! Up to them! Up to them!

BOUNDARIES (9):
GREENING CITIZENSHIP,
CONSUMERS, AND ECO-AUDIENCES

For audience considerations we again start with viewing aimed at kids. In television, as in film, children are usually conceptualized as a distinct audience and have a distinct set of eco-texts directed toward them. According to Wartella (1990), American children's television

is constrained by externalities—chief among them the regulatory framework and environment, the economic superstructure, and the industry structure of networks, cable networks, and independent producers—as well as internal constraints. Among these are producers' notions of their audience—what children are, what they like, how they watch, what they can and do learn—and the practices—technical and technological, creative, and political—producers use to make children's programs. (p. 39)

An animated cartoon television series, *Captain Planet and the Planeteers* (Boxer & Meugniot, 1990), attempts a different fusion of entertainment and education through blending typical comic-style heroes with Gaian-type ideologies. From its very first episode, the simplistic versions of the former win out over the latter with an explanatory opening giving way to this final five-planeteer rap: "We're the Planeteers, you can be one too, 'cause saving our planet is the thing to do, looting and polluting is not the way, hear what Captain Planet has to say." Nor does the series go for much in the way of innovative philosophy. In later episodes, ecological concerns, often shorn of any Gaian dimension, are equally crudely tagged onto other major social issues, such as drug abuse. The typical mix that results can be gathered from the following synopsis of narrative and *Planet Alerts* from an episode set in Washington, DC:

> Linka visits a Russian cousin now living in Washington who, because he has trouble fitting into this new community, falls prey to the evil Scum, a dealer of the drug, "bliss." The youth of the city become dependent and turn into "zombies" who will do anything for a fix. The Planeteers alone cannot deal with this problem on their own and require considerable help from Captain Planet to solve it. The story includes two planetary alerts:
>
> 1. "Some drugs are good for you, but many can be harmful. Only use ones given to you by your doctor and your parents. These can keep you healthy. Illegal drugs are dangerous and can damage your mind as well as your heart, your lungs, your whole body. It is only a fool who thinks drugs are cool. If you've got a drug problem get help—you can choose not to take drugs. The power is YOURS!"
> 2. "The health of the planet relies on the health of its people. To reach the highest heights and win the fight to save our planet we must have the strength, endurance and courage. Our minds and our bodies must be in shape. The power is YOURS!" (Boxer & Meugniot, 1990)[3]

The heavily didactic messages chime in with the reductive Nancy Reagan-supported "Just Say No" drugs campaign and clearly make no attempt to engage with the complexities of addiction or of its relation to the environment. The ease with which the ecological and social messages are stuck together demonstrates little more than new environmental content stuck into a familiar, and patronizing, didactic form. Frequently, in the planetary alert morals, the use of *we* and what *we* can do is unreflexively Western and well-off in a way that excludes other audiences:

> We often think of water as something that comes out of a tap whenever we want, but clean drinkable water is a precious resource. To conserve water don't let the hose run while washing your car. If you live in a dry climate use plants that don't need a lot of watering. That way when you turn on a tap you'll always know there is water for you. The power is YOURS! (Boxer & Meugniot, 1990)

Although it is easy to criticize the simplistic didacticism of *Captain Planet and the Planeteers,* there is little audience research on such eco-projects to gauge their actual influence. Existing literature on children as television viewers (Hodge & Tripp, 1986; Palmer, 1986) suggests that they view more actively and creatively than the series' passive textual positionings of them would imply. In terms of intergenerational environmental perspectives, children's texts offer a shared viewing point for many adults and children. Anyone who has watched *Bambi,* or a similar Disney movie, with a young child is usually aware, at least at times, of a different sensibility at work. The subject of human-animal relations and future planetary degradation clearly raises possibilities for cross-generational dialogues.

In the area of children's eco-texts as well as elsewhere, future research might take a lead from the single most impressive piece of audience work with an ecological content: Corner, Richardson, and Fenton's (1990) *Nuclear Reactions: A Study in Public Issue Television.* Interested "in television's centrality to modern public knowledge" (p. 1), they examined how viewers made sense of

nuclear energy debates in a research study of obvious environmental relevance. Methodologically, they follow that broadly ethnographic turn in audience research initiated by David Morley's
(1980) *The "Nationwide" Audience* (see Moores, 1993, for a useful
overview) and develop it in relation to nuclear programs and their
audience reception.

ECO-AUDIENCE WORK
AND EMOTIONAL REACTIONS

To elucidate these questions, Corner et al. (1990) selected
diverse programs around the nuclear theme. These covered the
political spectrum: from the nuclear industry's own promotional
videotape designed "to win back public opinion after the massive
loss of confidence occasioned by the Chernobyl disaster"; through
a critical investigation of "the health risks consequent upon the
nuclear industry's day to day operations and its problems with
waste disposal" (which featured speakers from both the industry
and its critics); to a trade union and labor movement dramatized
documentary that "developed a scenario about a disaster" at a
local nuclear power station "making imaginative and direct use
of the Chernobyl precedent and coming to strongly negative
conclusions about the industry" (pp. 9-10).

For the reception stage of the research, Corner et al. (1990)
selected audiences in terms of diverse "interest groups" seeking
to emphasize "the most relevant aspects of their social identities"
(p. 48). Accordingly, they involved participants from opposing
political parties, a local rotary club, unemployed people from a
resource center, "a women's discussion group, a group of comprehensive school pupils, a group of medical students, some
Friends of the Earth members and a set of workers at the
Heysham nuclear power plant" (pp. 48-49). Then, in the researchers' own words,

> We tried to elicit reactions on aspects of interest to us whilst at
> the same time allowing the groups to develop themes according
> to their own agendas. . . . The relative advantages of group-based

and individual-based respondent sessions has been a subject of much discussion in the literature. For the present study, the advantage of the group-based approach was the opportunity it offered for participants to negotiate with one another their often conflicting responses to the programmes screened. This keeps in focus the potential for divergence as well as convergence within sets of people who were participating as representatives of organizations. We are of course sensitive to the possibility that in some cases this may work to produce more consensus than might otherwise be the case. (Corner et al., 1990, p. 49)

Characterizing their general approach as *ethnodiscursive,* Corner et al. (1990) deploy an ethnographic base in conjunction with close attention to "the language used by the respondents in articulating and negotiating their responses to the programmes" (p. 50). They expressed specific interest in the way "debate was characterized by having at its centre, a number of highly esoteric technological, scientific and medical questions" that made "public comprehension, let alone judgement, difficult" and gave "mediation functions a particular salience" (p. 2). Because of its thoroughness, its interweaving of semiotic and ethnographic methods, and its engagement with complex debates, Corner et al.'s study offers an excellent model for testing different eco-audience responses to other environmental issues. Their researches need to be replicated and extended across a broad range of environmental impacts. This broadening might allow projects to address such central paradoxes of survival as the current gap between public perceptions of high eco-risk and public support for maintaining the status quo that creates the risks.

In their conclusion to the nuclear topic, Corner et al. (1990) emphasize three factors of wider environmental relevance: first, "that respondents' own prior doubts and anxieties about the industry were widely shared; . . . programmes were playing into an interpretative context of deep uncertainty;" second, "that uncertainty would often be *overlaid* by confidence, in either direction—the kind of confidence which is a matter of faith or hope, rather then specific factual knowledge;" and third, that different groups attached differential value to the affective properties of televisual texts—potent visualizations, dramatic simulations, eloquent personal narratives. For some groups the nuclear issue positively requires such strategies, to win the viewers' involvement. Others argued the danger of allowing emotions, not reason, to decide the issue. Yet this striking divergence should not be allowed to obscure the more important convergence—the power of the affective dimension, even on groups who reject its legitimacy, comes through in many ways. This may be of considerable significance in the shaping of public opinion about the issue. (p. 108)

BOUNDARIES (10): CS DISCIPLINES, FOOD, AND THE PHYSICAL

In the previous chapter, we attacked the Western intellectual tradition's dismissal of premodern and indigenous knowledges. We conclude this one by affirming another barrier of difference between those other knowledges and our fields' difficulty in handling a central " 'problem' of the physical substance" (Berland & Slack, 1994, p. 1): food. For example, one indigenous tribe in Canada claims simply that "the river is our dinner table" (as quoted in Leane, 1995). How far we in the West are from the worldview intrinsic in that perspective was brought home to us via a television documentary on *Meat* (Johnson & Cooper, 1990). The documentary ends with a series of surreal images that bring food futures only too sensuously to life: butchers chop pumpkins to reveal a core of steak; and carrots that enter a conventional-looking mincing machine emerge as fatty, red minced meat. Simultaneously, the soundtrack voice-over narrates scientific predictions of genetic research that might create "hibernating sheep to save on energy costs; asexual cattle to ensure all their energy goes into meat, not mating; and animal-like flesh inside plants—plant meat." However economically rational, these processes diverge dramatically from natural generation of our food.

They do not approximate, even vaguely, to that state of mind that allows rivers themselves respect as dinner tables (which in most cultures have gathered a host of traditional, symbolic, and even religious accretions).

Meat's images and ideas cut an industry-led edge into the politics of food. Corporate agribusiness drives much genetic research, and where it leads, markets tend to follow. Nevertheless, urban consumer compliance remains central to the whole process, and although unequal, the consumers-agribusiness alliance strengthens many of the boundaries considered in this chapter. *Meat* the program and *meat* the food raise many ecological issues. Green cuisine promotes vegetarianism, and meat, especially beef, has become symbolic of the excesses of Western diets. Ideas from the 1960s suggested that we are what we eat; 1990s ideas add that what we eat also shapes the planet. Nor, to add an existential edge, are individual choices negligible: "For every quarter-pound hamburger that comes from a steer raised in Central and South America, it is necessary to destroy approximately 75 kilograms (165 pounds) of living matter" (Rifkin, 1994, p. 198). That living matter typically includes "some of twenty to thirty different plant species" and "perhaps one hundred insect species, and dozens of bird, mammal, and reptile species" (Denslow & Padoch, 1988, p. 169). Nor do those losses take into account the use of rain forest wood as cheap timber for dining tables and other furniture. Indeed, outside of the environmental movement and feminist research, few studies address consumer contradictions in terms that allow much importance to the ecological consequences of what we buy (but see Nava, 1992).

We are far from acknowledging rivers as our dinner table or nonhuman life as a legitimate part of our ecological continuum. In practice, according to 1990 research, our beef habit generates more organic waste per 10,000 head of cattle than a city of over 100,000 people (see Rifkin, 1994, p. 220). The economics of diet seem to have been left behind by both right-wing (Bailey, 1995) and left-wing (Ross, 1994) dismissals of environmental calls for population reductions as nothing but Malthusianism. We argue against this trend because the unreflexive dietary regime of meat and dairy food choices by Western consumers remains central to issues of health, population, starvation, and planetary carrying capacity. According to Lappé's (1982) estimations, a shift of grain and soy resources from animals to humans would provide "the equivalent of one cup of grain for every single human being on earth every day for a year" (p. 71).

The typical absence of food politics from sociology, communication, and cultural studies further illustrates a general disciplinary failure to come to terms with physical substance. It is a failure compounded by a parallel gulf, tellingly identified by Penman (1994), between mainly city theorists and mainly rural producers. She demonstrates it through the discursive confusion (and emotional charge) surrounding vocabulary such as *biodiversity, sustainable,* and *environmentally safe* in those different locations. She goes on to discuss the attendant lack of systematic adequacy in our discursive language. Citing Mühlhäusler and Harré's (1994) example from *Tok Pisin* (the pidgin of Papua New Guinea), she sees the need for an equivalent distinction between "something that is *bagarup* or 'damaged' and 'something that is *bagarup pinis* or 'ruined beyond repair' " (Penman, 1994, p. 30). She makes the case for such distinctions in the context of discussions of *environmentally safe* because, in "our language, there is no distinction between something that is temporarily safe or safe *pinis,* safe in principle and perpetuity" (p. 30).

Whether we are located in city or country, First World or Third, the physical world is our source of material, emotional, intellectual, and spiritual nourishment. More ecocentric disciplines must bear that in mind: Controlling imagery that respects that source has to be cultivated; controlling imagery that denigrates that source has to be challenged. This chapter has suggested how an eco-friendlier media canon might build on earlier work, especially feminist-influenced work, and be more open to the wisdom of other knowledge traditions (especially premodern and indigenous ones). The chapter has also suggested some ways of bridging gaps that retard engagements with eco-impacts. In examining ecologically influenced constructions of the biosphere as physical system, our next chapter continues bridge building and border crossing.

NOTES

1. This is not to suggest that work has not kept advancing, as Van Zoonen's (1994) recent development and summary demonstrates.

2. This is slightly unfair to Hayward (1994) who does allow, if only in an end note, that not all eco-feminism can be characterized as "neo-romantic or biologolistic." He also appears to validate some eco-feminists, "particularly materialist eco-feminists" (p. 227) through quoting Salleh's view that they "are engaged in a subtle deconstruction of the patriarchal 'Mother Nature' ideology while trying to re-theorize our human embeddedness in what is called 'nature' " (Salleh, 1991, p. 130).

3. We gratefully acknowledge Helen Singleton's (1995) unpublished master's thesis, *Science on Television: A Representational Site for Mediating Ideology*, for drawing our attention to these episodes and for the use of its time-saving script summaries.

8

Contours of Knowledge

Science and the Death of Economics

This chapter traces where knowledge-power about the world is situated as a key communication, cultural, and environmental question. With assistance from popular science, we examine relations between Snow's (1964) "two cultures," especially, in their different mappings of contemporary issues, such as diversity, cosmology, and the post-Chaos (see Briggs & Peat, 1989; Cohen & Stewart, 1994) sciences of Complexity (see Coveney & Highfield, 1995; Waldrop, 1993) and of the health of the biosphere itself. Moving from that biospheric bottom line to a financial one, we then explore ecological potentials in the reported death of economics. Finally, considering neoclassical economics in line with post changes in the sciences and elsewhere, we contemplate the potential for a metamorphosis influenced by Chaos and Complexity (both capitalized to distinguish their specialist usage as scientific fields) to make space for women, the environment, and other exclusions of the neoclassical paradigm.

SPHERES OF INFLUENCE: REINTRODUCING EARTH

As part of the move from the media semiosphere of the previous two chapters to scientifically constructed accounts of the physical biosphere, we recross Snow's (1964) binary chasm. Although humans generate both science and culture, the nature of the world they map, or the way they map the same world, invests that illusionary divide with material consequences. The resultant mappings fissure the organization of knowledge about the earth. Social theory surveyors interested in science, for example, have, for many years, staked out at least a section of scientific territory as the sociology of science—see Mulkay (1991) for what he calls his 20-year pilgrimage. We contend that the fields of communication and cultural studies share far less common ground with scientific disciplines than such sociologists. Nor do these two fields make much of an attempt to keep in touch with recent developments on the science side of the divide. Nevertheless, some environmentalists (Merchant, 1980, 1989), ecoculturalists (Slack & Whitt, 1994), and scientists (Haraway, 1991, 1995) attempt cross-chasm dialogues and address eco-impacts biospherically and semiospherically.

Snow's binary divide also finds a reflection in attempts to map the biosphere in popular science and scientific textbooks. No one is likely to confuse the material of Carl Sagan's (1980) *Cosmos* with Jean Baudrillard's simulacra, although many might wonder if they inhabit the same discursive galaxy. Even in introductory student textbooks, scientific perspectives define a clear disciplinary difference in their approach to representing the globe. Pickering and Owen's (1994) undergraduate text, *An Introduction to Global Environmental Issues,* for example, has the following 10 chapter titles:

How many environmentally oriented books in our fields would allocate those topics chapter-length consideration? Along with most other social, communication, and cultural theorists, we obviously do not. And yet we believe that those biospheric concerns must somehow contribute to the debate: Pickering and Owen's appendix, "Summary of Principal Fluxes and Bio-Geo-chemical Cycles on Earth," may not be exciting reading but neither was meteorology, which has turned out to be economically and ecologically important as well as proving amenable to cultural analysis (e.g., Berland, 1994; Ross, 1991).

One possibility would be for our fields to routinely seek out, sift, and assess the value of scientific perceptions and findings and to include them as part of ongoing dialogues about semiosphere-biosphere interactions. We do not mean jumping the divide with one mighty leap and mastering such subjects as mathematics, physics, chemistry, and geology but instead consulting, and working with, scientifically informed constructions of the planet. After all, Carson's (1962) *Silent Spring* made science-based environmental advocacy an accessible bestseller. Some student textbooks, and the majority of popular science texts, today offer a high degree of accessibility not beyond the comprehension of readers steeped in Derridian deconstruction and Foucauldian genealogy. Through their introductory textbook, which has an attractive colored cover and plates and is clearly designed to be student-friendly, Pickering and Owen give an example of how to proceed. In attempting to bridge the divide, their preface opens with a familiar historic positioning of the recent increasing awareness of environmental issues over the past few decades in relation to 1960s protests and *Silent Spring*. They recommend a book, *The Green Case: A Sociology of Environmental Issues, Arguments and Politics,* by Stephen Yearley (1991) for an outline of the "evolution and establishment of the 'green' movement" (Pickering & Owen, 1994, p. xix). In another overlap with cultural theory and an illustration that the diversity of ecological sociology is not extensive, Yearley (1992) will reappear in Chapter 9 in his role as a spokesperson on environmental challenges.

Pickering and Owen (1994) paint a broad picture in extending their history back into past scientists' awareness "of anthropogenic effects on the natural world" (p. xix). In this, particularly when examining how "Victorian postulates, paradigms, hypotheses, and theories challenged and altered perceptions about the natural world" (p. xix), they reprise debates on nature akin to those in our first chapter. They go on to update scientific environmental concerns and initiatives from the UNESCO Arid Zone Program (1951-1964) through the Brundtland (1987) *Our Common Future* report and its "agenda for sustainable growth" (p. xx) to the Earth Summit in Rio de Janeiro. Pickering and Owen's acknowledged aim is a book that "explores some of the basic science and structure behind the most important environmental issues and links these issues to contemporary socio-economic and political considerations" (p. xxii). Their laudable ambition contrasts favorably with the scarcity of attempts at equivalent gap bridging on the sociology, communication, and cultural studies side.

To attain their aim, Pickering and Owen (1994) assemble a mass of diverse figures. These range from "Relationship Between Lithosphere, Hydrosphere, Atmosphere, Biosphere and Ecosphere" (p. xiv), which sets up links rarely broached outside of science, to "Selected Air Pollutants in Developing Countries, 1990-2030" (p. xvii) and tables of data (from "sensitivity classes of ecosystems" [p. 120] to "biofuel emissions relative to conventional fuels" [pp. 214-215]). These tables fill out dimensions of biosphere alteration not frequently featured in semiosphere accounts. Their book concludes with five simple issues for discussion that range from asking, "is sustainable global economic growth feasible, and even desirable?" to considering "that the single biggest problem facing the survival of humankind is overpopulation" as well as "the North-South divide" of "wealth and life chances" and pondering "to what extent should international policy on environmental issues take cognizance of various cultural and religious groups?" (1994, pp. 328-329). In relation to our disciplines, knowledge about the degree of overlap and the areas where priorities are shared and where they differ all matter and might help in assessing eco-impacts and survival prospects.

CULTURAL STUDIES FIGHTS BACK

Areas of dispute and cross-disciplinary fertilizations are of particular importance. Andrew Ross (1994) is one of the few who have ventured into ecological considerations more usually found on the scientific side of the divide. In disputed regions, he has opted to oppose the mainstream of environmental scientists in ways that are revealing. Arguing against Pickering and Owen's (1994) issue of overpopulation as perhaps "the single biggest problem facing the survival of mankind" (p. 329), he upholds a 20th-century version of an anti-Malthusian line long popular in the humanities. Ross (1994) rightly attacks "Malthus's dismal picture of a natural economy defined and willed by God as an unequal ratio between population and perpetually scarce resources" (p. 259). In our view, however, his monolithic cultural framing devalues science-influenced estimations of carrying capacity. Ross continues, seemingly on the basis of an assumption that these estimates are dependent on classical postulates about the permanence of scarcity, by counterposing his own posts: postscarcity and postcapitalism. He reframes the debate around "whether the postscarcity future of abundance comes about (a) through the market creation of wealth, (b) through some grand postcapitalist transition in social development, (c) through a simple transcendence of the present structure of inequalities"

(p. 270). Prior to the postscarcity condition, such optimism of the will must be tempered with pessimism of the intellect. In particular, we have in mind knowledge accumulated through empirical research into existing, and projected, population growth impacts on the biosphere surface (see Brown et al., 1995).

This is not to concede all truth to scientists, particularly those who would claim it absolutely. Ronald Bailey's (1995) edited collection, *The True State of the Planet: Ten of the World's Premier Environmental Researchers in a Major Challenge to the Environmental Movement,* is a Competitive Enterprise Institute project seemingly aimed at delegitimizing the Worldwatch Institute's annual State of the World report. Because both sides rely on scientifically authenticated data and hypotheses, it is unlikely that scientists can guarantee an undisputed singular truth on these matters (despite the claims of eminently credentialed scientists to the contrary). Elsewhere, Ross (1991) has dealt in some detail with one of the main assertions, strongly contested in Bailey's (1995) collection, emerging from environmental science: that existing population growth has "accelerated environmental degradation, and . . . precipitated potentially serious global climate change" (Pickering & Owen, 1994, p. 277).

Ross challenged this assertion in two very different ways. His first was to undermine science's claim to objective truth by accumulating a list of publication dates and titles that demonstrated a drastic shift in scientific fashion away from global cooling to global warming. Thus, he traces the switch from such book titles as *The End: The Imminent Ice Age and How We Can Stop It* (Ephron, 1988), *The Weather Conspiracy: The Coming of the New Ice Age* (Impact Team, 1977), and *The Cooling* (Ponte, 1976) through the transitional hot or cold options of *The Winds of Change* (Kelly & Gribbin, 1989) and *Ice or Fire? Can We Survive Climate Change* (Halacy, 1978), to the current glut of high-temperature titles such as *Global Warming: Are We Entering the Greenhouse Century?* (Schneider, 1989) and *Hothouse Earth: The Greenhouse Effect and Gaia* (Gribbin, 1990). This is well done and requires a response—but a response as part of an ongoing dialogue with scientists and not a conclusive dismissal.

The fact that the sciences have some rapid trend shifts and modish fashions means that they have to be scrutinized carefully. It does not mean that their whole regime of truth can be so simply dismissed. At the same time as we reject right-wing agitation (e.g., Bailey, 1995) to delay action until their scientists agree that sufficient risk exists to warrant reducing the profit margin, we do not see Ross's intervention as justifying any reduction in eco-activist struggles to get individuals, businesses, and governments to reduce emissions. On this issue, we align instead with the communiqué of the 1990 Bergen Conference on Environment and Development: "Where there are threats of serious or irreversible damage, lack of full scientific certainty should not be used as a reason for postponing measures to protect environmental degradation" (as quoted in McMichael, 1993, p. 326).

Ross makes another challenge to scientific perception on another front. Moving into the area of cross-divide fertilization, he observes how semiospheric concerns can overwhelm seemingly factual biospheric matters. From the revealingly titled, *The Uncertainty Business: Risks and Opportunities in Weather and Climate,* he quotes the argument of its New Zealand meteorologist author that the atmosphere, a "variable and elite resource," must be "accepted as an integral part of the management package" for industry (Maunder, 1986, p. 265). Further exposing discursive colonializations of global warming threats by "terms usually reserved for the liberal market economy," Ross (1991) selects an equally telling quote from a climatologist ("we still have to learn to live according to our climactic income" [p. 198]). He concludes that the accompanying "moralizing burden" for this is "shifted on to humanity as a whole, further Christianized by the language of retribution and penitence" so that "global warming must be seen as 'the wages of industrialisation' " (p. 198). This hits a key critical spot and works to destabilize the controlling imagery of the economic as constitutive of the natural order. It helps undermine still-current classic economics thinking that there is no need to worry about future oil shortages because the current market price is low. For ecological sanity, something has to change. From our perspective, neither the death of that *homo economicus* nor the birth of a communication and cultural studies species in dialogue with the sciences can come too soon.

BEYOND MODERN RATIONALITY: BE AFRAID, HABERMASIANS, BE VERY AFRAID

Our subheading, adapted from publicity for David Cronenberg's 1986 remake of *The Fly*, kicks off from something Habermas (1983) wrote in *Modernity—An Incomplete Project:* "I fear that the idea of antimodernity, together with an additional touch of premodernity, are becoming popular in the circles of alternative culture" (p. 15). However, setting aside these anxieties of critical social theory for the moment, we develop our call for greater ground sharing across the two-cultures divide. This extends beyond the simple environmental utility of science research to take up Robyn Eckersley's (1992) challenge that "the credibility of any Western philosophical worldview is seriously compromised if it is not at least cognizant of, and broadly consistent with, current scientific knowledge" (p. 50).

We contend that with regard to current ideas and issues from science, even those readily available in popular science writings, communication and cultural studies lacks such credibility. We identify issues from the sciences, particularly the sciences of Complexity, cosmology, and eco-diversity, as being largely absent in our fields. Because of Ross-type interventions into science debates not being a routine feature, our fields miss out on a burgeoning source of fresh, accessible, and often ecologically (in the wide use of the term) relevant ideas from popular science publishing. In fact, the genre of popular science itself, despite huge purchase on the popular imagination, remains underexamined either as a popular genre or as a shaping force on ideas of communicative practice. Katherine Hayles (1990) provides a useful starting point for interdisciplinary interactions by reconceiving Eckersley's notion of equal cognizance as one of uneven disciplinary development:

Different disciplines are drawn to similar problems because the concerns underlying them are highly charged within a prevailing cultural context. Moreover, different disciplines base the theories they construct on similar presuppositions because these are the assumptions that guide the constitution of knowledge in a given episteme. This position implies, of course, that scientific theories and models are culturally conditioned, partaking of and rooted in assumptions that can be found at multiple sites throughout the culture. (p. xi)

Two features particularly excite us about her formulation: the notion of highly charged concerns crossing the two-cultures chasm opens up ways to colocate post-prefixed nonscience movements with recent sciences; and her positioning of these kinds of ideas in multiple sites throughout the culture lends support to our speculations on the importance of links between popular texts and scientific, social, and cultural disciplines. In the realm of popular science writing, physicist Heinz Pagels (1989) perceived the two cultures as no more than "a rift in the perceived order of reality" (p. 13). His version of the sciences of Complexity identifies computerized technology as "altering the architectonic of the sciences and the picture we have of material reality" (p. 13). Indeed, computers have stimulated simulations of such power that some scientists talk about it as a third form of science standing halfway between theory and experiment. Working with simple software and ideas in line with Complexity's foundational belief that a few simple rules lie at the root of all complex systems, James Lovelock created "Daisyworld"—a small-scale, self-generating near embodiment of Gaia theory (see Lewin, 1993a, pp. 108-119). That simple program has already, through its Gaian extensions, significantly affected conceptions of the biosphere and humanity's relationship to it.

Central to the whole Complexity field are notions of natural self-organization, whether it be bacteria, prebiotic life, business firms, or planets, that set up new relations between laws of nature and patterns of behavior. In the case of evolutionary biology, Stuart Kauffman's (1992) computer-assisted perceptions have researched mathematical models of so-called fitness landscapes, which describe biological populations in terms of highs and lows of adaptive success. As a result, he has made claims for laws of increasing complexity able to self-generate systems remarkably similar to actual species evolution. If computer "games of life" turn out to be able to simulate the evolution of actual life, then such a faking of the organism has revolutionary possibilities absent in our fields' absorption with the cybersex faking of the orgasm (see McKie, 1994d) and information superhighways.

The nature of Complexity's models, topics, and interdisciplinarity can usefully be compared and contrasted with recent work within communication and cultural studies, such as Diprose and Ferrell's (1991) edited collection on *Cartographies: Poststructuralism and the Mapping of Bodies and Spaces*. Undoubtedly, their collection generates surface complexity in chapters that variously challenge the distinction between material reality and representation from desert paintings to the EPCOT center at Florida's Disney world. Their book's back cover also claims to derive that complexity from the simple source of showing "how each discipline produces its object—truth, the sexed body, the diseased body, national identity, cultural 'others'—while constituting itself" (p. x). More specifically, the collection aims to extend "the import of post-structuralist interventions" to the sciences by arguing against the assumption "that scientific modes of representation are not constitutive of their objects" (p. x).

In arguing for constructivism, they ignore how scientific models, at least sometimes, already acknowledge how they constitute versions of reality. For example, Peter Bowler's (1992) history of *The Environmental Sciences* structures his account around Foucault's famous poststructuralist encounter with the animal categories from the mythic Chinese encyclopedia. In giving science directions, Diprose and Ferrell's (1991) cartographers navigate with a disproportionately heavy cargo of theoretical equipment current in communication and cultural studies. They neglect to take on board significant ideational compasses from the sociology of science (e.g., Bloor, 1976; Latour & Woolgar, 1979), let alone from recent science itself—less than 3% of their select bibliography might be considered works from the scientific side of the divide.

Nevertheless, their essays do intervene at the most rewarding level of science-culture relations, that of conscious interaction.

COMBINING CULTURAL DIVERSITY AND ECO-DIVERSITY

Conscious interactions, on the issue of diversity, remain so sparse that the chasm yawns as large as ever. Communication and cultural studies have demonstrated an ongoing engagement with a variety of cultural and theoretical diversities for some time. More recently, the fields have substantially addressed concerns about self-reflexivity and referentiality, but ecological diversity continues to be neglected, and its corollary, extinction, might as well never have lived. In contrast, recent popular science, where concerns with class, race, gender, and self-reflexivity remain scarce, has concentrated on ecological diversity (e.g., E. Wilson, 1992) and extinction (see Donovan, 1989; Hoage, 1985; Raug, 1991). Indeed, as Eldredge (1993) notes, "the literature on both mass extinctions of the geological past and the mounting threat of extinction facing the modern biota has been growing, seemingly exponentially, over the past decade or so" (p. 231). These contrasting foci set a different political agenda and spatiotemporal coordinates.

As well as proving a rare exception to the exclusion of eco-diversity within cultural studies, Slack and Whitt (1994) exemplify the reorientation and gains to be made through interactions. By bringing their field's perspectives on diversity into contact with scientific eco-diversity perspectives, they disown the Euro-enlightenment inheritance of unique "man" and decenter the decidedly anthropocentric orientation of current theory. The disinheritance of the former might edge Habermasian fear toward nightmare; the decentering of the latter might expand social relations to include the nonhuman. Slack and Whitt (1994) go on to track how mainstream social science separates human communities from their environments and alienates "them from one another by drawing a clear line between them" (p. 21). In sharp contrast, scientific ecologists typically exclude humans from their idea of community as "an assemblage of [other] species, occupy-ing a given area" (p. 17). Dismissing such rigid demarcation lines, Slack and Whitt reaffirm the impossibility of "community without an environment and environment without a community" and ask that we "responsibly reconfigure community/environmental re-lationships" (p. 22).

From the scientific side, E. O. Wilson (1984), in a supporting definition of biophilia as "the innate tendency to focus on life and lifelike processes" (p. 1), also decenters anthropocentrism on the basis that to the degree that we come to understand other organisms, we will place greater value on them and on ourselves. His later coedited collection, under the title of *The Biophilia Hypothesis* (Kellert & Wilson, 1993), attempts to amplify and refine the concept and even to make it pleasurable. Elizabeth Lawrence's (1993) contribution on animal symbolism as cognitive biophilia is given zest by the title, "The Sacred Bee, the Filthy Pig, and the Bat Out of Hell" (p. 301). There is nothing to stop our fields following these leads, and zest, to further the future of communication processes for all life on earth; we might also learn from a greater openness to other premodern knowledge traditions within scientific eco-diversity thought.

E. O. Wilson's (1992) *The Diversity of Life*, for example, drew on contemporary paintings from the South American shamanic tradition without any trace of embarrassment, let alone Haber-masian fear. Similarly, Harvard ethnobiologist Richard Schultes observed that every death of a tribal shaman, who has unique knowledge of the properties of plants in their region, "is as if a library had burned down" (quoted in Gell-Mann, 1994, p. 339). Gell-Mann himself tells how one younger ethnobiologist totally inverted modernity's hierarchy of knowledge by publishing his research experiences under the title of *Tales of a Shaman's Apprentice* (p. 339). Such scientists have come to acknowledge the essential interaction between biodiversity in general and specific cultural diversities, whether they are premodern or post-modern. Our fields tend to channel their researches through the perspectives of modernity and postmodernity. They have much to gain by diversifying, by imitating some scientists' openness to other knowledge traditions, and by integrating them with the ongoing scientific tradition of eco-diversity studies. We maintain that nonhuman eco-diversity merits a higher profile and higher priority in our fields.

A BRIEF HISTORY (OUT OF TIME): COSMOLOGICAL SPECULATIONS AND COMPLEXITY

In theory, for this age of margins, cosmology would seem to offer an alluring boundary "at the edge of what is considered science and what is not" (Brawer & Lightman, 1990, p. vi). In practice, however, in relation to cosmology, the binary gulf between our fields and the sciences actually widens. Science produces whole books on *The First Three Minutes* (Weinberg, 1993) and *The Last Three Minutes* (Davies, 1994) of the planet, but our fields occupy time segments distant from both speculative extremities. A huge and expanding popular science literature describes searches for the beginning of the universe, the nature of the cosmos, and sometimes, the mind of god (see McKie, 1994c). It has little counterpart in our fields, which are more prone to books on the 30 seconds of television advertising known as *The Spot* (Diamond & Bates, 1992). Given that science conventionally occupies the role of skeptic in relation to theological matters, the noise scientists are currently making around religion is almost as strange as the silence in cultural fields, such as communication, that would embrace all meaning making as part of its territory (see Sless & Shrensky, 1995).

A comparable lack of curiosity surrounds conceptions of humankind's place in the cosmos. Our fields' attention to Hollywood and White House stars rather than celestial bodies exhibits both a lack of curiosity toward our human genetic genealogy and an attachment to conceptualizing the social world isolated from its cosmic evolutionary context. Perhaps the emphases on beginnings and ends remind us too much that, like our planet and the rest of its inhabitants, we are not immortal. Species extinctions and supernova deaths alike toll distant bells with faint but discernible human echoes. Popular interest in such matters should alert us to some of the cultural capital at stake and remind us how origin narratives matter to all cultures. At a minimum, attention could be directed to representations of this scientific narrative to see what it trails in its semantic wake.

Both sides of the chasm, at their best, inform their research with acknowledged political projects: communication and cultural studies in their egalitarian modes parallel science's utopian and visionary aspirations. Both, to varying degrees, seek "knowledge potent for constructing worlds less organized by axes of domination" (Haraway, 1991, p. 192) and both are impossibly large, doomed to failure, and must persist imperfectly. Both participate in a common Western 20th-century intellectual journey and are still rounding similar corners: the linguistic turn where everything seemed to hang on language; the feminist sweep that transformed contents, methods, and paradigms; the self-reflexive curve where everyone had to demonstrate awareness of their own practices; and the postmodern bend where everything had to be relativized and decentered. In traveling such paths, communication and cultural studies have done more work than science, yet both need, to stay true to their respective projects' emancipatory roots, to come to terms with the environment and its ecological imperatives as the fourth dimension of social space.

Last, despite a partial polemic in favor of learning from science, we have no wish to restore it as the paradigm model for Western thought. There is considerable truth in MacKenzie Wark's (1994a) contention that science does not offer "a way beyond the 'crisis of the metanarratives' " because it "is totally caught up in both these narrative currents, either as a predictive discourse on the 'fate' of nature or as a prime mover in the development of third nature itself, in collaboration with military needs and objectives" (p. 126). Nevertheless, we see his own narrative as too exclusive of other currents and ideas in science. At the Santa Fe Institute, for example, one of Complexity's prime movers, Murray Gell-Mann (1994), launched a Global Sustainability project that foregrounded cultural diversity alongside "sustainable coexistence with the organisms with which we humans share the biosphere" (p. 375). Despite deep scientific suspicion of this project eluding the "predictive role" and "turning into some kind of global environmental activism," Gell-Mann (as quoted in Waldrop, 1993, p. 352) persisted with the project. He argued that "cultural diversity will be just as important in a sustainable world as genetic diversity is in biology" and that we "*need* cross-cultural ferment" (as quoted in Waldrop, 1993, p. 352).

If biodiversity and communication diversity are to flourish, then ongoing dialogues between developments in both cultures are needed. Beyond that generality is the actuality of specific, dangerous, and probably irreversible ecological changes instigated by our species and endangering our species. It makes ecological sense to cross over the science-culture divide to preserve semiosphere and biosphere linkages and to cross-fertilize restricted gene pools of ideas. In practice, neither of the two cultures is an intellectual island and the ocean they occupy is promotional culture. Before quoting Gell-Mann's (1994) call for an interlinked biosphere and semiosphere at length, we draw attention to how his discourse simultaneously economizes what he calls nature's income and advocates economic practices that encourage charging true costs:

The conservation of nature, safeguarding as much biological diversity as possible, is urgently required, but that kind of goal seems impossible to achieve in the long run unless it is viewed within the wider context of environmental problems in general, and those in turn must be considered together with the demographic, technological, economic, social, political, military, diplomatic, institutional, informational, and ideological problems facing humanity. In particular, the challenge in all of these fields can be viewed as the need to accomplish a set of interlinked transitions to a more sustainable situation. . . . Greater sustainability, if it can be attained, would mean a leveling off of population, globally and in most regions; economic practices that encourage charging true costs, growth in quality rather than quantity, and living on nature's income rather than its capital; technology that has comparatively low environmental impact; wealth somewhat more equitably shared, especially in the sense that extreme poverty would no longer be common; stronger global and transnational institutions to deal with the urgent global problems; a public much better informed about the multiple and interacting challenges of the future; and, perhaps most important and most difficult of all, the prevalence of attitudes that favor unity in diversity-cooperation and nonviolent competition among different cultural traditions and nation states—as well as . . . sustainable coexistence with the organisms with which we humans share the biosphere. (p. 375)

SHIFTING ECONOMICS: METAPHOR TECTONICS AND PARADIGM TEMPLATES

Just as science continues to be important to the greening of postmodernity, so too do economic bottom lines. Just as some scientists are moving toward the posts, so too are some economists, but Gell-Mann's plea to charge true environmental costs does not fall on impartial ears. According to the cover of Ben Elton's (1994) *This Other Eden,* in "marketing terms, the end of the world will be very big" and anyone "trying to save it should remember that." In the selling of the biosphere, even a doomed biosphere, many advertisers, many brokers, and many customers have significant stakes. Simultaneously scarred, defended, and prettified by so many diverse stakeholders, the economic-promotional terrain covers significant social, political, and knowledge fault lines whose tectonic plates buckle the credibility of official claims to a unified common future. At Rio, for example, the elected spokesperson of the youth groups, Kenyan Wagaki Mwangi, condemned the Earth Summit's outcome as having damned his generation:

Multinational corporations, the United States, Japan, the World Bank, The International Monetary Fund have got away with what they always wanted, carving out a better and more comfortable future for themselves. . . . UNCED [United Nations Conference on Environment and Development] has ensured increased domination by those who already have power. Worse still it has robbed the poor of the little power they had. It has made them victims of a market economy that has thus far threatened our planet. (as quoted in Chatterjee & Finger, 1994, p. 167)

This alliance of the major earth brokers marks the culmination of processes perhaps as long as the Scientific Revolution's will to intellectual dominance over nature (see Merchant, 1980, 1994; and Chapter 1). It certainly extends back at least to 1776 with Adam Smith's *An Inquiry Into the Nature and Causes of the Wealth of Nations*. After that, the Euro-enlightenment's economic colonization, although professing elegant theories of, usually invisible, evenhandedness, performed real vanishing tricks with resources to secure disproportionate wealth for some nations. Both processes have been accompanied by the increasingly global privatization and commercial commodification of the material world, from the fish of the sea through the minerals beneath the Antarctic to the patenting of an individual's DNA (see Wilkie, 1994). In identifying the controlling imagery of commerce and market, Mwangi highlights the ongoing role economics plays in maintaining societies and environments structured in dominance.

Nevertheless, although past socioconceptual movements have eroded the neoclassical knowledge edifice of economics, recent tectonic activities may yet undermine its very foundations. Environmentalists have been joined by physicists in doubting its ability to preserve the planet; feminists have found support from economic historians in questioning how it makes women, and the home, count for virtually nothing; and Complexity theorists have dubbed its models outmoded and out of touch with other disciplines. In effect, a rainbow coalition of discourse analysts, eco-feminists, economists (practicing, renegade, and retired), journalists, physicists, and postmodernists has made the so-called dismal science's exclusionary paradigm a prime suspect in the mooted death of nature and decline of society. In fitting our frame on economics, we survey the concept tremors, mainly through metaphor, to speculate on how such ongoing destabilizations and their aftershocks test aspects of the edifice. In particular, we wonder how much ferment under the crust of contemporary economics might precipitate the disappearance of "Rational Economic Man" and the emergence of a less theoretically quarantined, less sexist, and more planetary-based home economics?

POST-ECONOMICS:
THE END OF HOMO ECONOMICS
AND THE NEW HOME ECONOMICS?

As ecoculturalists, with a current attachment to postmodernism and allied paradigms structured around Chaos and Complexity theory, we began with a vested interest in what we perceived to be new economics. On further examination, we found that economics, far from having an easily accessible configuration, turned out to evade almost any grid with which we attempted to compass it. Nevertheless, in the spirit of postmodernism in relation to modernism, we offer a version of economics constructed in binary opposition to our version of the post-economic.

Economics	Post-Economics
Positions an economy as a separate, self-regulating realm with environmental and social factors as externalities	Positions an economy as a dynamic, interactive part of environmental and social systems in continuous transition
Approaches the world as a timeless machine and takes its engendered models, as well as its inspiration, from prequantum physics	Approaches the world as an organism evolving within time and takes diverse models from biology, climatology, and post-Chaos math
Engages with "Rational Economic Man" and a linear world tending toward equilibrium through market forces	Engages with nonlinear worlds of markets and people where uncertainty and fluctuating patterns are the norm

According to this construction, which has support in recent economics literature (Brockway, 1993; Hey, 1992; Omerod, 1994), neoclassical economics rests on a triple bedrock: that the economy is a separate realm of society that can be understood in its own terms; that individuals act rationally to maximize their own gains; and that economics can aspire to the objectivity, relative certainty, and predictive competence of physics. On those conceptual foundations, economists erect an immense edifice. Its features include a self-regulating market that produces its own harmony of earthly spheres, public and private for instance, and a measurable maximal use of resources. Why then, amid such theoretically harmonious convergence, is the field changing?

For answers, in keeping with Ben Elton's (1994) Eden theme, we go back and survey the territory from an original unity. *Economy* and *ecology* come from the same root, meaning house or home. The subsequent abstraction of a separate humankind and nature hangs on a hypothetical binary divide between economics and ecology (Williams, 1980). After that fall into abstraction, "economic man's" identity can be defined along the lines of a "hypothetical man supposed to be free from altruistic sentiments and motives interfering with a purely selfish pursuit of wealth and its enjoyment" (Brockway, 1993, p. 9). As with the actual seismic risks around Tokyo and Los Angeles, enough instabilities underlie this, and other, core sites of the conceptual and empiric foundations of economic man and "his" economics to suggest impending upheavals.

Economists increasingly adopt the apocalyptic house style of environmentalists in relation to nature with parallel book titles announcing *The End of Economic Man* (Brockway, 1993), *The Death of Money* (Kurtzman, 1993), and *The Death of Economics* (Omerod, 1994). Despite their shared pessimistic tone, both sets of pathways to extinction are complex and far from complete. In drawing attention to the metaphor clusters around the double demise of nature and economics, we concentrate on how the latter, in practice, often defines the parameters of possibility for what kind of world we might have. In assessing postindustrial possibilities in the United States, Fred Block (1990) notes how "public debate has come to hinge, not on what kind of society we are or want to be, but on what the needs of the economy are" (p. 3). In Australia, Hughes and Emy (1991) observe how politics converges more around economic management than ideological difference and how neoclassical economists, "in applying the formal language of market economics and rational choice theory to

.democracy, . . . are again conceptualising democracy as an adjunct of the market economy" (p. 104).

MASTERING NATURE, ECO-FEMINISM, AND PLUMWOOD'S FIVE FEATURES

Despite those powerful convergences, both economics and the environment sit atop a fragile line of fracture. Identifying its unevenly matched conceptual plates as reason and nature, eco-feminist philosopher Val Plumwood (1993) argues convincingly that their collisions mimic master-slave relationships in how the former's power assigns the latter to the status of inferior other. In her book, *Feminism and the Mastery of Nature*, she deconstructs Western reason to show how a narrow form of rationality achieves a mastery of nature using five associated features: backgrounding, radical exclusion, incorporation, instrumentalism, and stereotyping. When they are applied to economics, Plumwood's five features significantly widen already existing fissures.

For example, through her first feature, backgrounding, economics establishes common "ways to deny dependency" through disempowering an other "by denying the importance of the other's contribution or even his or her reality" (p. 48). From this perspective, as current systems of ownership and management occupy an even greater taken-for-granted status in the post-wall world, the low profile of land makes sense. Land remains the major source of food, without which even high-flying financiers cannot survive, but it has a low economic profile other than as a source of profit through rising real estate prices or resource exploitation. In contrast, for the now decade-old New Economics, "with its emphasis on personal and local self-reliance," land is "of prime importance" (Elkins, 1986, p. 171). Circulating around the margins or in other fields, such as environmental studies, that kind of critique remains, at best, backgrounded in current mainstream economics.

In general, economics still tends to consign land and environmental factors to the traditional category of externalities. This correlates with the economic and political fetishizing of the gross national product (GNP) or gross domestic product (GDP). As presently constructed, the GNP or GDP excludes essential women's work, as was so clearly documented by Marilyn Waring's (1988) *If Women Counted: A New Feminist Economics* and environmental costings, such as the Index of Sustainable Economic Welfare established by Daly and Cobb (as cited in Omerod, 1994). Such behavior also fits Plumwood's (1993) second feature, radical exclusion or hyperseparation, which "helps to establish separate 'natures' which explain and justify widely differing privileges and fates" (p. 49).

In their exclusion of women and the environment, such master perspectives, to use Plumwood's term, present themselves as natural and universal. They exclude other views that refuse their obsessive and sometimes clearly unreasonable calculations whereby car crashes add value to the GDP, whereas the depletion of finite resources does not count at all. By their polarizing, master perspectives "establish separate 'natures' " (p. 49), and the resulting hyperseparation has parallels with anthropological distinctions between sacred and profane. Economically, the sacred cows and untouchables line up along similar lines to the backgrounding so that Rational Economic Man becomes the measure that, once accepted, founds a whole order of values hyperseparating self-interest and altruism across all spheres, from slavery to the treatment of animals. At another level, however, it can be argued in economic calculations, at least according to the Index of Sustainable Economic Welfare (Omerod, 1994, pp. 31-32), that the jury on environmental cost exclusions is still out. Calculated to allow deductions for environmental degradation and resource depletion, the Index's figures, over a period of time, confirm that prosperity is increasing, if more slowly than by the conventional measurements.

On the positive side, this insertion of environmental factors into numeric economic discourse does open up possibilities for a like-to-like comparison that has some potential for women's work and other excluded features. On the negative side, it cannot accommodate radical critiques that "consumer markets will continue to inflate the price of sustainable commerce" without a more socially responsible revolution than "industrial auditing that takes account of social and environmental costs" (Ross, 1994, pp. 2-3). Nor, according to Australian CSIRO economist Mike Young (1992), will so-called light green adjustments accommodate criticisms of single-indicator accounting: "Neither GDP, nor GNP or any welfare indicator are ever likely to measure Gross National Happiness, or the ecological integrity of national ecosystems" (p. 125).

INCORPORATION:
POLITICS AND PROBLEMS

Reinforcement for hyperseparation can also be found in Plumwood's (1993) third feature—incorporation, or relational difference—which defines the other only in relation to the master. Familiar in feminism from De Beauvoir to Irigaray, its economic equivalent also disallows any gender difference that does not reflect "the master's desires, needs and lacks" (p. 52). Accordingly, whereas substantial bodies of work address women's wages by comparison with men's, little economics research, outside of feminism, scrutinizes the categorization of the unrewarded private labor of homeworkers against the remunerative public sphere of marketplace employment.

Contemplation of possible linkages between economic downturn in countries practicing conventional economics and their attachment to public-private divides should no longer be unthinkable. Gender economics and their relationship to sustainable food practices in Africa and other third world countries might provide equally useful models for the survival necessity of changing masters in developed parts of the globe. Rowbotham and Mitter's (1994) *Dignity and Daily Bread,* as its subtitle, *New Forms of Economic Organising Among Poor Women in the Third World and the First,* suggests, looks at just that kind of connection globally and historically. In allied fashion, Chris Beasley's (1994) radical challenge to what she terms *Sexual Economyths* reverses at-

tempts to make women's work count within masculinist economics and demonstrates instead how the competent household
economy contrasts favorably with the former's inadequacy.

These challenges reprise some issues raised academically over
100 years ago. Ellen Swallow, "The Woman Who Founded Ecology" (Clarke, 1973), traced the German word *Oekologie* to its
origin in the Greek word for house, *oik* and *oek*, for "everyone's
house" or environment. It was touch and go whether the discipline that came to be known as home economics be called home
ecology. Now, home workers and environmentalists can again
take up common cause. They could combine in rejecting economics' buttressing of Plumwood's (1993) fourth feature—instrumentalism—in which only the dominant have intrinsic value and the
other-as-inferior serve merely as a resource with no ends of their
own. This emerges most obviously in the almost unrestrained
domination of nature (from energy sources to pollution dumps),
the use of animals for experiment, and the destruction of habitats
of indigenous people and other species for development profits.
In gender terms, it emerges partially from Graeme D. Snooks's
(1994) *Portrait of the Family Within the Total Economy: A Study in
Longrun Dynamics, Australia 1788-1990:*

> In order to understand the role played by the household sector in
> the development of the Total Economy over the past 200 years we
> need to discover an economic man of real substance. Owing to
> their myopic and static theoretical analysis, economists have lost
> sight of the wellspring of economic change. (p. 46)

Owing to his own male myopia, Snooks negates gender difference, let alone the possibility of an economic woman of real
substance, by masculinizing the household economy's agents.
Something, incidentally, no marketing agency could afford to do
and survive. The role of economic women in the Total Economy
might yet be of significance in mainstream economics' aspirations
toward their theory of everything. By valuing the contribution of
traditional female territory, Snooks's crypto-holistic approach
exposes sizable cracks in the neoclassical facade.

STEREOTYPING AND
THE CLASSIFICATION
OF THE NEOCLASSICAL

Plumwood offers a fifth feature—stereotyping—by which narrow rationality achieves mastery. Stereotyping emphasizes difference differently so that all masters are very like other masters
and very unlike nonmasters. Experiments on first-year graduate
students suggest how economists occupy this particular dichotomy. Using the methodology of behavioral studies, researchers
Frank, Gilovich, and Regan's study (as cited in Omerod, 1994)
discovered that economics students "performed significantly
more in accord with the self-interest model" (p. 34) than did
noneconomics students. Even more tellingly when the best solution for everyone in dividing sums of money into public and
private accounts was a fully cooperative one, "students studying
economics contributed on average 20 per cent of their initial
money to the public account," whereas "the non-economists
contributed no less than 50 per cent" (p. 35).

Nevertheless, in ethical terms, mature proponents of the discipline exhibit comparable continuity. In a 1939 essay, "Ethics
and Economic Reform," Frank Knight (1947) confidently declared
that "the Economic man neither competes nor higgles—nor does
he co-operate, psychologically speaking" (p. 66). Writing a book
On Ethics and Economics Amartya Sen (1987) could still, 28 years
later, pose the "real issue" as "whether there is a plurality of
motivations, or whether self-interest alone drives human beings"
(p. 19). This stereotyping into economists as distinctively different
from ecologists and noneconomists, reenacts the original fall to
binary opposition, makes the benefits of cooperative action less
economically rational, and downplays the fundamental interdependence of humans, nonhumans, and their habitat.

Thankfully, state-of-the-art discipline reviews demonstrate
changes within economics itself. Classical critiques of the neoclassical construction can be found, for example, in the French-
produced Economic Thought Since Keynes: History and Dictionary
of Major Economists. Not unexpectedly, in that it was written by

two authors who hold chairs in economics departments, the book confirms the field's high status as "a world in unremitting expansion" that appears "as the most firmly structured of all social sciences, efficient through the multiplicity of its applications to limited domains" (Beaud & Dostaler, 1995, p. 141).

Less expected are the terms of their conclusion: "The Babel which constitutes the city of present-day economists may be characterized by three mythological figures: Penelope, Sisyphus and Icarus" (p. 141). Figure one, Penelope, represents writers whose works "opened breaches in the fortress of" neoclassical "orthodoxy" but who, in doing so, "gave rise to works which strengthen it" (p. 145); figure two, Sisyphus, attempts to perpetually reconstruct the heterodoxy and give back "historical, sociological and political dimensions to economics" but it is a never ending labor to "work at a historical economics always to be reconstructed" (p. 150); figure three, Icarus, "the broken flight of economic thought," questions whether "some economists sought to draw too close to the sun of global knowledge" (p. 153). Their book concludes with "the economist unarmed, with his knowledge fragmented, his analysis perfunctory, and helpless before the enormous void separating a theoretical edifice lacking coherence and a world in need of responses and solutions" (p. 154).

COMMUNICATION CIRCUITS, PARADIGM SHIFTS, AND QWERTY COMPLICATIONS

Despite similarly undermining much economic rationalism, in a book disenchantingly titled *Peddling Prosperity: Economic Sense and Nonsense in an Age of Diminished Expectations*, prize-winning economist Paul Krugman (1994) continues to exclude the environmental problems of that world. Although he offers different fault lines and different versions of rationality than Plumwood, nothing he writes invalidates her essential point that a certain kind of rationality masters nature. What he does, however, is reposition the academic and public spheres in relation to economics.

Defining himself as one of the professors, or academic economists, Krugman (1994) identifies their main enemy as politicians
under the sway of economic "policy entrepreneurs" who whip up
aberrations such as Reagan's "voodoo economics." The communications circuit of this treason of the pseudo clerks is fascinating, particularly given his, albeit temporary, insider status with
President Clinton, and offers a good case study of how "discourses
organize practices" (Hartley, 1991, p. 11) through institutional
power. Our concern with Krugman here is more concerned with
paradigms and particularly his positioning of economics in relation to T. S. Kuhnian-style scientific paradigm shifts.

Krugman (1994) starts with an admirable professional modesty
by admitting that economists simply don't know why the magic
economic growth stopped. He positions the profession in the
current promotional academy by observing that instead of pro-
gressing as "an economics professor by solving the real problems
of the real economy, . . . you progress by convincing your colleagues that you are clever" (p. 8). Despite the resulting "ego,
pettiness, and careerism," he maintains that the "enterprise . . .
steadily adds to our knowledge" (p. 9):

> It's a primitive science, of course. If you want a parallel, think of
> medicine at the turn of the century. . . . Economists know a lot
> about how the economy works, and can offer some useful advice
> on things like how to avoid hyperinflations (for sure) and depres-
> sions (usually). They can demonstrate . . . that folk remedies for
> economic distress like import quotas and price controls are about
> as useful as medical bleeding. But there's a lot they can't cure.
> Above all, they don't know how to make a poor country rich, or
> bring back the magic of economic growth when it seems to have
> gone away. (p. 9)

Through choosing medical science rather than physics for his
comparison, Krugman has avoided the prevalent physics envy of
economists that drives them toward harder data and firmer
controls. He nevertheless still aligns his field as a science—albeit
an embryonic rather than mature one. In doing so, he remains

within the Scientific Revolution's singular rationality, so critiqued by Carolyn Merchant (1980, 1994), and its associated mechanisms of subordination, so deftly analyzed by Plumwood. Later in the book, in a strategy similar to renegade economist Paul Omerod and Australian journalist Brian Toohey, Krugman (1994) aligns himself with the theorists of so-called new science of Complexity and tells his parable of the qwerty typewriter keyboard, which "opens our eyes to a whole different way of thinking about economics" (p. 223). Rejecting the economic maxim that the market is always right, Krugman has the keyboard stand as representative of increasing-return economics, where a lock-in effect can eventually lead to huge competitive advantages even against superior products. In practice, this is what happened with the inefficiently configured—in that it was expressly designed to slow down typists whose speed caused the keys of early models to jam—qwerty keyboard. Because, despite its designer inefficiency, so many people trained on it, it retains market leadership.

This new vision has international ramifications because neoclassical economics holds that, over time, the market allows the economic wealth of all nations the opportunity to converge toward Western standards of prosperity. In effect, increasing returns mean that to those who have strategic competitive advantage, more returns are likely to come. For Krugman, "just because the industrial revolution happened in Northern Europe, there's no guarantee Africa and South America will join in" (Omerod, as quoted in Haigh, 1995, p. 39). Nor is the ongoing international injustice Krugman identifies the only threat to a sustainable system. Others have argued, especially in the wake of the 1987 stock market crash, for even greater frailty resulting from finance's international interfacing with the qwerty-topped computers. Kurtzman's (1993) *The Death of Money*, for example, has the subtitle: *How the Electronic Economy Has Destabilized the World's Markets and Created Financial Chaos* and the specter of the new so-called economic real of the media vector haunting MacKenzie Wark (1994b) is "something terrible and sublime, vast and godless" (p. 193).

INFLUENCING BUTTERFLIES:
CHAOS, COMPLEXITY,
AND NONLINEAR ECONOMICS

Nonlinear critiques of economics further test the neoclassical bedrocks of Rational Economic Man and self-regulating separable markets. Chaos and Complexity theories do not just undermine neoclassical economics but its whole 19th-century science foundations. At the interdisciplinary Santa Fe Complexity Institute, according to economist Brian Arthur, they realized that "we can cut the Gordian knot of equilibrium and deal with open-ended evolution, because many of these problems have been dealt with by other disciplines" (as quoted in Waldrop, 1993, p. 325). Questions of the irreversibility of time in other sciences can then be related to more temporal approaches to economics and address such questions as "whether the price mechanism could always be relied on to save the world from running out of exhaustible resources" (Omerod, 1994, p. 75). Astonishingly, a negative answer only emerged when economic theorists used theoretical models that "allowed the future to exist" (p. 76).

In differently disempowering the past's nonlinear world, Brian Toohey (1994) usefully summarizes the importance of the paradigm shift: "The exciting scientific breakthroughs during the 20th century matter a great deal, not least because they have shown that much of the natural world does not behave as presumed by the old-style physics" (p. 241). As a result, he continues, "there is even less reason to believe that models built" on it "are really applicable to the more complex data underlying human society" (pp. 241-242) in general and neoclassical economics in particular. James Gleick (1987) earlier recorded how Chaos theory led to economists digging out old data from stock markets and trying "a new kind of analysis" where "the insights that emerged led directly into the natural world—the shapes of clouds, the paths of lightning . . . the galactic clustering of stars" (p. 4).

In following these leads here, our main concern is with metaphor generation and interdisciplinarity. The Santa Fe Complexity Institute's program brought together leading economists and prominent physicists and biologists, some of whom (Arrow, Anderson, & Pines, 1988) subsequently produced a book titled *The Economy as a Evolving Complex System*. One of the leading economist participants, Brian Arthur, subsequently proposed

> that economists replace the concept of fully rational economic agents with one of "adaptive, intelligent creatures constantly seeing and imagining patterns, testing ideas, acting upon them, discarding them again, always evolving and learning." "If you do economics this way," he says, "then there might be no equilibrium in the economy at all. The economy could be like the biosphere: always evolving, always changing, always exploring new territory." (as quoted in Toohey, 1994, p. 255)

In drawing metaphors and models from the natural world, Arthur and his noneconomist colleagues begin to rejoin economics and ecology and contemplate econometrics alongside evolutionary theories. Earlier economist Joan Robinson advised that to "learn from the economists regarded as scientists, . . . separate what is valid in the description of the system from the propaganda that they make, overtly or unconsciously" (Robinson, as quoted in Waring, 1988, p. 44). In today's discourse-saturated times, even economists write books titled *The Rhetoric of Economics* (McCloskey, 1985), which claim that their "mathematical models and statistical tests and market arguments" may be seen "as figures of speech" (p. xvii). The discursive disentanglement is not so straightforward and *Metaphors We Live By,* to use the title of Lakoff and Johnson's (1980) influential work, have also to become acknowledged as the metaphors authorizing economics and perhaps survival.

Nevertheless, the question of how far economics has destabilized, and how this might be gauged, remains. Convinced that discourses organize practices, we see them as requiring scrutiny as much as statistics. Believing, in some cases, that they might even be constitutive—discourses creating practices—we see metaphor sourcing as worthy of special attention. Instead of the kind of highly abstract and technologically influenced language favored by Wark (1994a) or the classical myth figures chosen by

Beaud and Dostaler (1995), we favor the Chaos and Complexity theorists' choice of models and metaphors from the natural world. We see this as helping to keep economics and ecology interwoven, to keep different disciplines connected, and to validate flexible approaches to an uncertain future. Existing economic systems that deny their dependency on eco-systems are likely to face difficulties in adjusting to rapid climate change and increasingly variable environmental conditions.

For future tracking of economics, therefore, we propose a set of biological mutations recycled from media studies. Originally, and brilliantly, applied to the absorption and indigenization of foreign media cultures in Hong Kong, Paul Lee (1991) identifies four patterns of adaptation: the parrot pattern, the wholesale imitation of foreign cultural forms and contents; the amoeba pattern, which keeps the content but changes the form, just like an amoeba that retains the same substance; the coral pattern, which keeps the form but changes the content; and last, the butterfly pattern, which takes longer to evolve and metamorphoses into something else altogether.

SUMMARY

When applied to economics, Lee's (1991) patterns help to classify existing discursive shifts, destabilizations, and reconfigurations as well as, perhaps, prefiguring future transformation. In adapting his scheme, some of the challenges to neoclassical economics previously discussed, such as the Penelope figure, can be seen as following the parrot pattern. Others follow the amoeba pattern, as when the intact structure is adjusted to take some account of the new content as with, for example, the Index of Sustainable Economic Welfare's environmental factors. Others, such as Snooks (1994), follow the coral pattern, which persists with Rational Economic Man despite situating him in the new context of the household.

Discussions of sustainable economics cut across all the patterns and have reproduced some of the sharpest ecological value clashes. Radical perspectives view *sustainable* from an ecological point of view as "the maintenance of the integrity" of the environment "in the interaction between individual human beings and in their interaction with natural resources" (Idris, 1990, p. 16). At the other end of the spectrum lie so-called nonecological elites, such as traditional economists, for whom sustainable means "how to continue to sustain the supply of raw materials when the existing supply of raw materials runs out" (p. 16). In the 1990s, from Australia to Sweden, the Third World, and the United States, there has been a sizable stream of literature on environmental economics, from elementary textbooks to scholarly journals, right across that spectrum—see Bennett and Block (1991) *Reconciling Economics and the Environment;* Coker and Richards (1992) *Valuing the Environment: Economic Approaches to Environmental Evaluation;* Bateman, Pearce, and Turner (1994) *Environmental Economics: An Elementary Introduction;* Jansson, Hammer, Folke, and Costanza (1994) *Investing in Natural Capital: The Ecological Economics Approach to Sustainability;* and Norton (1995) in the journal, *Ecological Economics.*

Last, there is the possibility of a Chaos-influenced and Complexity-influenced metamorphosis, as the 19th-century physics model (equilibrium, stability, deterministic dynamics) shifts to a more biologically based model (pattern, self-organization, life cycles). Combining Complexity's engagement with the nonlinear real world with Chaos's typical concern for the everyday, the latter model might make space for women, the environment, and the other exclusions of neoclassical economics. Its images, language, and practice also promote a healthy diversity in tune with postmodern practices elsewhere: "The more diverse economic production systems . . . are capable of responding quickly, flexibly, and positively to change" (Young, as quoted in Toohey, 1994, pp. 339-340).

This potential metamorphosis is appropriately classified as *butterfly* in three ways: first, because the sciences associated with Complexity and Chaos (with its famous butterfly effect) offer to many, both inside and outside economics, a way of bringing the field into productive dialogue with outside conditions, especially environmental conditions, and thinkers, especially noneconomist thinkers; second, because the brilliant colors reflect the rainbow coalition that keeps moving the conceptual ground beneath neo-classical economics toward a less exclusionary, post-Enlightenment framework; and last, because these metaphor-concepts open less predictable, more diversely creative, and more ecologically con-cerned pathways for bridging the enormous void to the problem-filled world than the current broken flight (Beaud & Dostaler, 1995) of mainstream economic thought.

9

Decentering Cartography

Scientific Futuremaps
and Ecocultural Projections

Throughout the book, we have argued that two communities feature too infrequently in communication and cultural studies' interactions: the first is the scientific and the second is the nonhuman. In this chapter, we connect the two through ideas and maps derived from a popular science account of cartography for the next millennium. Using these future charts, we reassess mapmaking's role in the academic imperialism of the Birmingham Centre for Contemporary Cultural Studies (CCCS) to develop an ecological and postmodern decentering project. By taking additional bearings from the Human Genome Project (HGP), genetic engineering, and science fiction, we also extend future projections beyond the confines of traditional politics and the limits of high-tech, antiorganic cyborg configurations. Aligned with both ecoculturalist and scientific cartography, this final plotting of all these diverse coordinates further dethrones the human subject, widens our fields' community relations to compass aspects of the nonhuman, and reprises the main trajectory of our greening.

DYING SUBJECTS AND
SCIENTIFIC REVOLUTIONS

Postmodern and poststructuralist discourse on the death of the subject generally allows little space for the part played by science. The scientific revolution "begun by Copernicus and finished by Darwin" did much in the "marginalizing" of human beings so that people "were no longer cast at the center of the great scheme" (Davies, 1992, pp. 20-21). Despite incorporating threatening geological notions of a so-called deep-time planetary history with human "habitation restricted to a millimicrosecond at the very end" (Gould, 1988, p. 2), the scientific revolution still constructs the process as a partial dethroning rather than a symbolic dying. Nor has the process stopped. According to the cover of Stephen S. Hall's (1993) *Mapping the Next Millennium,* computer-driven cartography continues "revolutionizing" the "face of science."

Hall's (1993) book itself claims that "everyone from archaeologists to zoologists has been able to discover, explore, chart, and visualize physical domains so remote and fantastic that the effort involves nothing less than the reinvention of the idiom of geography" (pp. 4-5). He draws parallels with how earlier map makers extended the mental, as well as the geographical, boundaries of previous worldviews. He suggests that in surveying their new terrains, contemporary scientific mapmakers similarly expand perceptual limits. He tracks how their present-day vessels of cartographic discovery, which vary from multispectral scanners on satellites to X-ray crystallography of DNA, launch into novel worlds of remote sensing. On all their journeys, whether extraterrestrial or intracellular, Hall observes how computers participate as key instrumentation. From any standpoint, the new cartography's territorial reach is impressive:

> By relying on computers to plot data points with "geographic" integrity, scientists have learned to convert almost any kind of data into a landscape, whether it is the position of galaxies in the northern celestial hemisphere or the position of hydrogen atoms in a bacterial enzyme. . . . These brilliant-hued maps, called "false-color" because the computer arbitrarily assigns color where it does not exist in nature, predate the computer, of course, but the ease with which they can now be created has produced a dazzling atlas of images from the worlds of astronomy, biology, and chemistry, readily apparent in almost any recent issue of *Science* or *Nature*. (p. 13)

Nevertheless, salutary lessons remain. U.S. National Aeronautics and Space Administration (NASA) scientists and engineers compromised geographic integrity by failing to represent the ozone hole above the Antarctic accurately enough. With such a wealth of new information, they couldn't, in the words of one of them, "focus on anything" (as quoted in Hall, 1993, p. 134). Having set inadequate parameters for satellite data, their resulting landscape charts disregarded important measurements and falsely reduced the size of the hole. Salutary lesson number two is that, whereas adjusted satellite charts might help save the ozone, different adjustments might equally help to penetrate the Antarctic icecap and precipitate commercial mining of its mineral riches. Salutary lesson number three is that neither misinterpretation nor abundance have stopped the usual power-knowledge brokers from attempting to restrict the information wealth to some people in some nations. In the words of one senior cartographic expert (a former military officer loaned to NASA), "the military and the National Security Council didn't like the idea of the civilian community looking at the earth at all. That was their prerogative. They wanted to keep this classified" (as quoted in Hall, 1993, p. 60). In time, however, despite these objections, any "citizen from any nation" was able to "obtain one of the original Landsat images of any spot on earth for $1.25" (Hall, 1993, p. 69).

All citizens of all nations stand to benefit environmentally from the provision of photomap grids of terrestrial and extraterrestrial change by remote sensing devices. As well as enabling previously impossible prosecutions for large-scale ocean pollution, Landsat information, supplemented by TOMS (total ozone mapping spectrometer), allows a much more informed monitoring of planetary degradation. At the perceptual level, these kinds of detailed discoveries about earth and space also foster shifts and provide essential bearings for contemporary cultural navigators:

> For by virtue of the satellite panoptikon, the image of the globe is now summonable as an iconic ode to world peace, ecological interdependency, and love for a newly fragile planet, Gaia, a concept Lovelock himself attributed to the new photographic view of earth from space. (Berland, 1996, p. 129)

For future cultural projections, we contend that the possibilities of such new mappings require exploration in conjunction with the key ecoculturalist issue of human-nonhuman relations.

The politics of who should have knowledge about these contours of coverage of earth and space connect with concerns familiar to cultural theorists. The Landsat scientists' fight to survive the Reagan-Bush privatization program, for example, links with an array of public-versus-private debates. Its siting within a scientific institution, however, made it less likely than, say, struggles for government funding for education or wilderness protection to draw support from cultural or environmental activists. Common cause on issues of democratic accountability might more likely have converged around anxieties about the heavy military use of Landsat. The latter example would have fitted comfortably with existing libertarian agendas that have a long history of opposition to the antidemocratic practices of establishment power; the former might have involved some unfamiliar conceptual and political realignments. It is not easy to imagine environmentalists and social activists agitating internationally for public funds for a NASA program. At the least, work has to be done to open up such newly discovered data to those outside closed government and corporate communities and wealthy Western nations.

MAPPING OTHER FIELDS: COLONIZING OTHER TERRITORIES

On his opening page, Stephen Hall (1993) recalls *Mapping the Next Millennium's* genesis as the moment when he held a historic atlas in his hands:

> I felt certain I beheld one of the most beautiful objects ever crafted by human hands. By that I do mean hands, plural and metaphoric; for as I think back on that experience, I realize that every map is the sum not only of the cartographer's skills, but of the many explorers who win the territory in the first place. Thus the map is both aesthetic and informational, as individual as any work of art but also communal and consensual, the product of cultural values (especially the value of exploration itself) and accumulated wisdoms. (p. xii)

Although this initial account conveys the physical possession so central to most mapping, Hall, until later in the book, effectively depoliticizes the process by aestheticizing it and by associating it with heroic explorations and an increase in wisdom that is assumed to be of universal benefit.

In actuality, for colonizers, mapmaking acts as a prelude to possession. A traditional feature of practices as diverse as British cultural studies and Western imperialism are their opening gambits of mapping, and often thereby getting their hands on, or beginning to lay claim to, fields of study or actual land. Approaching maps as virtual territories, David Turnbull (1989) argues that major differences between Western and indigenous, sometimes contrasted as *scientific* and *primitive,* mapmaking come down to a territorializing function. The "real distinguishing characteristic of Western maps is that they are more powerful than aboriginal maps" because, through "disciplines like cartography and the

concept of land ownership they can be subject to juridical processes" and "enable forms of association that make possible the
building of empires" (Turnbull, 1989, p. 55). Ranging over examples from Australian Aboriginals to North American Inuit, Turnbull records an occasional land rights victory for indigenous
mapping practices. Overwhelmingly, though, his study indicates
how, in territorial terms, Western cartography functioned to
support Western powers' imperial expansions.

In more principled, and bloodless, fashion, the Birmingham
CCCS generated its own subject maps. Originally positioned in
the narrow academic margin of a university English department
and with a small number of staff and students, CCCS has
gradually extended its academic empire. As Australians speaking
from the southern hemisphere, and, therefore, well aware of how
traditional Mercator projections map the northern hemisphere as
disproportionately large,[1] we should make it clear that in selecting
CCCS for particular attention we are not claiming that it is the
font of cultural studies—see, for example, Brantlinger (1990) for
the United States in relation to Britain; Frow and Morris (1993)
for *Australian Cultural Studies;* and Blundall, Shepherd, and
Taylor (1993) for *Relocating Cultural Studies.* Nor do we position
CCCS as the continuing representative of cultural studies globally—see the geographic spread of contributors to During's (1993)
The Cultural Studies Reader and the multiple contestations in
Grossberg et al.'s (1992) *Cultural Studies* collection. In this chapter, CCCS is deployed more as an influential, and relatively
identifiable, trajectory—from the early genealogies of Stuart Hall
(1980) and Richard Johnson (1983) through the family tree drawn
up by distant Australian cousin Graeme Turner (1990) to the
plethora of recent anthologies. As academics who both partially
support and have benefited from much of CCCS's international
academic spread, we readily acknowledge our ongoing debt to, as
well as continuing argument with, its publications. On this point,
we'd like to endorse the both the specific thrust and general
tendency of Bruce Robbins's comment, "that if CCCS imperialism
means reading Stuart Hall rather F. R. Leavis, then I'm for it."[2]

Nonetheless, CCCS's mapping policy merits scrutiny in the
light of Stephen Hall's (1993) observation that every map "pre-

sages some form of exploitation" (p. 383). After all, academic surveying projects also partake of the double meaning of the term *survey:* they simultaneously set out how they view the region as a whole, and they assume their vantage point to be a superior viewing position. In *Policing the Crisis: Mugging, the State, and Law and Order,* Hall, Critcher, Jefferson, Clarke, and Roberts (1978) plotted coordinates for "the social history of a social panic" (p. 3). In the field of audience studies, David Morley's (1980) *The "Nationwide" Audience* began by surveying "the main trends" within "mainstream sociological research in mass communications" (p. 1) and *Culture, Media, Language* titled one piece, "Literature/Society: Mapping the Field" (Hall, Hobson, Lowe, & Willis, 1980, p. 227). Sometimes, these writers plotted their position in relation to earlier geographers. On other occasions, in moves akin to imperialist territorial measurements, they offered theirs as the sole reliable assessment of the region—most notoriously in Stuart Hall's (1980) restrictive description of the structuralist and culturalist enterprises as the only "names of the game" (p. 72) in cultural studies. By 1990, the success of cultural studies had drawn the acronym accolade of YUMDie, for "young upwardly mobile discipline" (Hebdige, 1990, p. ix) and substantial international dispersion for their ideas, methods, and personnel.

Perhaps the major location of CCCS diasporas has emerged in Britain's Open University. Its recent publication, *Modernity and Its Futures* (Hall, Held, & McGrew, 1992), maintains the ambiguity in *survey.* Despite welcome moves toward greater self-reflexivity, Stuart Hall et al. (1992) retain cartographic ambitions. Explicitly disassociating themselves from any " 'total theory' which would map society as a whole" (p. 10), the writers still offer a seemingly neutral grid, at the same time constructing worldview longitudes and latitudes based on central fixes from their own, firmly human centered, ideologically centered, and geographically centered location. Accordingly, they dwell at length on the unsettled geopolitical state of post-wall Europe but pay little attention to the destabilizing of anthropocentricism involved in eco-cartographic shifts. They omit, for example, such bioregional considerations as global warming's possible submersion of small Pacific Island nations and the transnational spread of desertification. Barely discernible on the post-Birmingham projections, such perceptual shifts show up on a range of atlases from the Gaia series, especially Myers's (1985) The *Gaia: Atlas of Planet Management* and Myers's (1990) *The Gaia Atlas of Future Worlds* to Joni Seager's (1990) *The State of the Earth: An Atlas of Environmental Concern.* These thematic maps demonstrate conceptual categories of nonhuman reality, whereas Stuart Hall et al.'s (1992) foci renders the nonhuman virtually invisible.

"UNTENABLE CENTRISMS"
AND A TALE OF TWO HALLS

In tracking these anthropocentric fixes through future charts, we aim, for the rest of this journey, to steer between the rock of depoliticized cartography and the hard place of mapping's implication in imperialist practices. We take bearings from approximate parallels between past and present mapmaking, as per Stephen S. Hall, and the brief history of cultural studies since the intervention of Stuart Hall. We identify, as a key perspective, the former Hall's view of "the history of cartography" as "the story of civilization, shedding a succession of untenable centrisms" (S. S. Hall, 1993, p. 21). His version of the story tells how the "terracentric world of Aristotle and the ancients" (p. 21) gave way: first, to Ptolemy's geocentric view, then to what he terms the heliocentric view associated with Copernicus, and, finally, on beyond what he sees as the galactocentric view, which placed the Milky Way ("our" galaxy) at the center, toward the possibility that "ours is not the only universe" (p. 21). If this decentering process has some rough equivalence with movements in communication and cultural studies, then perhaps we may find ways of shedding some of the modern Euro-centered and human centered colonizing baggage associated with mapmaking.

Cultural studies' revolutions, for example, have also decentered, but they are clearly not so mutually exclusive. Nor are they, as women, from the early CCCS (Women's Study Group, 1978) *Women Take Issue* to the (still) *Off-Centre: Feminism and Cultural Studies* of Franklin, Lury, and Stacey (1991), and people of color

(Gilroy, 1987, 1993) repeatedly testify, so complete in their supersession of preceding sexist and racist paradigms. Nevertheless, as we argued in earlier chapters, cultural studies, in line with social theory generally, can be seen as moving from a social class-centered position to accommodate, first, race and a less Euro-centered outlook, then gender and a less sexist approach. Academic mapmaking, like all mapmaking, always retains some imperialistic possibilities and specific partial bearings based on self-location and self-interest. At the least, the relativizing in both shifts should alert us to that fact and the concomitant need for as much reflexivity as we can build in.

From our reading of computer-driven maps, their fresh bearings indicate anthropocentrism as the current untenable centrism of cultural studies. In the extraterrestrial regions, these charts cross into discipline territories that cultural studies could not hope to colonize. The field nevertheless has to be prepared to learn in order to respond adequately to ecological changes. At the opposite end of the spectrum from intergalactic space, Stephen Hall (1993) identifies, through cartography, a common connection with genetic exploration:

> The unstated long-term aim running through genetics has been spatial, if not downright geographic: to plot out inheritance by discovering its organic terrain, surveying it, measuring it, staking out specific landmarks, and then painstakingly assigning genes to specific regions. (p. 177)

On this infinitesimal terrain, just as on the extraterrestrial surveys, the scientific charts point to perceptual reconsiderations of the distance, or rather lack of it, between humans and the rest of the planet. A cultural studies that stays stuck in anthropocentrism is unprepared to address the possible consequences of these shifting dimensions.

In logging the locations of bacterial DNA, according to Stephen Hall (1993), biological cartographers confirm that, "the secrets culled from lilliputian creatures have a biochemical universality that applies to all organisms, up and down the line" (p. 177). Charts from developmental biology similarly confirm that, even

after "six hundred million years" of separation (p. 213), humanity's organic terrain is still not so startlingly different from fruit
fly territory: "William McGinnis recently substituted a human
homeobox gene for its analogous fruit fly gene and watched as
the insect embryo developed normally" (p. 90). Nor, to geophysi-
cists, is charting the internal structure of earth's terrain dissimi-
lar to "the X rays that doctors use in computed tomography, or
CT scans, to image the internal structure of the human body"
(p. 90). There is a striking commonality in such genetic maps and
these other interior mapping practices. In content and methodology, they lend support to Gaian-type scientific research; in
blurring human-nonhuman boundary differences to foreground
commonalities, they lend support to ecoculturalist moves to
decenter anthropocentric perspectives.

CYBERBIAS AND
THE TRANSGENIC OTHER

With a few notable exceptions (e.g., Haraway), the fields of
sociology, communication, and cultural studies neglect, or oppose, more ecocentric movements in so far as they contain an
ecological ethic of "internal relatedness" whereby "all organisms
are not simply interrelated with their environment but also
constituted by those very environmental relationships" (Eckersley,
1992, p. 49). The neglect of nonhuman factors, and the associated
internal linkages that are part of the one environment, helps
explain the fields' implication in modernity's technophilia. This
technophilia is a disturbing eccentricity in the biosphere-
semiosphere matrix. Rather than promoting biodiversity and
extended systems, the cyborgs of the new military-industrial-
entertainment complex are "techno-junkies." The radical potential of an extended systems theory shared by deep ecology and
feminism is now in danger of retreating to a sterile 1950s-style
modernism. Evelyn Fox Keller (1994), for example, in tracking
what she calls a possible early prototypic definition of a cyborg,
quotes a Progress Report of the Air Defense Systems Engineering
Committee dated 1 May, 1950:

The Air Defense System has points in common with . . . different kinds of systems. But it is also a member of a particular category of systems: the category of organisms. This word, still according to Webster, means "a structure composed of distinct parts so constituted that the functioning of the parts and their relationship to one another is governed by their relation to the whole." . . . The Air Defense System then, is an organism. . . . What then are organisms? They are of three kinds: animate organism which comprise animals and groups of animals, including men [sic]; partly animate organisms which involve animals together with inanimate devices such as is the ADS; and inanimate organisms such as vending machines. All these organisms possess in common: sensory components, communication facilities, data analyzing devices, centers of judgment, directors of action, and effecters, or executing agencies. (George Vallee Committee, C50-10788-AF, as quoted in Keller, 1994)

By the 1990s, the military adoption of systems and cyborgs as part of a continuum with biological organisms has expanded into society. Katherine Hayles (1993), perceiving that "elisions between physical and textual bodies are entangled with complex mediations that merge actual and virtual realities, ecological and technological constructions," calls it the "transformation from biomorphism to technomorphism" (pp. 173-174). This transformation is observable in the anti-organic cyberbias of contemporary culture and cultural critics. In this area, Donna Haraway, who started "cyborgology" as "an academic attitude" (Gray, Mentor, & Figueroa-Sarriera, 1995, p. 8), stands as a significant exception. Since her seminal essay, "Manifesto for Cyborgs," Haraway (1985) has consistently colocated a range of organic and technological phenomena as cyborgian. Her latest includes Gaia herself, "the blue- and green-hued, whole, living, self-sustaining, adaptive, auto-poietic earth" alongside "the Terminators—the jelled-metal, shape-shifting, cyber-enhanced warriors" (Haraway, 1995, p. xi). Despite her insistence "on the inextricable weave of the organic, technical, textual, mythic, economic, and political threads that make up the world" (p. xii), the earlier sense of cyborgs as cybernetic systems-biological organisms has been hijacked by high-tech and high-tech representations of the Terminator variety.

Nowhere is this clearer than in the neglected origins of the world's first recorded use of the word *cyborg*. It described a white laboratory rat with an "ingenious osmotic pressure pump," about half the size of the rat itself, designed "to permit continuous injections of chemicals at a slow controlled rate" stuck into its rear (Clynes & Kline, 1960/1995, pp. 30-31). Subsequently, these organic but nonhuman parts of the origins have barely circulated. From the smart bombs of the Gulf War through interactive cybersex simulations to the replicants of 1982's *Blade Runner* and the liquid polyalloy body of cyborg T-1000 in *Terminator 2: Judgment Day* in 1990, cyborgs appear either as intelligent technological hardware or as technologically enhanced human hybrids. In neither case do they have significant others with nonhuman biology.

In their reception of cyborgs, social and cultural studies' theorists follow technoscience production and popular culture. Cyborgs colonize book and blockbuster film dystopias alike, have had their manifesto critically acclaimed and debated, and have had at least one recent handbook (Gray, 1995) devoted to them. Cyberpunk cartography charts ambiguous fictional futures in print and it features on critical charts in return. In commonly concentrating on the "implications of human/machine co-evolution" (Gray et al., 1995, p. 6), all of these ignore the special case of actual biological transformation when organisms "transformed by introducing novel DNA" are said, in biological science, "to be *transgenic*" (Tudge, 1993, p. 212). Transgens, or genetically transformed organisms, have inspired equally imaginative narratives with their own distinctive projections, but they fail to attract comparable critical attention. To redress this imbalance in novelistic future projections, we argue for supplementing the technophilic science fiction work of William Gibson with the more organocentric texts of David Brin.

Hailed by Jameson (1991) as "the supreme literary expression if not of postmodernism, then of late capitalism itself" (p. 419), Gibson's cyberpunk had an effect far outside the science fiction circuit. Numerous other social commentators have commended the way his cyberpunk futures extrapolate from contemporary features. On what he terms *the technophilic body*, David Tomas (1989) admires Gibson's fictions from "the point of view of the cultural complexity of their technological and ecological vision" (p. 113). He positions them "at the imaginative threshold of potential post-industrial techno-dystopian cultures" (p. 113). Peter Fitting (1991) similarly views "Gibson's concept of cyberspace as an attempt to grasp the complexity of the whole world system" as a "visualization" of Jameson's "notion of cognitive mapping" (p. 311). But cognitive mapping, as we suggested in Chapter 2, is neither sufficiently reflexive nor eco-friendly. Nor do Gibson's maps hold the same ecocentric possibilities as Brin's.

Andrew Ross (1991) is another who logs cyberspace's significant features: "the contours of the new maps of power and wealth with which the information economy was colonizing the global landscape" (p. 147). Maintaining his geographic metaphor, Ross goes on to critique these futuremaps more harshly as "the heady cartographic fantasy of the powerful, aestheticized by Gibson to the point of taking on mystico-metaphysical dimensions" in its "ecology of corporate space" (p. 148). He concludes with a memorable dismissal of how the genre's "idea of a counterpolitics— youthful male heroes with working-class chips on their shoulders and postmodern biochips in their brains—seems to have little to do with the burgeoning power of the great social movements of our day: feminism, ecology, peace, sexual liberation, and civil rights" (p. 152).

BEYOND *NEUROMANCER*: DOLPHIN DREAMING AND PARTIAL BIOCENTRISM

Agreeing wholeheartedly, we want to pick up on the biochips reference to identify an associated masculinized technophilia that is implanted in cyberbiased future projections. It is the technological prosthetics noted by Tomas and others that weld cyberpunk's rejection of actually existing bodies to modernity's "contempt for the world of nature" (Fuller, 1988, p. 129). Both rejections align with the current technoscience goal of the "transhuman" condition as "complete omnipotence: the power to remake humanity, earth, the universe at large" and to "*get rid of the flesh*" (Regis, 1991, p. 7). In Western cultures, we favor the technological over the organic. Cultural theorists who acquiesce in that preference steer cyberattention away from transgenetic developments.

Admittedly, Tomas (1989) does, at one or two points, acknowledge that a "cyborg culture ensures that technology and genetic engineering are the nodal points of human interaction" (p. 117). More powerful, however, is the dominance, in his arguments and elsewhere, of the compound change from cyborg to cyberpunk. That change divests the nonhuman organic component by semantically welding the human of *punk* to the steering of *cyber* with an associated concentration on technology. Tomas therefore accurately reads Gibson's "console cowboys" as "exemplary technophiles whose brand of technicity is cerebrally cyberpsychic" (p. 125) and so notes:

> It is possible to plot relative social patterns of aesthetic and functional cyborg uses of techniques and technologies within postulated post-industrial cultures, *and that these uses condense around questions of technological advantage, an advantage that can also form the basis of claims to technological kinship.* (p. 118)

Tomas (1989) concludes rightly that "examinations of fictional cyborg cultures can sensitize us to the possibility of explosive social/biological mutations produced by rapidly changing technoscapes" (p. 127). Unfortunately, he then chooses to operate only in the deorganicized cyberpunk terrain of "Gibson's Cartesian distinction between a cerebral cyberpsychic universe and a world of cyborged flesh" (p. 121). By his choice, Tomas denies himself access to the fictional material offering those other, less human, organic cyberpossibilities in this "age of genetic engineering" (Tudge, 1993, p. 206). With fear rather than excitement about what he greets as "Barbarism Modernized: The Eugenic Age," sociologist Ulrich Beck (1993) looks backward to Nazi experimentation to comprehend these brave new worlds: "In

Germany as elsewhere, human cloning and the creation of man-beast hybrids are criminal offenses. On the other side stand the world wide pioneers of human-genetic reproduction engineering" (p. 18).

In their coverage of both science and science fiction, social and cultural theorists allot inadequate space to the potential of a more organic-based change. As well as analyzing future projections of corporate power, they need to engage with a DNA revolution in biological science that can "envisage the creation of entire new kingdoms of organisms" (Tudge, 1993, p. 252):

> "Kingdom" is the latest recognized grouping of living things. All plants collectively form a kingdom; so do all animals; so, too, all fungi; and so do all bacteria. . . . Suppose, however, we combined qualities of different kingdoms in one organism—not just in a small way (as scientists do when they place animal genes in bacteria, say), but to create qualitatively different creatures? . . . [W]e would have plants able to survive in an acrid and fiercely hot environment: the kind of conditions we might theoretically envisage in a few million years, as the atmosphere continues to evolve. Thus, as life becomes intolerable for human beings and for most present-day life forms, we might none the less leave big and noble organisms behind us. (Tudge, 1993, pp. 252-253)

Such speculations, especially in their vast timescale and planetary altruism, lie light years away from cybertowns, communication, and cultural studies' territories alike. Yet any chart for future evolution will need to allow space for them. In marked contrast to Gibson, David Brin's (1983) *Startide Rising* weights his cybercompounds in favor of the transgenic. He mixes kingdoms to the extent of crewing an intergalactic spaceship with dolphins capable of interspecies communication and of making wisecracks about human beings: "They had always found men terribly funny. The fact that humanity had meddled with their genes and taught them engineering hadn't done much to change their attitude" (1983, p. 1). The example is typical of how the novel's ironic anthropomorphizing decenters anthropocentric assumptions.

Brin (1983) goes on to imagine a spacefaring future where, "'Old Earth' was still home to ninety percent of humanity, not to mention the other terrestrial sapient races" (p. 13). He constructs an evolutionary system called *uplift* where nearly all "species had patrons" and "Orphan Earth," a rare exception, appeared like "a planetary laboratory, upon which a series of senseless and bizarre experiments were tried" (p. 141). Equally rare in this imaginary galaxy, further developed in his sequel, *The Uplift War,* is the people of earth's nonexploitative attitude to its "client" races, "chimps and dolphins" (Brin, 1987, pp. vii-ix) and other-than-human life. That this fictional future world almost diametrically reverses actually existing human treatment of animals is significant. It matters less than Brin's provision of an entertainingly accessible form to speculate about the implications of the DNA revolution and evolutionary potentials.

For example, Charles Dart, a neochimpanzee planetologist, after being rescued from captivity by a human, poses a hypothetical situation to his rescuer: if "this was one of those 20th-century 'zoo' ships'" loaded with "a bunch of pre-sentient chimps" en route "from Africa to some laboratory or circus" would he still have attempted "to rescue them?" (Brin, 1987, p. 405). His questionings, with their implied assault on current perceptual boundaries between human and nonhuman, are akin to those suggested by some of the new scientific cartography. Brin, however, brings the moral dimension into sharper focus:

> Prior to uplift, the concept of the food chain as a mystical hierarchy had been central to cetacean morality. . . . [H]umans used to wonder why dolphins and many whales remained friendly to man after experiencing wholesale slaughter at his hands. . . . [A] cetacean did not blame a member of another race for killing him, not when that other race was higher on the food-chain. For centuries cetaceans simply assumed that man was at the topmost rung, and begrudged only the most senseless of his killing sprees. It was a code of honor which, when humans learned about it, made most of them more, not less ashamed of what had been done. (pp. 343-344)

In supporting Brin's decenterings of anthropocentrism, we take him as offering texts of "the break." We share his rejection of extreme "biocentrism" with "its antihumanistic image of human beings as interchangeable with rodents or ants" (Bookchin, 1990, pp. 10-11). Like him, we also dissociate ourselves from the "view which says that the Earth and all her creatures would be much better off without us" (Brin, 1983, p. 637). Closer to animals and more interwoven in the planetary web of life than communication and cultural studies currently acknowledge, humans remain distinctly different and valuable in their own right. In returning to the present and his own voice, Brin's (1987) postscripts maintain that we "do not have to see ourselves as monsters in order to teach an ethic of environmentalism" and that it "is now well known that our very survival depends on maintaining complex ecological networks and genetic diversity" (p. 637). In support of this ethic, Brin (1983) creates narratives of "Darwinian heretics" who see other species able "to bootstrap themselves" (p. 287). These serve to further his belief in the possibility that "some of our fellow mammals will one day be our partners" (pp. 461-462). Claiming that we owe it to that possible future to let their potential survive, his later postscript concludes with the reflection that "some day we may be judged by just how well we served, when we alone were Earth's caretakers" (Brin, 1987, pp. 637-638).

GENE MEDDLING, FUTURE PATHWAYS, AND DISCIPLINARY LEOPARDS

In the earlier novel, Brin (1983) depicted one of the dolphin crew, an illegal Orca gene-graft, turning into a vicious killer but made an explicit contrast with "a true killer whale," which "does not kill out of spite" (p. 338). Through other incidents along similar lines, Brin's organically hybrid world critiques irresponsible gene meddling. Such potentials are already implicit in some of the maps in Stephen Hall's millennium atlas. They become explicit in the familiar language of male exploration-colonization by the book titles of supporters of the HGP: William Cookson's

(1994) *The Gene Hunters: Hacking Through the Genome Jungle* assumes the latest white male scientist's burden in appropriate fashion; Robert Shapiro's (1992) *The Human Blueprint: The Race to Unlock the Secrets of our Genetic Script* has connotations of a Raiders of the Lost Ark-style search; and Bishop and Waldholz's (1990) title says it all, *Genome: The Story of the Most Astonishing Scientific Adventure of Our Time—The Attempt to Map All the Genes in the Human Body*. Bodmer and McKie's (1994) *The Book of Man: The Quest to Discover Our Genetic Heritage* similarly narrates the story of "one of mankind's [sic] greatest odysseys" through the Human Genome Project's "quest" to delineate "the exact molecular composition of the genes that make up Homo sapiens" in "biology's answer to the Apollo Space Program" (p. vii). These examples do not include the potential genetic biowarriers (see Piller & Yamamoto, 1988).

It is significant that Stephen Hall nowhere presages this genetic mapping as a form of exploitation. In the more ominously titled *Perilous Knowledge: The Human Genome Project and Its Implications*, another science commentator points out the HGP's potential to create "a subcaste of genetic lepers who are refused jobs, insurance cover, . . . the right to marry" (Wilkie, 1994, p. 11). Wilkie concludes that although one effect of the HGP "may be to blur further the distinction between humans and animals, it is possible that a second consequence may be to accentuate the differences between humans" (p. 178). Paul Davies (1994) concurs that we "may soon be able to design human beings with prescribed attributes and physical characteristics by direct genetic manipulation" (p. 103).

Given these predictions, it is significant that nowhere do Stuart Hall et al. (1992) begin to sound out their implications for human-nonhuman relations, let alone citizenship and future society. This is despite a response spectrum stretching from fear about the dystopic potential in genetic cartography to the futuristic utopianism that "we might eventually create an organism from scratch . . . ending up with super-crops, or dinosaurs, or replicate human beings, or what you will" (Tudge, 1993, p. 253). Nor are commentators like Tudge and Wilkie isolated or recent phenomena. They offer updates on well-established charts drafted by many optimistic and pessimistic predecessors on biological revolutions (e.g., Judson, 1979), DNA (e.g., Olby, 1974), eugenics (e.g., Kelves, 1986), genetics (e.g., Lewontin, Rose, & Kamin, 1984), genetics and ethics (e.g., Knudtson & Suzuki, 1990) and the Human Genome Project (e.g., Kelves & Hood, 1992).

The territorial explorations of Brin and Gibson, as their subsequent inspirations indicate, also continue to follow very different pathways to the future. Gibson (1993) acknowledges the source of his post-cyberpunk title *Virtual Light* as a term "coined by scientist Stephen Beck to describe a form of instrumentation that produces 'optical sensations directly in the eye without the use of photons' *(Mondo 2000)*" (p. 324). Compared with his earlier cyberpunk fiction, Gibson does display some increase in social awareness. In *Virtual Light*, he projects ideas about the privatization of Californian public space (probably derived from his other acknowledged source, Mike Davis's [1990] *City of Quartz*) into a high-tech future. Human bodies, too, including an interesting AIDS variation, retain more recognizable flesh than in his cyberpunk fiction. Despite this, neither Gibson nor his critics make space for nonhuman organisms.

In *Earth*, on the other hand, Brin (1990) extends his voice beyond sentient beings in that rare kind of postcolonialism that encompasses the planet itself (see McKie, 1993). More recently, in *Glory Season* (Brin, 1993), he fictionalized the computer Game of Life, which is famous in science, popular science, and artificial life literature (see Levy, 1993, pp. 49-58). But even in this case, Brin (1993) contrasts with Gibson in foregrounding genetic material. Connecting genes with gender issues through the sciences of Complexity, he opens up the whole question of autonomy and organisms. Inspired, according to his afterword, by "a contemplation of lizards. . . . that reproduce parthenogenetically—mothers giving birth to daughter clones" (p. 559), Brin chooses to avoid the fictionally widespread idea of cloning "in terms of medical technology involving complex machinery" (p. 559). Instead, he hypothesizes self-cloning as "just another of the many startling capabilities of the human womb" (p. 560). This might, as he sees it, require certain social adjustments because "there are no scientific reasons not to show males relegated to the sidelines of history, a peripheral social class, as has been the lot of women in our own civilization" (p. 560). In their divergent inspirational sources and directions of development, Brin and Gibson gravitate toward the biological and the technological, respectively. Brin, however, links more directly with current issues in science.

Disputes about the nature of "biological 'reality' " (Goodwin, 1994, p. xii) occupy scientists as well as science fiction writers. Taking his initial focus from nature and theoretical science rather than technology, Brin connects with a Complexity-inspired paradigm challenge within biology. In another recentering, rather than a decentering, move, Brian Goodwin's (1994) *How the Leopard Changed Its Spots* argues for the science of biology (the leopard in his title) undergoing a major theoretical change. He wants to change its disciplinary spots to what he calls an *organo-centric* perspective: "Nothing of value in contemporary biology is lost in this shift of perspective: it simply gets reframed, reintegrated from a different viewpoint" (p. 3).

Goodwin's (1994) reorientation recognizes the "fundamental nature of organisms" as connecting "directly with our own natures as irreducible beings" with "significant consequences regarding our attitude to the living realm" (p. xii). This is the kind of perceptual shift we desire in our fields. By an equivalent relaxing of their anthropocentric viewpoint, for example, sociology and communication and cultural studies might similarly integrate traditional social perspectives with ecology as the fourth dimension. They might then take on board, as part of their disciplinary spot changing, the need to address the prospects of actual leopards, other endangered species, and the biosphere itself. After all, as Carolyn Merchant (1994) has recently observed, "domination" has proved "one of our century's most fruitful concepts for understanding human-human and human-nature relationships" (p. 1). But, she concludes, the problem of analyzing and overcoming it remains, along with "much disagreement over why and how nature and humans are linked and what to do about changing those linkages" (p. 1).

This is evident in the ease with which even the more eco-conscious supporters of the potential of a transgenic revolution ignore the issues of genetic rights. Serious concerns about the collection of "endangered" human DNA from "unique" indigenous human "species," and the possible patenting of that DNA for Western drug companies profits, have been slow to surface (see Lewin, 1993b). So, too, have been concerns about the vast unknown into which genetically engineered ecosystems and new organisms are hurtling in search of bioengineered wealth. In this area, there also needs to be space for the always more conservative, in relation to the "natural," voices of deep ecology and the counterculture. Humanity has a huge inner journey to contemplate before the natural stability of genetic sequencing, which has evolved over long time frames, is rapidly superseded by the facile optimism of the gene junkies and other bio-technophiles. As Damasio (1994a) expresses it in relation to other organisms, "survival depends on a collection of biological processes that maintain the integrity of cells and tissues throughout its structure" (p. 114).

DISPOSITIONS FOR SURVIVAL

Strangely, given its title of *Modernity and Its Futures*, Stuart Hall et al.'s (1992) book charts very little in the way of forthcoming scientific developments, few prospective socioscientific changes, and no science fictional extrapolations. Neither Hall, his coeditors, nor their six selected contributors, offer navigational help in any of these areas, let alone, with one exception, Merchant's other linkages. Nor do they acknowledge the existence of the new cartography, its terrains, and its implications. For future cultural mapmakers, we contend that, in conjunction with the environmental movement and its atlases, organocentric science and science fiction (McKie, 1995) and the new scientific cartography (especially in relation to DNA) offer essential reference points. Extrapolating from existing science, they indicate a more environmentally aware agenda grounded in less exploitative planetary relations. Ecologically sensitive and informed by ideas from the scientific community, their future projections decenter anthropocentrism, dethrone the human kingdom, and dismantle rigid demarcation lines with other-than-human communities.

In imagining future grids, few cultural theorists have followed Raymond Williams's (1983) lead, in *Towards 2000*, in placing "life forms and land forms" and their "intricate interdependence" (p. 261) high on agendas of social anticipation. Hall et al.'s (1992) *Modernity and Its Futures* is more representative of current sociological surveys of the topographies of tomorrow. Other prominent communication and cultural studies futurology—for example, Bird, Putnam, Robertson, and Tickner's (1993) *Mapping the Futures: Local Cultures, Global Change*—is equally neglectful of linkages with the nonhuman, current science, and the charts of the new cartography. Moreover, although typical in many of its exclusions, Hall et al.'s *Modernity and Its Futures* is untypical in devoting a whole chapter, by sociologist Steven Yearley (1992), to "Environmental Challenges." That chapter's conclusions take us back to where we began in Chapter 1, with the impending death of nature where "the ecological hazards of pollution and resource depletion" pose "a potentially catastrophic threat" (p. 150). Yearley expresses serious doubts that the existing "reformist path is sustainable" or can "penetrate deeply enough to overcome the global threats of pollution, species extinction and habitat loss" (p. 152). Alongside that possible demise are the emotional, knowledge, and political gaps that hinder us in taking adequate action to engage with those threats and the possible end, not only of the Enlightenment project, but of human life on earth. According to Yearley, radical green thinking, such as deep ecology, "does challenge the Enlightenment project" but "lacks a firm social basis" (p. 152), whereas those sociologically and politically informed Greens who do try "to accommodate the Enlightenment" cannot "guarantee" that "they can pull this trick off" (p. 152).

No one in that book actually suggests how the magic trick might be performed. Contesting Yearley's concluding summary, we end with a less mutually exclusive reading of the multiple maps of environmentalism—possibilities and responses we have registered as eco-impacts. We readily admit that our own personal histories, cultural formations, and geographic locations have all helped to configure the social and intellectual routes we follow and the cartographies we favor. As offspring of the 1960s, we retain that period's embryonic promise of interlinked inner and outer emancipation. In engaging with eco-impacts, we advocate freedoms that continue the 1960s, search for integration between self and environment, between personal and political, between male and female, and between body and intellect with as much celebratory energy as serious study. In our meditations, we have been influenced by the natural world and by non-Western and indigenous traditions. As more conventional activists and practicing academics, we have been informed by both Western Marxism and the Euro-Enlightenment tradition. As well as remaining sympathetic to some of their liberation impulses, we remain open to postmodern sciences without certainties.

In every case, we give much greater weighting to environmental questions. In accepting criticisms that perennial philosophies, such as Taoism and Zen, pay little attention to sociopolitical structures, we suggest that sociopolitical movements pay little attention to traditional technologies for evolving nondualist consciousness and to quests for spiritual values. In poking fun at the Western intellectual tradition, although we cannot deny how it shapes us, we contend that too much social, communication, and cultural studies' theory still revolves around a remarkably unrelativized Enlightenment-modernity axis and a politics with a "virtually complete reliance" on "the program set by modernity" (Bauman, 1991, p. 263). We see that program as too dismissive of other knowledge traditions, interlinked indigenous practices, and their more sustainable relationships to the nonhuman and material world.

In our deployment of a dialectical holism that is open, playful, and postmodern, we seek, above all, to transgress anti-ecological divides. We emphasize that, in our critique of *Modernity and Its Futures* and in our arguments for the greening of our disciplines, we do not claim to have the answers. We do, however, hope to persuade our co-workers that sociology, communication studies, and cultural studies can help generate more environmentally helpful maps:

By engaging with eco-impacts centrally as the interlinked fourth dimension of academic and social space;

By confronting the many deaths in a declining biosphere through the integration of emotional, mental, and environmental factors;

By developing cultural mapping techniques that expose differences, margins, edges, and cores;

By locating postmodernity as the "age of ecology" and prioritizing canon formations and political projects accordingly;

By contrasting the cultural diversity of environmentalism with the narrow economism and human chauvinism of institutionally entrenched left critical theory;

By fostering an ecologically extended sense of self and retheorizing the self-subjectivity-identity nexus;

By extending temporal frames to situate humans as part, albeit an exceptional part, of longer evolutionary processes;

By intensifying interdisciplinarity and interrelating biosphere maps from science with semiosphere maps from culture;

By contesting outmoded controlling imagery and promoting more ecologically friendly discourse; and

By reducing anthropocentrism to make space for more ecocentric perspectives.

NOTES

1. See, for example, the Arno Peters projection map, which represents countries accurately according to their surface areas and so provides a helpful corrective to the Eurocentric distortions of traditional maps "by setting all countries in their true size and location" and allowing "each one its actual position in the world" (New Internationalist, n.d.).

2. He made the comment on an earlier version of this chapter delivered to the Intellectuals and Communities Conference of the Cultural Studies Association of Australia at the University of Technology, Sydney, December 1994.

References

Achbar, M., Symansky, A., & Wintonick, P. (Producers). (1992). *Manufacturing consent: Noam Chomsky and the media* [Videocassette]. Montreal: National Film Board of Canada.

Alexander, C. (1992). Aborigines in capitalist Australia: What it means to become civilized. In T. Jagtenberg & P. D'Alton (Eds.), *Four dimensional social space: Class, gender, ethnicity and nature: A reader in Australian social sciences* (2nd ed., pp. 482-486). Sydney: Harper.

Anderson, A. (1991). Source strategies and the communication of environmental affairs. *Media, Culture and Society, 13*(4), 459-476.

Anderson, P. (1988). Modernity and revolution. In L. Grossberg & C. Nelson (Eds.), *Marxism and the interpretation of culture* (pp. 317-338). London: Macmillan.

Appignanesi, L., & Lawson, H. (Eds.). (1989). *Dismantling truth: Reality in the post-modern world*. New York: St. Martin's.

Angier, J. (Executive Producer & Director). (1990). *Race to save the planet*. WGBH Science Unit in association with Chedd-Angier, Film Australia, the University Grants, Commission of India/Gujarat University.

Appleby, P. (Producer). (1993). *Two seconds to midnight*. London: BBC/Discovery Channel.

263

Aries, P. (1974). *Western attitudes toward death: From the middle ages to the present* (P. M. Ranum, Trans.). Baltimore, MD: Johns Hopkins University Press.

Arrow, K., Anderson, P., & Pines, D. (1988). *The economy as an evolving complex system.* Redwood City, CA: Addison-Wesley.

Atkisson, A. (1990). The unity of global thinking. *In Context, 25,* 55-57.

Attenborough, D. (1987). *The first Eden: The Mediterranean world and man.* London: Collins & BBC Books.

Austen, H. I. (1990). *The heart of the goddess: Art, myth and meditations of the world's sacred feminine.* Berkeley, CA: Wingbow.

Bailey, R. (Ed.). (1995). *The true state of the planet: Ten of the world's premier environmental researchers in a major challenge to the environmental movement.* New York: Free Press.

Barthes, R. (1977). *Image-music-text* (S. Heath, Trans.). London: Fontana.

Baskin, R., Bernstein, A, & Witt, P. J. (Executive Producers), & Baskin, R., & Hemion, D. (Directors). (1990). *The Earth Day special.* United States: Time Warner and People of the Earth Foundation.

Bataille, G. M., & Silet, C. L. P. (Eds.). (1980). *The pretend Indians: Images of Native Americans in the movies.* Ames: Iowa State University Press.

Bateman, I., Pearce, D., & Turner, R. K. (1994). *Environmental economics: An elementary introduction.* London: Harvester Wheatsheaf.

Baudrillard, J. (1983). *Simulations* (P. Foss, P. Patton, & P. Beitchman, Trans.). New York: Semiotext(e). (Original work published 1981)

Baudrillard, J. (1987). The ecstasy of communication. In H. Foster (Ed.), *Postmodern culture* (pp. 126-134). Sydney: Pluto.

Baudrillard, J. (1988). *Selected works* (Various Trans., M. Poster, Ed.). Cambridge, MA: Polity.

Baudrillard, J. (1990). *Seduction* (B. Singer, Trans.). London: Macmillan. (Original work published 1980)

Baudrillard, J. (1995). *The Gulf War did not take place* (P. Patton, Trans.). Sydney: Power Publications. (Original work published 1991)

Bauman, Z. (1991). *Modernity and ambivalence.* Cambridge, MA: Polity.

Bauman, Z. (1992). *Intimations of postmodernity.* London: Routledge.

Beasley, C. (1994). *Sexual economyths: Conceiving a feminist economics.* Sydney: Allen & Unwin.

Beaud, M., & Dostaler, G. (1995). *Economic thought since Keynes: History and dictionary of major economists.* New York: Elgar. (Original work published 1993)

Beck, U. (1992). *Risk society: Towards a new modernity.* London: Sage.

Bell, D. (1976). *The cultural contradictions of capitalism.* New York: Basic Books.

Bell, P., Boehringer, K., & Crofts, S. (1982). *Programmed politics: A study of Australian television.* Sydney: Sable.

Benedikt, M. (Ed.). (1992). *Cyberspace: First steps.* Cambridge: MIT Press.

Bennett, J., & Block, W. (Eds.). (1991). *Reconciling economics and the environment.* Perth, Western Australia: Australian Institute for Public Affairs.

Benton, T. (1993). *Natural relations: Ecology, animal rights and social justice.* London: Verso.

Berger, P. L., & Luckmann, T. (1972). *The social construction of reality: A treatise in the sociology of knowledge.* Harmondsworth, UK: Penguin.

Berland, J. (1992). Angels dancing: Cultural technologies and the production of space. In L. Grossberg, C. Nelson, & P. A. Treichler (Eds.), *Cultural studies* (pp. 38-55). London: Routledge.

Berland, J. (1994). On reading the weather. *Cultural Studies, 8*(1), 99-114.

Berland, J. (1996). Mapping space: Imaging technologies and the planetary body. In S. Aronowitz, B. Martinsons, & M. Menser (Eds.), *Technoscience and cyberculture* (pp. 123-137). New York: Routledge.

Berland, J., & Slack, J. D. (Eds.). (1994). On environmental matters. *Cultural Studies, 8*(1), 1-4. [special issue]

Berman, M. (1982). *All that is solid melts into air.* New York: Simon & Schuster.

Berman, M. (1984). *The reenchantment of the world.* Sydney: Bantam.

Berry, W. (1977). *The unsettling of America: Culture and agriculture.* New York: Avon Books.

Berry, W. (1981). *The gift of good land.* San Francisco: North Point.

Berry, W. (1989, September). The futility of global thinking. *Harper's*, pp. 16-21.

Best, S., & Kellner, D. (Eds.). (1991). *Postmodern theory: Critical interrogations.* London: Macmillan.

Biehl, J. (1991). *Rethinking ecofeminist politics.* Boston: South End.

Birch, C. (1990). *On purpose.* Sydney: New South Wales University Press.

Bird, J., Putnam, T., Robertson, G., & Tickner, L. (Eds.). (1993). *Mapping the futures: Local cultures, global change.* London: Routledge.

Bishop, J., & Waldholz, M. (1990). *Genome: The story of the most astonishing scientific adventure of our time—The attempt to map all the genes in the human body.* New York: Simon & Schuster.

Block, F. (1990). *Postindustrial possibilities: A critique of economic discourse.* Berkeley: University of California Press.

Bloor, D. (1976). *Knowledge and social imagery.* London: Routledge & Kegan Paul.

Blundall, V., Shepherd, J., & Taylor, I. (Eds.). (1993). *Relocating cultural studies: Developments in theory and research.* London: Routledge.

Bodmer, W., & McKie, R. (1994). *The book of man: The quest to discover our genetic heritage.* London: Little, Brown.

Bolen, J. S. (1990). Foreword. In H. I. Austen, *The heart of the goddess: Art, myth and meditations of the world's sacred feminine* (pp. xiii-xiv). Berkeley, CA: Wingbow.

Bolter, D. J. (1986). *Turing's man: Western culture in the computer age.* Harmondsworth, UK: Penguin.

Bolton, E. (1981). *Spoils and spoilers: Australians make their environment, 1788-1980.* Sydney: Allen & Unwin.

Bonner, J. T. (1980). *The evolution of culture in animals.* Princeton, NJ: Princeton University Press.

Bonney, B., & Wilson, H. (1983). *Australia's commercial media.* Melbourne: Macmillan.

Bookchin, M. (1982). *The ecology of freedom.* Palo Alto, CA: Chesire.

Bookchin, M. (1990). *Remaking society: Pathways to a green future.* Boston: South End.

Bookchin, M. (1991). *The ecology of freedom* (2nd ed.). Montreal: Black Rose.

Bourdieu, P. (1986). *Distinction: A social critique of the judgement of taste* (R. Nice, Trans.). London: Routledge. (Original work published 1979)

Bourdieu, P. (1988). *Homo academicus* (P. Collier, Trans.). Cambridge, MA: Polity. (Original work published 1984)

Bowler, P. J. (1992). *The Fontana history of the environmental sciences.* London: Fontana.

Boxer, N., Meugniot, W. (Executive Producers), Boxer, N., & Meugniot, W. (Directors). (1990). *Captain Planet and the Planeteers.* United States: TBS Productions.

Bramwell, A. (1989). *Ecology in the twentieth century: A history.* Oxford, UK: Oxford University Press.

Brand, J., & Falsey, J. (Executive Producers). (1991). *Northern exposure.* United States: CBS.

Brantlinger, P. (1990). *Crusoe's footprints: Cultural studies in Britain and America.* New York: Routledge.

Brawer, R., & Lightman, A. (Eds.). (1990). *Origins: The lives and worlds of modern cosmologists.* Cambridge, MA: Harvard University Press.

Briggs, J., & Peat, F. D. (1989). *Turbulent mirror: An illustrated guide to chaos theory and the science of wholeness.* New York: Harper & Row.

Brin, D. (1983). *Startide rising.* New York: Bantam.

Brin, D. (1987). *The uplift war.* New York: Bantam.

Brin, D. (1990). *Earth.* New York: Bantam.

Brin, D. (1993). *Glory season.* New York: Bantam.

Brockway, G. P. (1993). *The end of economic man: Principles of any future economics* (rev. ed.). New York: Norton.

Brooks, W. D., & Heath, R. W. (1993). *Speech communication.* Dubuque, IA: Brown & Benchmark.

Brown, L., Denniston, D., Flavin, C., French, H., Kane, H., Lenssen, N. Renner, M., Roodman, D. M., Ryan, M., Sachs, A., Starke, L., Weber, P., & Young, J. (1995). *State of the world 1995: A Worldwatch Institute report on progress toward a sustainable society.* London: Earthscan.

Brown, M. E. (1987). The politics of soaps: Pleasure and feminine empowerment. *Australian Journal of Cultural Studies, 4*(2), 1-25.

Brundtland, H. (1987). *Our common future: Report for the World Commission on Environment and Development.* Oxford: Oxford University Press.

Bryant, G. (1985). *Positivism in social theory and research.* London: Macmillan.

Burger, J., with campaigning groups and native peoples worldwide. (1990). *The Gaia atlas of first peoples: A future for the indigenous world.* London: Gaia.

Burgess, J., Harrison, C., & Maiteny, P. (1991). Contested meanings: The consumption of news about nature conservation. *Media, Culture and Society, 13*(4), 499-519.

Burgmann, V. (1993). *Power and protest: Movements for change in Australian society.* Sydney: Allen & Unwin.

Burkitt, I. (1991). Social selves. *Current Sociology, 39*(3), 1-225.

Burnam, B. (1992). Aboriginal Australia and the green movement. In D. Hutton (Ed.), *Green politics in Australia* (pp. 91-104). Sydney: Angus & Robertson.

Byrne, D. (Director), & Kurfirst, G. (Producer). (1986). *True stories* [Videocassette]. Los Angeles: Warner Bros.

Caine, B., de Lepervanche, M., & Grosz, E. A. (Eds.). (1988). *Crossing boundaries: Feminisms and the critique of knowledges.* Sydney: Allen & Unwin.

Campbell, J. (1984). *The way of the animal powers.* London: Times.

Carey, J. (1989). *Communication as culture: Essays on media and society*. Boston: Unwin Hyman.

Carey, J. (1993, July). *Everything that rises must converge: Notes on communication, technology and culture*. Paper presented at the Australian Communication Association Conference, Communication and Identity: Local, Regional, Global, Victoria University of Technology, Melbourne, Victoria.

Carpini, M. X. D., & Williams, B. A. (1994). "Fictional" and "non-fictional" television celebrates Earth Day: Or, politics is comedy plus pretense. *Cultural Studies, 8*(1), 74-88.

Carroll, L. (1967). The hunting of the snark. In M. Gardener (Ed.), *The annotated snark* (pp. 41-96). Harmondsworth, UK: Penguin.

Carson, R. (1962). *Silent spring*. Boston: Houghton Mifflin.

Castaneda, C. (1971). *A separate reality*. New York: Simon & Schuster.

Chambers, I. (1986). Waiting on the end of the world? *Journal of Communication Inquiry, 10*(2), 100-108.

Chatterjee, P., & Finger, M. (1994). *The earth brokers: Power, politics and world development*. London: Routledge.

Chesneaux, J. (1992). *Brave modern world*. London: Thames & Hudson.

Chibnall, S. (1977). *Law-and-order news: An analysis of crime reporting in the British press*. London: Tavistock.

Chomsky, N., & Herman, E. S. (1988). *Manufacturing consent: The political economy of the mass media*. New York: Pantheon.

Clarke, R. (1973). *Ellen Swallow: The woman who founded ecology*. Chicago: Follett.

Clynes, M. E., & Kline, N. S. (1995). Cyborgs and space. In C. H. Gray (Ed.), *The cyborg handbook* (pp. 29-33). London: Routledge. (Original work published 1960)

Cohen, B. (1994). Technological colonialism and the politics of water. *Cultural Studies, 8*(1), 32-55.

Cohen, J., & Stewart, I. (1994). *The collapse of chaos: Discovering simplicity in a complex world*. New York: Viking.

Coker, A., & Richards, C. (Eds.). (1992). *Valuing the environment: Economic approaches to environmental evaluation*. Proceedings of a workshop held at Ludgrove Hall, Middlesex Polytechnic, on 13th and 14th of June, 1990. London: Belhaven.

Collins, J. (1992). Postmodernism and television. In R. C. Allen (Ed.), *Channels of discourse, reassembled* (pp. 327-353). London: Routledge.

Cookson, W. (1994). *The gene hunters: Hacking through the genome jungle*. London: Aurum.

Corner, J. (1991). Meaning, genre and context: The problematics of "public knowledge" in the new audience studies. In J. Curran & M. Gurevitch (Eds.), *Mass media and society* (pp. 267-284). London: Edward Arnold.

Corner, J., Richardson, K., & Fenton, N. (1990). *Nuclear reactions: A study in public issue television*. London: John Libbey.

Corner, J., & Schlesinger, P. (1991a). Editorial. *Media, Culture and Society, 13*(4), 435-441.

Corner, J., & Schlesinger, P. (Eds.). (1991b). Media and the environment [Special issue]. *Media, Culture and Society, 13*(4).

Cotgrove, S. (1982). *Catastrophe or cornucopia: The environmentalist, politics, and the future.* Chichester, UK: John Wiley.

Cottle, S. (1994). Mediating the environment. In A. Hansen (Ed.), *The mass media and environment issues* (pp. 107-133). London: Leicester University Press.

Coveney, P., & Highfield, R. (1995). *Frontiers of complexity: The search for order in a chaotic world.* London: Faber & Faber.

Cowan, J. (1993). *Messengers of the gods: Tribal elders reveal the ancient wisdom of the earth.* Sydney: Random House.

Cranny-Francis, A. (1992). *Engendered fictions: Analysing gender in the production and reception of texts.* Sydney: New South Wales University Press.

Crook, S., & Pakulski, J. (1995). Shades of green: Public opinion on environmental issues in Australia. *Australian Journal of Political Science, 30*(1), 39-95.

Crook, S., Pakulski, J., & Waters, M. (1992). *Postmodernization: Change in advanced society.* London: Sage.

Cuff, E., Sharrock, W., & Francis, D. (1992). *Perspectives in sociology* (3rd ed.). London: Routledge.

Daly, M. (1978). *Gyn/ecology: The metaethics of radical feminism.* London: Women's Press.

Damasio, A. R. (1994a). *Descartes' error: Emotion, reason, and the human brain.* New York: Grosset/G. P. Putnam.

Damasio, A. R. (1994b, October). Descartes' error and the future of human life. *Scientific American, 271*(4), 116.

Davidson, A. (1993). *Endangered peoples.* San Francisco: Sierra Club.

Davies, P. (1992). *The mind of god: The scientific basis for a rational world.* New York: Simon & Schuster.

Davies, P. (1994). *The last three minutes.* London: Weidenfeld & Nicolson.

Davies, P., & Gribbin, J. (1992). *The matter myth: Beyond chaos and complexity.* Harmondsworth, UK: Penguin.

Davis, M. (1990). *City of quartz: Excavating the future in Los Angeles.* London: Verso.

Dawkins, R. (1976). *The selfish gene.* Oxford, UK: Oxford University Press.

De Landa, M. (1991). *War in the age of intelligent machines.* New York: Zone.

Deleuze, G., & Guattari, F. (1987). *A thousand plateaus* (B. Massumi, Trans.). Minneapolis: University of Minnesota Press. (Original work published 1980)

Denslow, J., & Padoch, C. (1988). *People of the tropical rainforest.* Berkeley: University of California Press.

Denzin, N. (1989). *Interpretive biography.* Newbury Park, CA: Sage.

Denzin, N. (1992). *Symbolic interactionism and cultural studies: The politics of interpretation.* Oxford, UK: Basil Blackwell.

Devall, B. (1990). *Simple in means, rich in ends: Practicing deep ecology.* London: Green Print.

Devall, B., & Sessions, G. (1985). *Deep ecology: Living as if nature mattered.* Layton, UT: Gibbs M. Smith.

Dewdney, A. K. (1989, July). Computer recreations. *Scientific American.*

Diamond, E., & Bates, S. (1992). *The spot: The rise of political advertising on television* (3rd ed.). Cambridge: MIT Press.

Diamond, I., & Feman-Orenstein, G. (Eds.). (1990). *Reweaving the world: The emergence of ecofeminism.* San Francisco: Sierra Club.

Diamond, J. (1992). *The rise and fall of the third chimpanzee.* London: Vintage.

Dickens, P. (1992). *Society and nature: Towards a green social theory.* Philadelphia: Temple University Press.

Dickson, D. (1988). *The new politics of science.* Chicago: University of Chicago Press.

Diprose, R., & Ferrell, R. (Eds.). (1991). *Cartographies: Poststructuralism and the mapping of bodies and spaces.* Sydney: Allen & Unwin..

Docker, J. (1994). *Postmodernism and popular culture.* Cambridge, UK: Cambridge University Press.

Donovan, S. K. (Ed.). (1989). *Mass extinctions: Processes and evidence.* New York: Columbia University Press.

Druyan, A., & Sagan, C. (1992). *Shadows of forgotten ancestors: A search for who we are.* Sydney: Random House.

During, S. (Ed.). (1993). *The cultural studies reader.* London: Routledge.

Easlea, B. (1983). *Fathering the unthinkable.* London: Pluto.

Eckersley, R. (1992). *Environmentalism and political theory: Towards an ecocentric approach.* New York: SUNY Press.

Eco, U. (1987). *Travels in hyperreality* (W. Weaver, Trans.). London: Picador. (Original work published 1967)

Edgar, P. (Ed.). (1980). *The news in focus: The journalism of exception.* Melbourne: Macmillan.

Ehrlich, P. A., & Ehrlich, A. H. (1991). *Healing the planet: Strategies for resolving the environmental crisis.* Reading, MA: Addison-Wesley,.

Eldredge, N. (1993). *The miner's canary: Unravelling the mysteries of extinction.* London: Virgin.

Elkins, P. (Ed.). (1986). *The living economy: A new economics in the making.* London: Routledge.

Elton, B. (1994). *This other Eden.* London: Simon & Schuster.

Ephron, L. (1988). *The end: The imminent ice age and how we can stop it.* Berkeley, CA: Celestial Arts.

Ericson, R. V., Baranek, P. M., & Chan, J. B. L. (1987). *Visualizing deviance: A study of news organisations.* Milton Keynes, UK: Open University Press.

Estés, C. P. (1992). *Women who run with the wolves: Contacting the power of the wild woman.* London: Rider.

Ferguson, R., Gever, M., Minh-ha, T. T., & West, C. (Eds.). (1990). *Out there: Marginalization and contemporary cultures.* Cambridge: MIT Press.

Ferré, F. (1976). *Shaping the Future: Resources for the postmodern world.* New York: Harper & Row.

Feuer, J. (1992). Genre study and television. In R. C. Allen (Ed.), *Channels of discourse, reassembled* (2nd ed., pp. 138-160). London: Routledge.

Finn, G. (1993). Why are there no great women postmodernists? In V. Blundell, J. Shepherd & J. Taylor (Eds.), *Relocating cultural studies: Developments in theory and research* (pp. 123-151). London: Routledge.

Fiske, J. (1987). *Television culture.* London: Routledge.

Fiske, J. (1990). *Introduction to communication studies* (2nd ed). London: Routledge.

Fitting, P. (1991). The lessons of cyberpunk. In C. Penley & A. Ross (Eds.), *Technoculture* (pp. 295-315). Minneapolis: University of Minnesota Press.

Forman, P. (1993, November). *Physics, modernity, and our flight from responsibility.* Paper presented at Santa Fe History of Science Society meeting, Santa Fe, NM.

Forman, P. (1994, April). *On the postmodern mode of knowledge production: Instrumental, incommensurable, responsible.* Paper delivered at the Boston Colloquium of Science, "Are There Post-Modern Effects in Science?" session, Boston University, Boston.

Fox, W. (1984). Deep ecology: A new philosophy of our time? *The Ecologist, 14,* 194-204.

Fox, W. (1990). *Toward a transpersonal ecology: Developing new foundations for environmentalism.* Boston: Shambhala.

Franklin, S., Lury, C., & Stacey, J. (1993). *Off-center: Feminism and cultural studies.* New York: HarperCollins.

Frow, J., & Morris, M. (Eds.). (1993). *Australian cultural studies: A reader.* Sydney: Allen & Unwin.

Fuller, P. (1988). The search for a postmodern aesthetic. In J. Thackara (Ed.), *Design after modernism: Beyond the object* (pp. 117-134). London: Thames & Hudson.

Gaard, G. (Ed.). (1993). *Ecofeminism: Women, animals, nature.* Philadelphia: Temple University Press.

Gablik, S. (1991). *The reenchantment of art.* London: Thames & Hudson.

Galvin, M. (1995, July). *The computer as obscure object of desire.* Paper presented at the National Conference of Australian and New Zealand Communication Association, Edith Cowan University, Perth, Western Australia.

Game, A. (1991). *Undoing the social: Towards a deconstructive sociology.* Milton Keynes, UK: Open University Press.

Gay, P. (1973). *The Enlightenment: An interpretation: 2. The science of freedom.* London: Wildwood House.

Gell-Mann, M. (1994). *The quark and the jaguar: Adventures in the simple and the complex.* New York: Freeman.

Gibson, W. (1984). *Neuromancer.* Great Britain: Victor Gollancz.

Gibson, W. (1993). *Virtual light.* New York: Bantam.

Giddens, A. (1991). *Modernity and self identity.* Cambridge, MA: Polity.

Giddens, A. (1992). *The transformation of intimacy: Sexuality, love and eroticism in modern societies.* Cambridge, MA: Polity.

Gilbert, S. (1994, April). *Resurrecting the body: Has postmodernism had any effect on biology?* Paper delivered at the Boston Colloquium of Science, "Are There Post-Modern Effects in Science?" session, Boston University, Boston.

Gilroy, P. (1987). *There ain't no black in the union jack.* London: Hutchinson.

Gilroy, P. (1993). *The black Atlantic.* London: Verso.

Glasgow University Media Group. (1976). *Bad news.* London: Routledge & Kegan Paul.

Glasgow University Media Group. (1980). *More bad news.* London: Routledge & Kegan Paul.

Glasgow University Media Group. (1982). *Really bad news.* London: Writers & Readers.

Glass, F. (1989). The "new bad future": Robocop and 1980s sci-fi films. *Science as Culture, 5,* 7-49.

Gleick, J. (1987). *Chaos: Making a new science.* London: Cardinal.

Gleick, J. (1992). *Genius: Richard Feynman and modern physics.* London: Abacus.

Goffman, E. (1959). *The presentation of self in everyday life.* Garden City, NY: Doubleday.

Goffman, E. (1961). *Asylums: Essays on the social situation of mental patients and other inmates.* Garden City, NY: Doubleday.

Golding, P., & Murdock, G. (1991). Culture, communications, and political economy. In J. Curran & M. Gurevitch (Eds.), *Mass media and society* (pp. 15-32). London: Edward Arnold.

Goodwin, B. (1994). *How the leopard changed its spots: The evolution of complexity.* London: Weidenfeld & Nicolson.

Gorz, A. (1980). *Ecology as politics.* Boston: South End.

Gould, S. J. (1988). *Time's arrow, time's cycle: Myth and metaphor in the discovery of geological time.* Harmondsworth, UK: Penguin.

Gould, S. J. (1991). *Bully for brontosaurus: Reflections on natural history.* London: Hutchinson Radius.

Gould, S. J. (1993). *Eight little piggies: Reflections in natural history.* London: Jonathan Cape.

Gray, C. H. (Ed.), with the assistance of Figueroa-Sarriera, H. J., & Mentor, S. (1995). *The cyborg handbook.* London: Routledge.

Gray, C. H., Mentor, S., & Figueroa-Sarriera, H. J., (1995). Cyborgology: Constructing the knowledge of cybernetic organisms. In C. H. Gray (Ed.), with the assistance of Figueroa-Sarriera, H. J., & Mentor, S., *The cyborg handbook* (pp. 1-14). London: Routledge.

Gribbin, J. (1990). *Hothouse earth: The greenhouse effect and Gaia.* London: Black Swan.

Griffin, D. R. (Ed.). (1988). *The re-enchantment of science: Postmodern proposals.* New York: SUNY Press.

Grof, S., & Halifax, J. (1977). *The human encounter with death.* New York: E. P. Dutton.

Grossberg, L., Nelson, C., & Treichler, P. A. (Eds.). (1992). *Cultural studies.* New York: Routledge.

Grosz, E. A. (1989). *Sexual subversions: Three French feminists.* Sydney: Allen & Unwin.

Habermas, J. (1981, Fall). New social movements. *Telos, 49,* 33-37.

Habermas, J. (1983). Modernity—An incomplete project. In H. Foster (Ed.), *Postmodern culture* (pp. 3-15). London: Pluto.

Haigh, G. (1995, March 6). The new heretic is unrepentant. *The Australian,* p. 39.

Halacy, D. S. (1978). *Ice or fire? Can we survive climate change.* New York: Harper & Row.

Hall, S. (1980). Cultural studies: Two paradigms. *Media, Culture and Society, 2*(2), 57-72.

Hall, S. (1991a). Ethnicity: Identity and difference. *Radical America, 23*(4), 9-20.

Hall, S. (1991b). The local and the global: Globalization and ethnicity. In A. D. King (Ed.), *Culture, globalization, and the world system: Contemporary conditions for the representation of identity* (pp. 19-40). New York: Macmillan.

Hall, S. (1994). The question of cultural identity. In A. Giddens, D. Held, H. Hubert, S. Loyal, D. Seymore, & J. Thompson (Eds.), *The Polity reader in cultural theory* (pp. 119-125). Cambridge, MA: Polity.

Hall, S., Critcher, C., Jefferson, T., Clarke, J., & Roberts, B. (1978). *Policing the crisis: Mugging, the state, and law and order.* London: Macmillan.

Hall, S., Held, D., & McGrew, T. (Eds.). (1992). *Modernity and its futures.* Cambridge, MA: Polity.

Hall, S., Hobson, D., Lowe, A., & Willis, P. (Eds.). (1980). *Culture, media, language.* London: Hutchinson.

Hall, S. S. (1993). *Mapping the next millennium.* New York: Random House.

Hamilton, P. (1992). The Enlightenment and the birth of social science. In S. Hall & B. Gieben (Eds.), *Formations of modernity* (pp. 17-69). Cambridge, MA: Polity.

Hansen, A. (1991). The media and the social construction of the environment. *Media, Culture and Society, 13*(4), 443-458.

Hansen, A. (Ed.). (1994). *The mass media and environment issues.* London: Leicester University Press.

Haralambos, M., & Holborn, M. (1990). *Sociology: Themes and perspectives* (3rd ed.). London: Unwin Hyman.

Haraway, D. J. (1985). Manifesto for cyborgs: Science, technology, and socialist feminism in the 1980s. *Socialist Review, 80,* 65-108.

Haraway, D. J. (1989). *Primate visions: Gender, race and nature in the world of modern science.* New York: Routledge.

Haraway, D. J. (1991). *Simians, cyborgs, and women: The reinvention of nature.* London: Routledge.

Haraway, D. J. (1992a). Otherworldly conversations; terran topics; local terms. *Science as Culture, 3*(1), 64-98.

Haraway, D. J. (1992b). The promises of monsters: A regenerative politics for inappropriate/d others. In L. Grossberg, C. Nelson, & P. A. Treichler (Eds.), *Cultural studies* (pp. 295-337). London: Routledge.

Haraway, D. J. (1995). Cyborgs and symbionts: Living together in the new world order. In C. H. Gray (Ed.), *The cyborg handbook* (pp. 1-14). London: Routledge.

Hardin, G. (1968). The tragedy of the commons. *Science, 162,* 1243-1248.

Hardin, G. (1974). Living on a lifeboat. *Bioscience, 24,* 561-568.

Hardin, G. (1989). There is no global population. *The Humanist, 49,* 11-14.

Hare, B. (1992). Ecological sustainable development. In T. Jagtenberg & P. D'Alton (Eds.), *Four dimensional social space: Class, gender, ethnicity and nature: A reader in Australian social sciences* (2nd ed., pp. 555-560). Sydney: Harper..

Hartley, J. (1991). Popular reality: A (hair)brush with cultural studies. *Continuum, 4*(2), 5-18.

Hartley, J. (1992). *The politics of pictures.* London: Routledge.

Hartley, J. (1994). Discourse. In T. O'Sullivan, J. Hartley, D. Saunders, M. Montgomery, & J. Fiske, *Key concepts in communication and cultural studies* (2nd ed., pp. 92-94). London: Routledge..

Harvey, D. (1989). *The condition of postmodernity.* Oxford: Blackwell.

Harvey, D. (1993). The nature of the environment: Dialectics of social and environmental change. In R. Miliband & L. Panitch (Eds.), *The socialist register—1993* (pp. 1-51). London: Merlin.

Hawking, S. (1988). *A brief history of time: From the Big Bang to black holes.* New York: Bantam.

Hayles, N. K. (1989). Chaos as orderly disorder: Shifting ground in contemporary literature and science. *New Literary History, 20*(2), 305-322.

Hayles, N. K. (1990). *Chaos bound: Orderly disorder in contemporary literature and science.* Ithaca, NY: Cornell University Press.

Hayles, N. K. (1991). Complex dynamics in literature and science. In N. K. Hayles (Ed.), *Chaos and order: Complex dynamics in literature and science* (pp. 1-33). Chicago: University of Chicago Press.

Hayles, N. K. (1993). The seductions of cyberspace. In V. A. Conley (Ed.), on behalf of the Miami Theory Collective, *Rethinking technologies* (pp. 173-190). Minneapolis: University of Minnesota Press.

Hayward, T. (1994). *Ecological thought: An introduction.* Cambridge, MA: Polity.

Hebdige, D. (1988). *Hiding in the light: On images and things.* London & New York: Routledge.

Hebdige, D. (1990, Summer). Subjects in space. *New Formations, 11*, v-x.

Hecht, S., & Cockburn, A. (1990). *The fate of the forest: Developers, destroyers, and defenders of the Amazon.* New York: Harper & Row.

Hedlund, P. (1992, Spring). Virtual reality warriors: Native American culture in cyberspace. *High Performance,* 31-35.

Hey, J. D. (Ed.). (1992). *The future of economics.* Oxford, UK: Basil Blackwell.

Hoage, R. J. (Ed.). (1985). *Animal extinctions: What everyone should know.* Washington, DC: Smithsonian Institution.

Hodge, B., & Tripp, D. (1986). *Children and television.* Cambridge, MA: Polity.

Hodge, R., & Kress, G. (1988). *Social semiotics.* Ithaca, NY: Cornell University Press.

Hughes, O. E., & Emy, H. V. (1991). *Australian politics: Realities in conflict.* Melbourne: Macmillan.

Hutcheon, L. (1988). *A poetics of postmodernism: History, theory, fiction.* London: Routledge.

Hutcheon, L. (1989). *The politics of postmodernism.* London: Routledge.

Hutton, D. (1987). *Green politics in Australia.* Sydney: Angus & Robertson.

Huyssen, A. (1984, Fall). Mapping the postmodern. *New German Critique, 33,* 5-52.

Huyssen, A. (1986). *After the great divide: Modernism, mass culture, postmodernism.* Bloomington: Indiana University Press.

Idris, S. M. M. (1990, October). Going green—a Third World perspective. *Chain Reaction, 62,* 16-17.

Impact Team. (1977). *The weather conspiracy: The coming of the new ice age.* New York: Ballantine.

Jagtenberg, T. (1983). *The social construction of science.* Dordrecht, Holland: Reidel.

Jagtenberg, T. (1992). Four dimensional social space: Towards a global view. In T. Jagtenberg & P. D'Alton (Eds.), *Four dimensional social space: Class, gender, ethnicity and nature: A reader in Australian social sciences* (2nd ed., pp. 560-568). Sydney: Harper.

Jagtenberg, T. (1993, July). *The death of nature.* Paper presented at the National Conference of the Cultural Studies Association of Australia, Victoria University of Technology, Melbourne, Australia.

Jagtenberg, T. (1994). The end of nature. *Australian Journal of Communication, 21*(3), 14-25. [special issue]

Jagtenberg, T., & D'Alton, P. (Eds.). (1992). *Four dimensional social space: Class, gender, ethnicity and nature: A reader in Australian social sciences* (2nd ed.). Sydney: Harper.

Jameson, F. (1984). Postmodernism, or, the cultural logic of late capitalism. *New Left Review, 146*, 53-92.

Jameson, F. (1988). Cognitive mapping. In C. Nelson & L. Grossberg (Eds.), *Marxism and the interpretation of culture* (pp. 347-360). London: Macmillan.

Jameson, F. (1991). *Postmodernism, or, the cultural logic of late capitalism.* London: Verso.

Jansson, A., Hammer, M., Folke, C., & Costanza, R. (Eds.). (1994). *Investing in natural capital: The ecological economics approach to sustainability.* Washington, DC: Island Press..

Jay, M. (1984). *Adorno.* London: Fontana.

Johnson, R. (1983). *What is cultural studies anyway?* Birmingham, UK: Birmingham University CCCS stencilled paper No. 74.

Johnson, S. (Producer), & Cooper, D. (Writer). (1990). *Meat* [Television broadcast]. Bristol, UK: BBC.

Jones, D. (1994). Nga Kaitaki and the managers: Bicultural communication and resource management in Aotearoa/New Zealand. *Australian Journal of Communication, 21*(3), 105-16.

Judson, H. F. (1979). *The eighth day of creation: Makers of the revolution in biology.* New York: Simon & Schuster.

Kaplan, E. A. (1983). *Women and film: Both sides of the camera.* London: Methuen.

Kaplan, E. A. (1984). Is the gaze male? In A. Snitow, C. Stansell, & S. Thompson (Eds.), *Desire: The politics of sexuality* (pp. 321-338). London: Virago.

Kauffman, S. (1992). *The origins of order: Self-organisation and selection in evolution.* Oxford, UK: Oxford University Press.

Keane, J. (1991). *The media and democracy.* Cambridge, MA: Polity.

Keller, E. F. (1994, April). *Situating the organism between telegraphs and computers.* Paper delivered at the Boston Colloquium of Science, "Are There Post-Modern Effects in Science?" session, Boston University, Boston.

Kellert, S. R., & Wilson, E. O. (Eds.). (1993). *The biophilia hypothesis.* Washington, DC: Island Press.

Kelly, M., & Gribbin, J. (1989). *The winds of change.* London: Headway.

Kelly, P. (1984). *Fighting for hope.* London: Chatto & Windus.

Kelves, D. J. (1986). *In the name of eugenics: Genetics and the uses of human heredity.* Berkeley: University of California Press.

Kelves, D. J., & Hood, L. (Eds.). (1992). *The code of codes: Scientific and social issues in the human genome project.* Cambridge, MA: Harvard University Press.

Kennedy, D. (1981). *Commercialization of academic biomedical research: Hearings before the Subcommittee on Investigations and Oversight and Subcommittee on Science, Research and Technology of the House Committee on Science and Technology,* 97th Cong., 1st Sess.

Knight, F. H. (1947). *Freedom and reform: Essays in economics and social philosophy.* New York: Harper.

Knudtson, P., & Suzuki, D. (1988). *Genethics: The ethics of engineering life.* London: Allen & Unwin.

Knudtson, P., & Suzuki, D. (1992). *Wisdom of the elders.* Sydney: Allen & Unwin.

Kolakowski, L. (1972). *Positivism.* London: Penguin.

Kress, G. (Ed.). (1988). *Communication and culture: An introduction.* Sydney: New South Wales University Press.

Krishnamurti, J. (1969). *Freedom from the known.* New York: Harper & Row.

Krugman, P. (1994). *Peddling prosperity: Economic sense and nonsense in an age of diminished expectations.* New York: Norton.

Kübler-Ross, E. (1969). *Death: The final stage of growth.* Englewood Cliffs, NJ: Prentice Hall.

Kuhn, A. (1982). *Women's pictures: Feminism and cinema.* London: Routledge & Kegan Paul.

Kuhn, A. (Ed.). (1990). *Alien zone: Cultural theory and contemporary science fiction cinema.* London: Verso.

Kuhn, T. S. (1962). *The structure of scientific revolutions.* Chicago: University of Chicago Press.

Kumar, K. (1995). *From post-industrial to post-modern society: New theories of the contemporary world.* Oxford, UK: Basil Blackwell.

Kurtzman, J. (1993). *The death of money: How the electronic economy has destabilized the world's markets and created financial chaos.* New York: Simon & Schuster.

Kutzera, D. (1992, March). Adjusting for *Northern Exposure. American Cinematographer,* 74-78.

LaChapelle, D. (1985). Sacred land, sacred sex. In M. Tobias (Ed.), *Deep ecology* (pp. 102-21). San Diego, CA: Avant.

Laing, R. D. (1967). *The politics of experience and the bird of paradise.* Harmondsworth, UK: Penguin.

Lakoff, G., & Johnson, M. (1980). *Metaphors we live by.* Chicago: University of Chicago.

Lappé, F. M. (1982). *Diet for a small planet.* New York: Ballantine.

Lasch, C. (1980). *The culture of narcissism.* London: Abacus.

Lash, S. (1990). *The sociology of postmodernism.* London: Routledge.

Latour, B., & Woolgar, S. (1979). *Laboratory life: The social construction of scientific facts.* Beverly Hills, CA: Sage.

Lauwerier, H. (1991). *Fractals: Images of chaos.* Harmondsworth, UK: Penguin.

Lawrence, E. A. (1993). The sacred bee, the filthy pig, and the bat out of Hell: Animal symbolism as cognitive biophilia. In S. R. Kellert & E. O. Wilson (Eds.), *The biophilia hypothesis* (301-341). Washington, DC: Island Press.

Lawson, H. (1985). *Reflexivity: The post-modern predicament.* London: Hutchinson.

Layder, D. (1994). *Understanding social theory.* London: Sage.

Leane, G. (1995, December). *Indians fishing for justice: A Canadian case study in conflicting environmental paradigms.* Paper presented at the Law and Society Conference, Ballina, New South Wales.

Lee, P. (1991). The absorption and indigenization of foreign media cultures: A study on a cultural meeting point of the East and West—Hong Kong. *Asian Journal of Communication, 1*(2), 52-72.

Lévi-Strauss, C. (1969). *The raw and the cooked.* London: Cape.

Levy, S. (1993). *Artificial life: The quest for a new creation.* Harmondsworth, UK: Penguin.

Lewin, R. (1993a). *Complexity: Life on the edge of chaos.* London: Phoenix.

Lewin, R. (1993b, May 8). Genes from a disappearing world. *New Scientist,* 36-39.

Lewis, M. (Director). (1987). *Cane toads: An unnatural history* [Videocassette]. Sydney: Film Australia.

Lewontin, R. C., Rose, S., & Kamin, L. (1984). *Not in our genes: Biology, ideology and human nature.* New York: Pantheon.

Lovelock, J. F. (1979). *Gaia: A new look at life on earth.* Oxford, UK: Oxford University Press.

Lovelock, J. F. (1987). Gaia: A model for planetary and cellular dynamics. In W. I. Thompson (Ed.), *Gaia: A way of knowing* (pp. 83-97). Great Barrington, MA: Lindisfarne.

Lovelock, J. F. (1992). *Gaia: The practical science of planetary medicine.* Sydney: Allen & Unwin.

Lucas, A. (1994). Lucas Heights revisited: The framing of a major scientific controversy by the *Sydney Morning Herald: Australian Journal of Communication, 21*(3), 72-91. [special issue]

Luckmann, T. (Ed.). (1978). *Phenomenology and sociology.* Harmondsworth, UK: Penguin.

Luper-Foy, S. (1995). International justice and the environmental movement. In D. E. Cooper & J. Palmer (Eds.), *Just environments: Intergenerational, international and interspecies issues* (pp. 91-107). London: Routledge.

Lyotard, J.-F. (1984). *The postmodern condition: A report on knowledge* (G. Bennington & B. Massumi, Trans.). Manchester, UK: Manchester University Press.

Mandelbrot, B. (1982). *The fractal geometry of nature.* San Francisco: Freeman.

Mander, J. (1991). *In the absence of the sacred: The failure of technology and the survival of the Indian Nations.* San Francisco: Sierra Club.

March, A. (1982). Female invisibility in androcentric sociological theory. *Insurgent Sociologist 11*(2), 99-107.

Margulis, L., & Sagan, D. (1986). *Microcosmos.* New York: Summit.

Marika, W. (1995). *Wandjuk Marika: Life story* (As told to J. Isaacs). St. Lucia, Australia: University of Queensland Press.

Marshall, P. (1992). *Nature's web: An exploration of ecological thinking.* London: Simon & Schuster.

Martell, L. (1994). *Ecology and society: An introduction.* Amherst: University of Massachusetts Press.

Marx, K., & Engels, F. (1967). *The communist manifesto* (S. Moore, Trans.). Harmondsworth, UK: Penguin. (Original work published 1888)

Mathews, F. (1991). *The ecological self.* London: Routledge.

Mathews, F. (1993). To know the world: Approaches to science in feminist theory. In F. Kelly (Ed.), *On the edge of discovery: Australian women in science* (pp. 199-227). Melbourne: University of Melbourne.

Mathews, F. (1994). Ecofeminism and deep ecology. In C. Merchant (Ed.), *Ecology* (pp. 235-245). Atlantic Highlands, NJ: Humanities Press.

Matson, F. W. (1964). *The broken image: Man, science, and society.* Garden City, NY: Doubleday.

Matthews, R. (1993). *Unravelling the mind of God: Mysteries at the frontier of science.* London: Virgin.

Maunder, W. J. (1986). *The uncertainty business: Risks and opportunities in weather and climate.* London: Methuen.

McCloskey, D. M. (1985). *The rhetoric of economics.* Madison: University of Wisconsin Press.

McHale, B. (1992). *Constructing postmodernism.* London: Routledge.

McKenzie, D., & Wajcman, J. (1985). *The social shaping of technology—How the refrigerator got its hum.* Milton Keynes, UK: Open University Press.

McKibben, B. (1990). *The end of nature.* London: Viking.

McKibben, B. (1993). *The age of missing information.* New York: Random House.

McKie, D. (1992). Communicating futures: *The Handmaid's Tale* or *Terminator 2: Judgement Day. Australian Journal of Communication, 19*(1), 1-8.

McKie, D. (1994a). Popular science, post culture and promotional power. *Media, Culture and Society, 16*(4), 693-697.

McKie, D. (1994b). Telling stories: Natural histories, unnatural histories and biopolitics. *Australian Journal of Communication, 21*(3), 92-104. [special issue]

McKie, D. (1994c). Virtual reality shapes the future: Cybersex, lies and computer games. In L. Green & R. Guinery (Eds.), *Framing technology: Society, choice and change* (pp. 15-28). Sydney: Allen & Unwin.

McKie, D. (1994d). Postcolonialism verses postmodernism: Premature births and premature burials in the latest capitalist environment. *Span, 36*(1), 25-34.

McKie, D. (Ed.). (1994d). The environment issue [Special issue]. *Australian Journal of Communication, 21*(3).

McKie, D. (1995). Popular futures: Techno-crime, policing, and social change. *Australian Journal of Communication, 22*(3), 1-12.

McKie, D., & Bennett, M. (1992, Summer). Chaos, cultural studies and cosmology. *Meanjin, 4,* 785-794.

McMichael, A. J. (1993). *Planetary overload: Global environmental change and the health of the human species.* Cambridge, UK: Cambridge University Press.

McNamara, N. (1990). Australian Aborigines—A question of identity. In B. Hocking (Ed.), *Australia Towards 2000* (pp. 95-99). London: Macmillan

Mead, G. H. (1934). *Mind, self, and society.* Chicago: University of Chicago Press.

Mellencamp, P. (1992). *High anxiety: Catastrophe, scandal, age, and comedy.* Bloomington: Indiana University Press.

Melucci, A. (1989). *Nomads of the present: Social movements and individual needs in contemporary society.* London: Century Hutchison.

Mercer, J. (1984). *Communes: A social history and guide.* Dorchester, UK: Prism.

Merchant, C. (1980). *The death of nature: Women, ecology, and the scientific revolution.* San Francisco: Harper & Row.

Merchant, C. (1989). *Ecological revolutions: Nature, gender, and science in New England.* Chapel Hill: University of North Carolina Press.

Merchant, C. (1992). *Radical ecology: The search for a livable world.* London: Routledge.

Merchant, C. (Ed.). (1994). *Ecology.* Atlantic Highlands, NJ: Humanities Press.

Metcalf, W., & Vanclay, F. (1987). *Social characteristics of alternative lifestyle participants in Australia* (2nd ed.). Nathan, Australia: Institute of Applied Environmental Research.

Metzner, R. (1971). *Maps of consciousness.* London: Collier-Macmillan.

Mies, M. (1993). Liberating the consumer. In M. Mies & V. Shiva (Eds.), *Ecofeminism* (pp. 251-263). Melbourne: Spinifex.

Mies, M., & Shiva, V. (Eds.). (1991). *Ecofeminism*. Melbourne: Spinifex.

Miller, B., Miller, G., & Mitchell, D. (Producers), & Noonan, C. (Director). (1995). *Babe*. Century City, CA: Universal Pictures.

Milner, A. (1991). *Contemporary cultural theory: An introduction*. Sydney: Allen & Unwin.

Moores, S. (1993). *Interpreting audiences: The ethnography of media consumption*. London: Sage.

Morley, D. (1980). *The "Nationwide" audience: Structure and decoding*. London: BFI.

Morris, M. (1988). *The pirate's fiancee: Feminism, reading, postmodernism*. London: Verso.

Morse, M. (1986). The television news personality and credibility: Reflections on the news in transition. In T. Modleski (Ed.), *Studies in entertainment: Critical approaches to mass culture* (pp. 55-79). Bloomington: Indiana University Press.

Mühlhäusler, P., & Harré, R. (1994). *Linguistic and philosophical aspects of environmentalism*. Unpublished manuscript.

Mulkay, M. (1991). *Sociology of science: A sociological pilgrimage*. Milton Keynes, UK: Open University Press.

Mundey, J. (1981). *Green bans and beyond*. Sydney: Angus & Robertson.

Munro-Clark, M. (1986). *Communes in rural Australia: The movement since 1970*. Sydney: Hale & Iremonger.

Murdock, G. (1992). Citizens, consumers, and public culture. In M. Skovmand & K. C. Skovmand (Eds.), *Media cultures: Reappraising transnational media* (pp. 17-41). London: Routledge.

Murray, S. (1995, December). Life lessons. *Cinema Papers, 107*, 6-13, 53-55.

Myers, N. (Ed.). (1985). *The Gaia atlas of planet management*. London: Pan.

Myers, N. (Ed.). (1990). *The Gaia atlas of future worlds: Challenge and opportunity in an age of change*. London: Robertson McCarta.

Naess, A. (1985). Identification as a source of deep ecological attitudes. In M. Tobias (Ed.), *Deep ecology* (pp. 256-270). San Diego, CA: Avant.

Nash, R. (1990). *The rights of nature: A history of environmental ethics*. Leichhardt, NSW, Australia: Primavera.

Nava, M. (1992). *Changing cultures: Feminism, youth and consumerism*. London: Sage.

Neale, S. (1990). Questions of genre. *Screen, 31*(1), 45-66.

New Internationalist. (n.d.). *Map of the world: Peters projection*. Oxford: Author.

Newby, H. (1991, May). One world, two cultures: Sociology and the environment. *BSA Bulletin Network, 50*, 1-8.

Nichols, B. (1991). *Representing reality: Issues and concepts in documentary*. Bloomington: Indiana University Press.

Nicholson, L. J. (Ed.). (1990). *Feminism/postmodernism*. London: Routledge.

Nicholson, L. J. (1992). On the postmodern barricades: Feminism, politics, and theory. In S. Seidman & D. G. Wagner (Eds.), *Postmodernism and social theory: The debate over general theory* (pp. 82-100). Oxford, UK: Basil Blackwell.

Nohrstedt, S. A. (1991). The information crisis in Sweden after Chernobyl. *Media, Culture and Society, 13*(4), 477-497.

Norton, B. (1995). Elevating ecosystem states: Two contemporary paradigms. *Ecological Economics, 14*, 113-127.

O'Brien, M. (1981). *The politics of reproduction.* London: Routledge & Kegan Paul.

O'Sullivan, T., Hartley, J., Saunders, D., Montgomery, M., & Fiske, J. (1994). *Key concepts in communication and cultural studies* (2nd ed.). London: Routledge.

Offe, C. (1985). New social movements: Challenging the boundaries of institutional politics. *Social Research, 52*(4), 817-868.

Olby, R. (1974). *The path of the double helix.* Seattle: University of Washington Press.

Omerod, P. (1994). *The death of economics.* London: Faber & Faber.

Ornstein, R. (1986). *Multimind.* Boston: Houghton Mifflin.

Pace, D. (1986). *Claude Lévi-Strauss: The bearer of ashes.* London: Ark.

Paehlke, R. C. (1989). *Environmentalism and future of progressive politics.* New Haven, CT: Yale University Press.

Pagels, H. R. (1989). *The dream of reason: The computer and the rise of the sciences of complexity.* New York: Bantam.

Pakulski, J. (1991). *Social movements.* Melbourne: Longman Chesire.

Palmer, L. (1994, July). *The space buggy in my heart.* Paper presented at the National Conference of the Australian and New Zealand Communication Association, University of Technology, Sydney, Australia.

Palmer, P. (1986). *The lively audience: A study of children around the TV.* Sydney: Allen & Unwin.

Papadakis, E. (1993). *Politics and the environment: The Australian experience.* Sydney: Allen & Unwin.

Patton, P. (1995). Mabo, freedom and the politics of difference. *Australian Journal of Political Science, 30*(1), 9-13.

Peat, F. D. (1995). *Blackfoot physics: A journey into the Native American universe.* London: Fourth Estate.

Penman, R. (1994). Environmental matters and communication challenges. *Australian Journal of Communication, 21*(3), 26-39. [special issue]

Pickering, K. T., & Owen, L. A. (1994). *An introduction to global environmental issues.* London: Routledge.

Pickover, A. (1986). Computer displays of biological forms generated from mathematical feedback loops. *Computer Graphics Forum, 5,* 313-316.

Piller, C., & Yamamoto, K. (1988). *Gene wars: Military control over the new genetic technologies.* New York: William Morrow.

Plumwood, V. (1993). *Feminism and the mastery of nature.* London: Routledge.

Ponte, L. (1976). *The cooling.* Englewood Cliffs, NJ: Prentice Hall.

Ponting, C. (1991). *A green history of the world.* Harmondsworth, UK: Penguin.

Porritt, J. (1984). *Seeing green.* Oxford, UK: Basil Blackwell.

Porritt, J., & Winner, M. (1988). *The coming of the greens.* London: Fontana.

Prigogine, I., & Stengers, I. (1984). *Order out of chaos: Man's new dialogue with nature.* London: Fontana.

Raug, D. M. (1991). *Extinction: Bad genes or bad luck.* New York: Norton.

Redclift, M., & Benton, M. (Eds.). (1994). *Social theory and the global environment.* London: Routledge.

Regis, E. (1991). *Great mambo chicken and the transhuman condition: Science slightly over the edge.* London: Viking.

Remmling, G. (1973). *Towards the sociology of knowledge: Origin and develop-ment of a thought style*. London: Routledge & Kegan Paul.

Rheingold, H. (1992). *Virtual reality*. London: Mandarin.

Rheingold, H. (1994). *The virtual community: Finding connection in a computerized world*. London: Secker & Warburg.

Rifkin, J. (1991). *Biosphere politics: A new consciousness for a new century*. New York: Crown.

Rifkin, J. (1994). *Beyond beef: The rise and fall of the cattle culture*. London: Thorsons.

Robins, K. (1993). The war, the screen, the crazy dog and poor mankind. *Media, Culture and Society, 15*(2), 321-327.

Roos, M. (1994). *Introduction to cosmology*. Chichester, UK: John Wiley.

Rose, M. A. (1991). *The post-modern and the post-industrial: A critical analysis*. Cambridge, UK: Cambridge University Press.

Rosenau, P. M. (1992). *Post-modernism and the social sciences: Insights, inroads, and intrusions*. Princeton, NJ: Princeton University Press.

Ross, A. (1990). Ballots, bullets, or batmen: Can cultural studies do the right thing? *Screen, 31*(1), 26-44.

Ross, A. (1991). *Strange weather: Culture, science and technology in the age of limits*. London: Verso.

Ross, A. (1992). New Age technoculture. In L. Grossberg, C. Nelson, & P. A. Treichler (Eds.), *Cultural studies* (pp. 531-555). London: Routledge.

Ross, A. (1994). *The Chicago gangster theory of life: Nature's debt to society*. London: Verso.

Roszak, T. (1969). *The making of a counter culture*. Garden City, NY: Doubleday/ Anchor.

Roszak, T. (1973). *Where the wasteland ends*. New York: Doubleday.

Roszak, T. (1975). *Unfinished animal: The Aquarian frontier and the evolution of consciousness*. New York: Harper & Row.

Rowbotham, S., & Mitter, S. (Eds.). (1994). *Dignity and daily bread: New forms of economic organising among poor women in the Third World and the First*. London: Routledge.

Ruether, R. (1975). *New woman, new earth*. Minneapolis, MN: Seabury.

Rushkoff, D. (1994). *Media virus: Hidden agendas in popular culture*. New York: Random House.

Rutherford, P. (1994). The administration of life: Ecological discourse as intel-lectual machinery of government. *Australian Journal of Communication, 21*(3), 40-55. [special issue]

Sagan, C. (1980). *Cosmos*. New York: Ballantine.

Sagan, D. (1991). *Biospheres: Metamorphosis of planet earth*. London: Arkana.

Sahlins, M. (1976). *The use and abuse of biology: An anthropological critique of sociology*. Ann Arbor: University of Michigan Press.

Salleh, A. (1984). Deeper than deep ecology. *Environmental Ethics, 6*, 339-345.

Salleh, A. (1991). Discussion: Eco-socialism/eco-feminism. *Capitalism, Nature, Socialism, 6*, 129-134.

Sardar, Z. (1988). *The revenge of Athena: Science, exploitation and the Third World*. London: Mansell.

Schlesinger, P. (1987). Putting "reality" together: BBC news. London: Methuen.

Schlesinger, P. (1990). Rethinking the sociology of journalism: Source strategies and the limits of media centrism. In M. Ferguson (Ed.), *Public communication: The new imperatives* (pp. 61-83). London: Sage.

Schneider, S. H. (1989). *Global warming: Are we entering the greenhouse century?* San Francisco: Sierra Club.

Schneider, S. H. (1990). Debating Gaia. *Environment, 32*(4), 5-32.

Schneider, S. H., & Boston, P. J. (Eds.). (1991).´ *Scientists on Gaia.* Cambridge: MIT Press.

Schur, E. (1976). *The awareness trap: Self absorption instead of social change.* New York: McGraw-Hill.

Schutz, A., & Luckmann, T. (1974). *The structures of the life-world.* London: Heinemann Educational.

Seager, J. (1990). *The state of the earth: An atlas of environmental concern.* London: Unwin Hyman.

Sen, A. (1987). *On ethics and economics.* Oxford, UK: Basil Blackwell.

Shapiro, R. (1992). *The human blueprint: The race to unlock the secrets of our genetic script.* London: Cassell.

Shiva, V. (1988). *Women, ecology and development.* London: Zed.

Shiva, V. (1993). The Chipko women's concept of freedom. In M. Mies & V. Shiva (Eds.), *Ecofeminism* (pp. 246-250). Melbourne: Spinifex.

Singer, M. (1993). *The making of Heaven and Earth.* Sydney: Tower.

Singleton, H. (1995). *Science on television: A representational site for mediating ideology.* Unpublished master's thesis, Edith Cowan University, Western Australia.

Slack, J. (1994). The environment matters: Complicity, ethics, theoretical rigour, intervention. *Australian Journal of Communication, 21*(3), 1-13. [special issue]

Slack, J. D., & Whitt, L. A. (1992). Ethics and cultural studies. In L. Grossberg, C. Nelson, & P. A. Treichler (Eds.), *Cultural studies* (pp. 571-592). London: Routledge.

Slack, J. D., & Whitt, L. A. (1994). Communities, environments and cultural studies. *Cultural Studies, 8*(1), 5-31.

Sless, D. (1991). Communication and certainty. *Australian Journal of Communication, 18*(3), 19-31.

Sless, D. (1994). Who am I, where am I, what do I understand? In H. Borland (Ed.), *Communication and identity: Local, regional, global: Selected papers from the 1993 National Conference of the Australian Communication Association* (pp. 6-16). Canberra, Australian Capital Territory: ANZCA.

Sless, D., & Shrensky, R. (1995). The boundary of communication. *Australian Journal of Communication, 22*(2), 31-47.

Snooks, G. D. (1994). *Portrait of the family within the total economy: A study in longrun dynamics, Australia 1788-1990.* Cambridge, UK: Cambridge University Press.

Snow, C. P. (1964). *The two cultures and a second look: An expanded version of the two cultures and the scientific revolution.* Cambridge, UK: Cambridge University Press.

Soja, E. W. (1989). *Postmodern geographies. The reassertion of space in critical social theory.* New York: Verso.

282 ECO-IMPACTS: THE GREENING OF POSTMODERNITY

Soper, K. (1979). Marxism, materialism and biology. In J. Mepham & D.-H. Ruben (Eds.), *Issues in Marxist philosophy: Vol. 11. Materialism* (pp. 61-99). London: Harvester Wheatsheaf.

Soper, K. (1992). Discussion: Eco-feminism and eco-socialism. *Capitalism, Nature, Socialism, 11*, 111-114.

Spretnak, C. (1991). *States of grace: The recovery of meaning in the postmodern age.* San Francisco: HarperCollins.

Stabile, C. A. (1994). A garden enclosed is my sister: Ecofeminism and ecovalences. *Cultural Studies, 8*(1), 56-73.

Stephanson, A. (1987). Regarding postmodernism—A conversation with Frederic Jameson. *Social Text, 17*, 29-54.

Stevens, J. (1989). *Storming heaven: LSD and the American dream.* London: Paladin Grafton.

Stratford, E. (1994). Disciplining the feminine, the home, and nature in three Australian public health histories. *Australian Journal of Communication, 21*(3), 56-71. [special issue]

Strauss, L. (1953). *Natural rights and history.* Chicago: University of Chicago Press.

Suzuki, D. (1987). *Metamorphosis: Stages in a life.* Toronto: Stoddart.

Suzuki, D. T. (1956). *Zen Buddhism* (W. W. Barrett, Ed.). Garden City, NY: Doubleday Anchor.

Swimme, B. (1988). The cosmic creation story. In D. R. Griffin (Ed.), *The re-enchantment of science: Postmodern proposals* (pp. 47-56). New York: SUNY Press.

Sydie, R. A. (1987). *Natural women, cultured men: A feminist perspective on sociological theory.* Milton Keynes, UK: Open University Press.

Tafler, D., & d'Agostino, P. (1993, August). The techno/cultural interface. *Media Information Australia, 69*, 47-54.

Tauber, A. I. (1993). Darwinian aftershocks: Repercussions in late twentieth century medicine. *Journal of the Royal Society of Medicine, 87*, 27-31.

Tauber, A. I. (1994a). The immune self: Theory or metaphor? *Immunology Today, 15*(3), 134-136.

Tauber, A. I. (1994b, April). *Post-modernism and immune selfhood.* Paper presented at the Boston Colloquium of Science, "Are there Post-Modern Effects in Science?" session, Boston University, Boston.

Tauber, A. I., & Sarkar, S. (1994). The ideology of the Human Genome Project. *Journal of the Royal Society of Medicine, 86*, 537-540.

Thiele, B. (1986). Vanishing acts in social and political thought: Tricks of the trade. In C. Pateman & E. A. Grosz (Eds.), *Feminist challenges: Social and political theory* (pp. 30-43). Sydney: Allen & Unwin.

Thurman, R. A. F. (1991). Tibetan psychology: Sophisticated software for the human brain. In D. Goleman & R. A. F. Thurman (Eds.), *MindScience: An east-west dialogue* (pp. 51-73). Boston: Wisdom Publications.

Tobias, M. (Ed.). (1985). *Deep ecology.* San Diego, CA: Avant.

Todorov, T. (1981). *An introduction to poetics.* Brighton, UK: Harvester.

Tomas, D. (1989, Summer). The technophiliac body: On technicity in William Gibson's cyborg culture. *New Formations, 8*, 113-129.

Toohey, B. (1994). *Tumbling dice.* Melbourne: William Heinemann.

Toulmin, S. (1982a). The construal of reality: Criticism in modern and postmodern science. *Critical Inquiry, 9*(1), 93-111.

Toulmin, S. (1982b). *The return to cosmology: Postmodern science and the theology of nature.* Berkeley: University of California Press.

Touraine, A. (1985). An introduction to the study of social movements. *Social Research, 52,* 749-787.

Trimble, S. (Ed.). (1989). *Words from the land: Encounters with natural history writing.* Salt Lake City, UT: Peregrine Smith.

Tuchman, G. (1978). *Making news: A study of the construction of reality.* New York: Free Press.

Tudge, C. (1993). *The engineer in the garden: Genes and genetics: From the idea of heredity to the creation of life.* London: Jonathan Cape.

Turnbull, D. (1989). *Maps are territories, science is an atlas: A portfolio of exhibits.* Victoria, Australia: Deakin University Press.

Turnbull, D. (1991). *Technoscience worlds.* Victoria, Australia: Deakin University Press.

Turner, B. S. (1994). *Orientalism, postmodernism, and globalism.* London: Routledge.

Turner, G. (1990). *British cultural studies: An introduction.* Boston: Unwin Hyman.

Van Zoonen, L. (1994). *Feminist media studies.* London: Sage.

Vandenbeld, J. (1988). *Nature of Australia: A portrait of the island continent.* Sydney: Collins & ABC Enterprises.

Waldrop, M. M. (1993). *Complexity: The emerging science at the edge of order and chaos.* London: Viking.

Walker, M. (1982). *Powers of the press: The world's great newspapers.* London: Quartet.

Waring, M. (1988). *If women counted: A new feminist economics.* San Francisco: Harper San Francisco.

Wark, M. (1994a). Third Nature. *Cultural Studies 8*(1), 115-132.

Wark, M. (1994b). *Virtual geography: Living with global media events.* Bloomington: Indiana University Press.

Warren, K. (Ed.). (1994). *Ecological feminism.* London: Routledge.

Wartella, E. A. (1990). Producing children's television programs. In J. S. Ettema & D. C. Whitney (Eds.), *Audiencemaking: How the media create an audience* (pp. 38-56). Newbury Park, CA: Sage.

Watts, A. (1973). *The book on the taboo of knowing who you are.* London: Sphere.

Weber, S. (1987). *Institution and interpretation.* Minneapolis, MN: University of Minneapolis.

Webster, A. (1988). *The changing structural relationship between public sector science and commercial enterprise* (Science Policy Support Group Concept Paper No. 4). Cambridge, UK: Cambridge College of Arts and Technology.

Weinberg, S. (1993). *The first three minutes: A modern view of the origin of the universe.* London: Flamingo.

Wernick, A. (1991). *Promotional culture: Advertising and ideology in late capitalism.* London: Sage.

Whitley, R. (1974). *Social processes of scientific development.* London: Routledge & Kegan Paul.

ECO-IMPACTS: THE GREENING OF POSTMODERNITY

Wilkie, T. (1994). *Perilous knowledge: The Human Genome Project and its implications.* London: Faber.

Williams, R. (1980). *Problems in materialism and culture.* London: Verso.

Williams, R. (1983). *Towards 2000.* Harmondsworth, UK: Penguin.

Williamson, J. (1978). *Decoding advertisements.* London: Marion Boyars.

Wilson, A. (1992). *The culture of nature: North American landscape from Disney to the Exxon Valdez.* Oxford, UK: Basil Blackwell.

Wilson, E. O. (1984). *Biophilia: The human bond with other species.* Cambridge, MA: Harvard University Press.

Wilson, E. O. (1992). *The diversity of life.* Cambridge, MA: Harvard University Press.

Winner, L. (1977). *Autonomous technology: Technics-out-of-control as a theme in political thought.* Cambridge: MIT Press.

Women's Study Group, Centre for Contemporary Cultural Studies, University of Birmingham. (1978). *Women take issue: Aspects of women's subordination.* London: Hutchinson.

Woolgar, S. (Ed.). (1988). *Knowledge and reflexivity: New frontiers in the sociology of knowledge.* London: Sage.

Worster, D. (1985). *Nature's economy: A history of ecological ideas.* Cambridge, UK: Cambridge University Press.

Wright, W. (1975). *Sixguns and society: A structural study of the Western.* Berkeley: University of California Press.

Yearley, S. (1991). *The green case: A sociology of environmental issues, arguments and politics.* London: Routledge.

Yearley, S. (1992). Environmental challenges. In S. Hall, D. Held, & T. McGrew (Eds.), *Modernity and its futures* (pp. 117-153). Cambridge, MA: Polity.

Young, D. (1991). *FernGully.* Sydney: Ashton.

Young, M. D. (1992). *Sustainable investment and resource use.* Paris: UNESCO and Parthenon.

Younger, W., & Faiman, P. (Producers), & Kroyer, B. (Director). (1992). *FernGully: The last rainforest* [Videocassette]. United States: Twentieth Century Fox.

Zablocki, B. D. (1971). *The joyful community: An account of the Bruderhof, a communal movement now in its third generation.* Baltimore, MD: Penguin.

Zablocki, B. D. (1980). *Alienation and charisma.* New York: Free Press.

Zimmerman, M. E. (1994). *Contesting Earth's future: Radical ecology and postmodernity.* Berkeley: University of California Press.

Index

About the Authors

Tom Jagtenberg, PhD, is a senior lecturer in the Department of Sociology, University of Wollongong, in Australia. He is Coordinator of Communication Studies in the Faculty of Arts at the University of Wollongong and a founding member of the faculty's master's program in cultural studies. He has published widely, including two editions of *Four Dimensional Social Space: Class, Gender, Ethnicity and Nature; A Reader in Australian Social Sciences* (coedited with P. D'Alton); and *The Social Construction of Science.* He serves on the editorial board of *Continum: The Australian Journal of Media and Culture.* His research interests include ecoculturalism, the postmodernization of social theory and communication and cultural studies, interactionism, promotional culture, New Age and counterculture, and the mapping of Australian society and culture.

David McKie, PhD, a Scot by birth and an Australian by naturalization, is a senior lecturer in communications, media, and public relations at Edith Cowan University and a past President of the Australian and New Zealand Communication Association. He serves on the editorial boards of the *Australian Journal of Communication* and *Continuum: The Australian Journal of Media and Culture* and has published widely in the areas of communication and media studies. In addition to ecoculturalism, he has research interests in paradigmatology, television science, "the Post," public relations, organizational culture, promotional culture, 19th-century Scottish fiction, national identities, thrillers, and techno-futures.